CW01067006

The Language of Mental Health

Series editors
Michelle O'Reilly
The Greenwood Institute of Child Health
University of Leicester
Leicester, Leicestershire, UK

Jessica Nina Lester
School of Education
Indiana University Bloomington
Bloomington, Indiana, USA

This series brings together rich theoretical and empirical discussion at the intersection of mental health and discourse/conversation analysis. Situated broadly within a social constructionist perspective, the books included within this series will offer theoretical and empirical examples highlighting the discursive practices that surround mental health and make 'real' mental health constructs. Drawing upon a variety of discourse and conversation analysis perspectives, as well as data sources, the books will allow scholars and practitioners alike to better understand the role of language in the making of mental health.

More information about this series at
http://www.palgrave.com/series/15193

Michelle O'Reilly • Jessica Nina Lester
Tom Muskett
Editors

A Practical Guide to Social Interaction Research in Autism Spectrum Disorders

palgrave
macmillan

Editors
Michelle O'Reilly
University of Leicester
Leicester, UK

Jessica Nina Lester
Indiana University
Bloomington, Indiana, USA

Tom Muskett
Leeds Beckett University
Leeds, UK

The Language of Mental Health
ISBN 978-1-137-59235-4   ISBN 978-1-137-59236-1   (eBook)
https://doi.org/10.1057/978-1-137-59236-1

Library of Congress Control Number: 2017959549

Cover credit: Adrienne Bresnahan/gettyimages

Printed on acid-free paper

This Palgrave Macmillan imprint is published by Springer Nature
The registered company is Macmillan Publishers Ltd.
The registered company address is: The Campus, 4 Crinan Street, London, N1 9XW, United Kingdom

Acknowledgements

We thank all the people that contributed to this book and made it possible. As editors, we thank the publishers for supporting us through the process of writing, and our families for their patience. We also thank the scholars who were interviewed for in chapter three: Helen Cameron, Sushie Dobbinson, and Rachael Gabriel. Specifically, the quality of the chapters in this book has been assured through the peer review process. Several experts in autism spectrum disorder and/or discourse and conversation analysis provided feedback on initial drafts of the chapters. Their useful insights have helped the authors and editors of this book to develop and improve the text and ensure that it is reader-friendly. We list these reviewers in alphabetical order by surname.

Louise Bradley—Research Assistant, Centre for Research in Psychology, Behaviour, and Achievement, Coventry University

Gemma Dacey—Multisystemic Therapist within Coventry City Council and Coventry and Warwickshire Partnership Trust

Eryn Mann—Multisystemic Therapist within Coventry City Council and Coventry and Warwickshire Partnership Trust

Alison Davies—Independent Academic Consultant and Counselling Psychotherapist

Hannah Dorstal—Assistant Professor of Reading Education, University of Connecticut

Rachael Gabriel—Assistant Professor of Literacy Education, University of Connecticut

David Giles—Reader in Media Psychology, University of Winchester

Mary Horton-Salway—Academic Consultant in Psychology

Nikki Kiyimba—Chartered Clinical Psychologist, Cheshire and Wirral Partnership NHS Trust, and Senior Lecturer, Chester University.

Chad Lochmiller—Assistant Professor of Education Leadership and Policy Studies, Indiana university

Jessica Robles—Lecturer in Social Psychology, Loughborough University

Suraj Uttamchandani—PhD student, Learning Sciences, Indiana University

Editorial Board

We are very grateful to our expert editorial board who continue to provide support for the book series. They continue to provide support as we continue to edit the book series 'The Language of Mental Health'. We acknowledge them here in alphabetical order by surname.

Contents

Abbreviations

ASD	Autism Spectrum Disorder
ADHD	Attention Deficit Hyperactivity Disorder
ADI	Autism Diagnostic Inventory
ADOS	Autism Diagnostic Observation Schedule
BPS	British Psychological Society
CA	Conversation Analysis
CDP	Critical Discursive Psychology
DA	Discourse Analysis
DISCO	Diagnostic Interview for Social and Communication Disorders
DP	Discursive Psychology
DSM	Diagnostic and Statistical Manual of Mental Disorders
ESRC	Economic and Social Research Council
IDK	'I don't know' utterances
IPA	Interpretative Phenomenological Analysis
LD	Learning Disability
MDT	Multi-disciplinary Team
OCD	Obsessive Compulsive Disorder
QAA	Quality Assurance Agency
SALT	Speech and Language Therapist
SSK	Sociology of Scientific Knowledge
TCU	Turn Construction Unit

List of Figures

List of Tables

List of Boxes

1

Introduction: Mental Health, Mental Illness, and a Critical Position on Autism Spectrum Disorder

Michelle O'Reilly, Jessica Nina Lester, and Tom Muskett

Learning Objectives

By the end of this chapter, you will be able to:

- Describe the history of mental illness.
- Evaluate the criteria against which normality is measured.
- Critically assess the classification of autism spectrum disorder (ASD) as a mental health disorder.
- Appraise the critical turn to language.
- Recognise the value of this book.

M. O'Reilly (✉)
The Greenwood Institute, University of Leicester, Westcotes Drive, Leicester, UK

J.N. Lester
Indiana University, Bloomington, IN, USA

T. Muskett
Leeds Beckett University, Leeds, UK

© The Author(s) 2017
M. O'Reilly et al. (eds.), *A Practical Guide to Social Interaction Research in Autism Spectrum Disorders*, The Language of Mental Health,
https://doi.org/10.1057/978-1-137-59236-1_1

1

Introduction

A practical guide to doing social interaction research in Autism Spectrum Disorders (ASDs): Communication, discourse and conversation analysis is a co-edited volume that aims to provide readers with practical understandings of how to go about carrying out discourse and conversation analysis research in the field of autism. There is a huge amount of research, clinical and practice literature on language, communication and social interaction in ASD, which you may be familiar with. These topics are the focus of this book. However, the ideas and research work presented in this book differ from the majority of writings about communication in ASD. This difference is grounded in the methodologies that this book is based around: discourse and conversation analysis approaches begin from the position that language and communication are *interactional, social,* and/or *cultural* entities. As this book will demonstrate, examining language, communication, and interaction in ASD using such approaches can help people to understand phenomena that are typically overlooked, or even help to rethink existing theories.

As may be clear from the above, some of the ways that ASD is examined in this book may feel different to traditional research on the same issues. Therefore, in this introduction, we discuss this 'tradition' and try to convey, within a historical context, the way in which diagnoses such as ASD are usually discussed and presented. It is important to acknowledge at this point that whilst the majority of people would rightly not use terms such as 'mental illness' to discuss ASD, the diagnostic concept itself has emerged from the practices of psychiatry. In other words, the way in which ASD is defined and diagnosed is fundamentally the same as in other psychiatric conditions such as 'depression', 'anxiety', 'schizophrenia', and so forth. For this reason, we begin the chapter with a brief discussion of the history of mental illness to understand how particular ways of presenting conditions such as ASD may have emerged historically. To contextualise the different approaches taken in this book, we then discuss the impact of the so-called turn to language in the social sciences in understanding both ASD and topics related to mental health more broadly. Finally, we present the overarching aims and structure of the book.

Historical Overview of Mental Illness

The development of psychiatry and the way in which it has shaped how we conceive 'normality' and 'abnormality' is vast with a significant history, which to some extent has been contentious and critical. It is difficult to conceptualise such a complex history in a brief introduction; yet, it is nonetheless a useful endeavour to provide some contextual background for those planning to undertake research focused on ASD. For the sake of simplicity, we provide a partial history here to provide a benchmark for understanding the classification of 'normality' and 'abnormality'.

The very notions of mental distress, mental health, mental illness and its related concepts, such as madness, have a rich and chequered history. Indeed, arguments have been presented that 'madness may be as old as mankind' (Porter, 2002, p. 10).

> *For example:* In ancient Egypt, there were writings of 'hysterical disorders' and this predates 1900 BC. (Sigerist, 1951)

> *For example:* In ancient Greece, Hippocrates believed that mental illness could be treated through medicines which stood in contrast to the prevailing view of demonic possession common at that time. (Sigerist, 1951)

Perspectives about 'abnormality' and mental distress have changed over time, with a range of different beliefs having existed. During medieval times, distress was frequently attributed to the supernatural, for instance, caused by demonic possession (Clay, 1966). It is perhaps therefore unsurprising that many of those displaying symptoms of mental illness were persecuted (in part) because of such demonology. A good example of this is the thousands of (female) 'witches' who were executed due to their 'possession' (Russell, 1972). Despite this focus on superstitious beliefs, there is also historical evidence that some people in medieval times held a belief that mental illness was associated with natural causes and therefore could be cured with the right types of treatments.

For example: Some villages and towns paid for pilgrimages to religious sites for those who were suffering ill symptoms indicative of mental illness and this had the primary aim of curing those symptoms. (Rosen, 1968)

An important work in the descriptions of the history of 'abnormality' and mental illness is the seminal writing of Foucault (1965). In his work, he identified three significant historic periods in the construction of madness:

1. *Renaissance:* This period marked an era wherein reason and madness were considered in the sense that God was conceived of as reasonable, and madness was indicative of the discrepancy between what man was and what he hoped to be. Thus, during the 1400s and 1600s there was a focus on isolating those who were considered to be mad, with this period of history marked with inhumane treatments of the insane.
2. *Classical Age:* In the seventeenth and eighteenth centuries, a clear distinction was made between madness and reason. In this period, madness was constructed as being in opposition to reason, and social institutions were put in place to confine those who were thought to lack reason. During the late 1700s, there were some concerns voiced about the maltreatment of those mentally ill individuals, and madness became an object to be studied in medicine.
3. *Rise of the asylum*: The modern experience of mental illness managed to retain a focus on madness as an object of study. During the eighteenth and nineteenth centuries, there was the rise of asylums and psychiatric hospitals, which were considered to protect the public from the insane. However, it was also during this period that mental illness started to be studied more scientifically with the promotion of treatment for those with 'problems'. The growth of asylums led to a range of moral and medical therapies in Europe and the USA, although inmates were still subjected to isolation, cold showers, and electric shock treatments (Porter, 1997). The twentieth century included an extension of more moral treatments and the rise of psychological therapies, such as psychoanalysis. Yet, there were still some radical treat-

ments used, such as lobotomies. However, by the 1940s, some mental hospitals unlocked their doors and therapeutic communities were set up (Porter, 2002).

Important point

! Note that respectful and ethical treatment of individuals with mental illness is only fairly recent.

It is only since the 1970s that deinstitutionalisation began, due to the criticism within and outside of psychiatry (Mayes & Horwitz, 2005). Indeed, this deinstitutionalisation led to the discharge of many individuals who had been detained within institutions for many years (Grob, 1995).

Important point

! This shift in thinking within the field of psychiatry led to a change in the discipline being concerned with insanity, to one that is primarily concerned with normality (Horwitz, 2002).

Evidently, it was during the 1970s that the discipline sought more explicitly to position itself as a 'science', and this marked a shift in thinking which began to marginalise non-scientific approaches, including psychoanalysis (Shorter, 1997). This was marked most significantly by the rise in psychopharmacology, which promoted psychiatry as a branch of medicine (Porter, 2002). Thus, by the end of the twentieth century, the big 'P' in psychiatry was Prozac, and medical treatments in psychiatry flourished; however, in other areas of mental health, talking therapies still prevail (Shorter, 1997). For a helpful overview of the history of psychiatric hospitals and the institutionalisation of the mentally ill, refer to Bone and Marchant (2016). We invite you now to try the activity in the box below before you proceed with the chapter.

Activity
It is useful to carefully consider the history of mental health constructs that you might intend to study, as they are not ahistorical entities. Thus, take time to trace the history of a mental health disorder of interest (e.g., ASD). Consider the following questions: • When was this mental health construct first considered a 'disorder'? • How did the mental health construct come to be? • Who were the key players or scholars/clinicians involved in developing understandings of this mental health construct? • What historical perspectives shaped the meaning(s) of the mental health construct? • How has the meaning(s) of the mental health construct changed over time?

Psychiatric Determinants of Normal Behaviour

The historical changes and shifts in thinking have had a profound effect in how normal behaviour is currently classified. Indeed, notions of normality stand as the benchmark against which pathology could be measured. Historically, the discipline of psychiatry has provided the boundaries for normality and abnormality, while simultaneously defining who is and who is not eligible for services. Arguably, though, constructs such as 'normal' and 'mental disorder' are fluid and changeable, with no possibility of fixing the boundaries (Frances and Nardo 2013). Additionally, the very constructions of normality and abnormality can be conceived of as possible only when comparing the object of study to something else (Davis, 1995). Further, the very boundaries of normality are historically, culturally, socially, and economically bound (O'Reilly & Lester, 2016).

The focus by some psychologists, psychiatrists, and other health care professionals is therefore on the identification and treatment of individuals whose functioning is seen to be out of the 'normal' range. Indeed, the very view that human life can be measured against a benchmark of normality is a prevailing view in society. Such a perspective is embedded within traditional theories of child development and shaped what has come to be defined as a 'normally functioning adult'. For example, if a child fails to meet one or more developmental milestones, they are considered to be 'abnormally developing', with such a view being particularly prevalent in Western cultures. The focus therefore for many psychologists, psychiatrists, and other mental health professionals is on the identification and treatment of those individuals who are seen to be outside of the 'normal' range (O'Dell & Brownlow, 2015).

Important point

! When an individual is considered to have an illness, especially if that is an illness of the mind, their diagnosis is contingent upon what counts as 'normal' behaviour.

It is important to recognise that the boundaries of what constitutes normal and abnormal behaviour have shifted over time. Most often, what we understand to be normal or abnormal behaviour has been defined by biomedical explanations (Thomas & Bracken, 2004). It is through this understanding that the notion of an 'illness' and the 'mental health patient' have been constructed (Griffiths, 2001), with a focus on clusters of 'symptoms' that are grouped together to form a diagnosis (Walker, 2006). However, critical writers have argued that such a conceptualisation of normality has a negative impact on those deemed ill, with many different critiques proffered to reconceptualise how we might understand mental health differently. Such critiques have aimed to destabilise psychiatric knowledge and practice as ahistorical entities, and have opened alternatives and more empowering understandings of practice and ways of dealing with mental distress (Georgaca, 2012).

The Classification of a Mental Disorder

To fully appreciate a more critical perspective of mental distress, it is necessary to understand the mechanisms used in psychiatry and psychology to biomedically conceptualise the boundaries of normality and abnormality. Although there have been several critical arguments presented, in recent times classification systems have been developed to categorise the nature of mental illness and guide professional practice. It is these classification systems that are used by professionals to determine whether a person is mentally ill or not in an arguably more 'scientific' way.

Initially, the purpose of early classification systems was to statistically track rates of occurrence and pursue preventative medicine. Over time, a classification system was circulated and included a list of diseases and their causes. This system was eventually referred to as the *International Classification of Diseases* (ICD), which, alongside the *Diagnostic and Statistical Manual of Mental Disorders* (DSM), are now readily accepted as the two core toolkits for defining normality and abnormality. In contemporary mental health, then, it is these two classification systems that legitimise the pathology of certain conditions. Notably, these two systems do have some differences. ICD tends to be internationally recognised as a diagnostic tool for clinical purposes, as well as for epidemiology and health management, and has been specifically used to categorise and record diseases (World Health Organization, 2014). In fact, it was only with the publication of the sixth edition that mental health disorders were included in the ICD. However, DSM was constructed specifically for categorising mental disorders.

Interestingly, earlier versions of the classification systems had very few mental disorders listed. Prior to the Second World War, the DSM had only seven categories of mental disorder (American Psychiatric Association, 2013):

1. Mania
2. Monomania
3. Paresis
4. Melancholia
5. Dementia
6. Epilepsy
7. Dipsomania

This rather short list stands in contrast to modern classification systems where there is a significantly longer list of categories of disorder—a list that has gradually grown and changed over time. Some of the disorders posited on it have been more controversial than others.

For example: In earlier conceptions of DSM, homosexuality was considered to be a mental disorder which required treatment, and this included electroconvulsive therapy. However, there was a drive to make DSM more consistent with ICD and due to political pressure the status of homosexuality was changed in 1980, which triggered a paradigm shift in how society viewed mental illness. (Mayes & Horwitz, 2005)

For example: A contemporary controversy continues regarding the existence of ADHD as a mental disorder, with some saying that this reflects a 'naughty child' and poor parental discipline, and others more clinically conceptualising it as a mental health condition.

As aforementioned, the classification systems of mental disorders have a biomedical foundation, and for the DSM this is a consequence of its historical context (Lafrance & McKenzie-Mohr, 2013). There have been some key criticisms of this perspective, however, and these are outlined in Table 1.1.

The boundaries of normality and abnormality defined by these systems have been under constant review, resulting in several revisions over the last few decades. The most recently updated version of DSM (i.e., DSM-5), for instance, remains controversial. In fact, concerns regarding the validity and reliability of the categorisation system within the DSM-5 have been raised.

Table 1.1 Key criticisms of classification systems

Criticism	Description
Views illness as objective	The biomedical approach to mental health and mental illness assumes that the condition is an objective reality, residing within the ill person. However, the illness tends to be fluid and flexible and so is the response from society.
It is not value free	The classification systems have been critiqued with the argument that the DSM is an atheoretical document that is not value free (Caplan, 1995). In other words, the classification and categorisation of mental disorders by virtue of the category makes judgements about those classified.
An assumption of universality	The classification systems have an underpinning assumption that mental disorders have biochemical and psychological causes that are universal (Crowe, 2000). Such a universal position on mental disorders assigns fault and blame with the individual and excludes any possibility that the cause may be a response to external events.

For example: There have been changes in understanding childhood mental disorders with a newer classification in line with new scientific research and this has been heavily critiqued. (see, e.g., Timimi, 2008)

Some scholars have argued that the contemporary DSM, which moved to be more sensitive to psychiatric diagnostic processes, has resulted in limited specificity (Frances & Nardo, 2013). Indeed, it has even been argued by some that the ongoing changes to DSM have consequently led to the *pool of normality* shrinking to *a mere puddle* (Wykes & Callard, 2010, p. 302). We suggest you now try the activity in the box below to encourage you to think about the conceptualisation of normality.

Activity

There is some controversy regarding the ways in which normality and abnormality are conceptualised. Before you go any further with the book, it is useful to reflect on your own point of view and be clear about your own thoughts about diagnostic categories. Take some time now to write a brief reflective statement about what you think. To support and build this, we recommend you read:

- Canguilhem, G. (1989). *The normal and the pathological*. Brooklyn, NY: Zone Books.
- Davis, L. J. (1995). *Enforcing normalcy: Disability, deafness and the body*. New York, NY: Verso.
- Timimi, S. (2008). Child psychiatry and its relationship to the pharmaceutical industry: Theoretical and practical issues. *Advances in Psychiatric Treatment, 14*, 3–9.
- Wykes, T., & Callard, F. (2010). Diagnosis, diagnosis, diagnosis: Towards DSM-5. *Journal of Mental Health, 19(4)*, 301–304.

A Brief Introduction to Autism Spectrum Disorder

Any study of ASD should be contextualised against the broader historical backdrop of mental illness more generally. ASD is currently considered to be a neurodevelopmental condition and is formally classified as a mental disorder in psychiatry by both DSM-5 and ICD-10. To this point, in the chapter we have provided you with a brief history of mental illness and given you an overview of the two core classification systems that categorise disorders more generally. While Chap. 2 gives a more comprehensive description of ASD and the process of diagnosis, we very briefly introduce you to the condition here.

We are using the term ASD in this book due to the contemporary preference noted in DSM-5. However, it is important to recognise that in its history there have been a range of labels used to describe these individuals, including:

- Autism
- Classic autism
- High-functioning autism
- Pervasive developmental disorder
- Asperger syndrome
- Rett syndrome
- Autistic disorder

Notably, the term 'autism' was a condition first described by Leo Kanner in 1943 and this was followed in 1944 by a description of Asperger's by Hans Asperger to describe children with similar characteristics. It was, however, Lorna Wing (1981) who coined the term 'autistic spectrum disorder' and who classified a 'triad of impairments', which are outlined in Table 1.2.

Within clinical circles, it is now consensus that ASD is a complex neurodevelopmental condition, which presents with difficulties in daily

Table 1.2 Triad of impairments (Wing, 1981, 1996)

Impairment	Description
Social interaction	These individuals are shown to have trouble in a social situation and to be impaired in reciprocal social interaction.
Communication	These individuals are shown to have difficulty in communicating with others, in terms of speech and language skills and in reading the intonation and so forth of others.
Rigidity	These individuals are shown to have repetitive patterns of behaviour and a rigid style of thinking.

functioning (Karim, Ali, & O'Reilly, 2014). ASD, is defined behaviourally and the individual is clinically judged as demonstrating specific behavioural impairments across the triad (Baird et al., 2003). In modern mental health services, diagnostic criteria and classification systems, such as the ICD-10 and DSM-5, are considered crucial in determining the presence of ASD, particularly as there is no definitive test.

Most significantly has been the rise in prevalence of ASD diagnoses across the globe (Bailey, 2008). The reasons for this are contested and complex. Whilst it could reflect a genuine rise in incidence rates, it equally may reflect the evolving developing diagnostic criteria and improvements in public awareness (Williams et al., 2006). Alternatively, some critical theorists argue that the rise in prevalence may reflect broader socio-economic changes that are resulting in an ongoing broadening of the parameters of what is considered 'abnormal' (Timimi et al., 2011).

Questions about classifying Autism Spectrum Disorder as a mental disorder

By definition, ASD is a mental disorder; its very emergence as a category is dependent on psychiatric approaches to diagnosis and classification. However, more recently, a broader range of voices have emerged about ASD, and the term has begun to take on a wider set of meanings, many of which are less overtly 'negative' than might be implied by the psychiatric approach. Hence, although ASD is classified by both ICD-10 and DSM-5 as a 'mental disorder', and thus is commonly viewed as a disability in society, this perspective has been challenged in the disability literature, the mental health literature, and by autistic communities themselves.

When considering whether ASD is a disability or mental disorder, it is important to raise questions regarding what constitutes a disability, what makes any definition valid, and the function such labels have in society (O'Reilly, Lester, & Karim, 2015). In the context of ASD, making a claim that the condition is not a disability is contentious (Nauert, 2011). Typically, ASD is positioned within a deficit framework; yet, the construction of the autistic identity is complex and fluid (Lester & Paulus, 2012; Lester, Karim, & O'Reilly, 2015). Furthermore, individuals with

ASD and their families must engage in daily negotiations of what constitutes normal or autistic behaviour (Lester & O'Reilly, 2016).

There are some individuals who themselves are diagnosed with ASD who challenge the ideas that they have a mental disorder. In fact, there is a group of individuals, which refer to themselves as 'Aspies', who were diagnosed with Asperger Syndrome (before it was removed from DSM-5 somewhat controversially) and celebrate their individuality and the strengths associated with their diagnosis, whilst problematising the 'neurotypical' world they are part of. Evidently, therefore, there are individuals in society who embrace ASD as part of their identity (Baker, 2011) and actively oppose the search for a cure (Brownlow, 2010). Notably, this is not a universally held view by all who are diagnosed. There is also evidence from research that some individuals, and their family members, find the condition disabling and the effects stressful (Huws & Jones, 2008). These individuals tend to favour the development of interventions and may actively seek a cure (Bagatell, 2010).

Critical Perspectives in the Field of ASD

Clearly, there are tensions and diverse viewpoints regarding how ASD is classified. In the clinical field, however, ASD is very much viewed as a mental health disorder and this condition has been framed in an objectivist, positivist, and realist framework. These three concepts are closely related and are defined next:

Objectivist – a belief that *objective* approaches to creating knowledge are more valid than *subjective experience*.

Positivist – a belief that the most valid knowledge is that which can be *scientifically verified* (i.e., by collecting real-world measurements and testing hypotheses using these).

Realist – a belief that there is a 'real world' that exists independently from the observer, and that therefore the use of positivist research approaches will ultimately generate an independent, objective, accurate, and neutral single account of this world. This contrasts with beliefs that knowledge is always *constructed* by the observer within some kind of personal, social, and cultural context.

Such a framing has important implications for the ways in which ASD is viewed in society and how researchers undertake research projects to investigate it. To date and reflecting psychiatry's current orientation as a 'scientific discipline', most work on ASD has adopted the aforementioned beliefs. This is reflected by the great abundance of quantitative and statistical work on the diagnosis, including in relation to language. In turn, such work has strong relationships with a 'medicalised' view on ASD. From this perspective, any disability is viewed as a permanent, biological impairment, and individuals who cannot be 'fixed' by modern medicine are constructed as deficient (Gilson & DePoy, 2015). This medicalisation promotes the reduction of certain elements of disability to medically recognisable phenomena (Grue, 2011).

However, as we have argued earlier in the chapter, it is necessary when undertaking research with individuals with ASD to critically consider the situated (i.e., the relationship between what is known and the values and history of the 'knower') and therefore contextual nature of constructions of ASD (Nadesan, 2005), while also bearing in mind the financial and social consequences of being constructed as disabled (Lester & O'Reilly, 2016). There are a range of critical approaches to ASD, and this is not a 'critical ASD book' per se. However, as noted earlier, conversation and discourse analysis approaches start from a different socially oriented perspective on language to the quantitative, individually focused approaches that pervade research on ASD. Hence, the authors will also explicate and disentangle some of the critical theoretical perspectives, methodological approaches, and philosophical perspectives on the nature of ASD knowledge that critique the prevailing biomedical perspectives that dominate the evidence base in this field.

The Critical Turn to Language

The recognition of the power of language and labels is not new, with Foucault (1965) being a prominent figure challenging the coercion and power held by psychiatry. Before we consider this issue of labels and language further, we invite you to reflect on the power of language, and try the activity in the box below.

Activity

We will all be aware of pejorative terms that can be used in society to describe those diagnosed with mental disorders. The negative concepts can have a strong impact on those individuals who experience such language.

- Write down negative terms that have been used to describe individuals diagnosed with mental disorders.
- When you have completed your list, write down as many positive ways in which these populations are described.

We would imagine that your list of negative terms is longer than your list of positive ones.

While there is a plethora of negative terms associated with mental illness, there are also those who have oriented to mental health disorders in positive ways. For instance, as previously noted, Aspies have taken up and 'reclaimed' diagnostic language to conceptualise their identity positively. In this way, what some may presume is language evidencing pathology is re-appropriated within a positive framework. Across both positive and negative uses of labels, there is an underlying assumption that language functions to create certain identities. These identities are ones that carry consequence, whether intended or not, and thus bring with them political weight. How one comes to be named is indeed impactful, as language always plays a crucial role in our understanding of self and others.

The turn to language, often referred to as the 'discursive turn' in the social sciences and in other disciplines, reflects challenges to the traditional paradigmatic perspectives on the world. Through this turn to language, language became viewed as constitutive of social life, constructing minds and identities and is simply representing inner mental workings of the mind. Within this linguistic paradigm, there has been a call to pay more attention to how language creates reality. For the field of mental health where social scientific research and viewpoints are often applied, the implication of this turn to language is that clinicians no longer should consider mental illness as a discovered truth but instead as something socially constructed (Walker, 2006).

Aims and Objectives of the Book

This book aims to provide foundational understandings to those interested in doing discourse and conversation analysis research in ASD. More specifically, our book takes a social constructionist position to examine ASD—a perspective that assumes that psychiatric categories are made real in and through written and spoken language. We therefore aim to move the reader away from viewing ASD as an objective truth, and reintroduce the importance of language in constructing and deconstructing the assumptions that surround diagnosis and treatment of ASD (Fee, 2000).

Discourse and conversation analysis are methodological approaches that are growing in popularity and are employed by researchers, practitioners, and students from a range of disciplines including psychiatry, psychology, social science, education, and social care. Thus, throughout this book, we introduce you to the different types of discourse analysis and conversation analysis work related to ASD. We position these analytical approaches as useful language-focused approaches to the study of ASD.

The book is pedagogical in style and is thus filled with activities, 'important point' boxes, and useful tips to help you with your research project. A practical book focused on ASD research challenges is important as ASD is the most researched childhood disorder (Wolff, 2004) and is a condition that is increasing in prevalence (Bailey, 2008). Notably, the majority of research in ASD has been positioned within a discourse of disease and deficit, and methods to investigate it have generally been undertaken through a quantitative, 'scientific' lens, which evades the institutional history of ASD and has important implications for its construction as a mental disorder.

Structure of the Book

The book is structured to provide practical guidance and advice for doing discourse or conversation analysis research in ASD. The emphasis on practical skills is facilitated by the range of contributions from clinical practitioners who showcase the relevance of these methodological approaches to clinical practice and the potential implications for contributions to the evidence base. To illustrate the usefulness of these approaches and provide practical tips for engaging in this kind of work, the book is organised into two core parts.

The first part of the book focuses on providing pedagogical advice for the reader, illustrating the process of undertaking this kind of research. The contributors provide examples from their own work to illustrate exactly how to do this type of work in relation to ASD, and the chapters are filled with activity boxes, important points, and vignettes.

The second part of the book focuses on providing empirical examples from the field of ASD research and discourse analysis and conversation analysis studies to illuminate the processes in practices. The contributors provide real-world research examples to highlight how they conducted their own work in practice and to showcase the value of the findings.

The book is organised to guide the reader through some of the core decisions to be made in discourse and conversation analysis research in ASD, as well as illuminating some of the related theoretical discussions. Each chapter attends to the practical implications and recommendations for clinical practice and other areas such as education and social work. This practical focus is promoted by a practical highlights box at the end of each chapter along with additional recommended reading lists. There is also a glossary at the end of the book to explain some of the core terms used throughout the book. We provide an overview here of each of the chapters for ease of reference.

Abstracts

The book is made up of 13 chapters. As we noted earlier, in the first part of the book, these are designed to teach you about ASD and the social and interactional research approaches such as conversation analysis and discourse analysis. In the second part of the book, the chapters serve as empirical examples in the field to show you how it has been done by scholars in the field. Next, we list a summary of each chapter so you can see the main focus of each of them.

Chapter 2

Autism spectrum disorders (ASDs) are a group of neurodevelopmental conditions that have similar characteristics and thus categorised under the same rubric. Consequently, they can present very differently and the addition of further co-existing problems complicates this picture. While ASD was until recently described as having a triad of impairments, with problems in the development of social skills, communication impairments, and a lack of flexibility in thinking, in newer classifications, the social and communication dimensions are now conceptualised together. In this chapter, Karim provides an overview of ASD and particularly the impact that communication difficulties create for these individuals. Individuals with ASD experience multiple intrinsically linked challenges in their social interactions due to problems with expressive, receptive, and paralinguistic communication. In the chapter, Karim explores the role of research around communication in individuals with ASD, particularly on Conversation Analysis (CA) and Discourse Analysis (DA) approaches, and the benefits that have been demonstrated in previous studies in this area.

Chapter 3

In this chapter, O'Reilly and Lester highlight how a social constructionist perspective shapes the way in which analysts might employ discourse analysis for the study of ASD. Specifically, they divide this chapter into three sections, each building upon the other. First, O'Reilly and Lester offer a general overview of social constructionism, specifically highlighting how the linguistic turn shaped how scholars have come to view and ultimately study language. They point to some of the essential principles that undergird a social constructionist research agenda. The discussion of social constructionism lays the foundation for a more applied consideration of the usefulness of discourse analysis approaches to the study of language, and more specifically ASD. Thus, second, they highlight the usefulness of approaching the study of childhood mental health, specifically autism, from a variety of discourse perspectives. Finally, they discuss how social constructionist and discourse analysis perspectives inform the study of autism. In doing so, the varied ways in which ASD, as a construct, might be defined, as well as how various interactions can and have been studied from these particular epistemological and analytical lenses. Throughout, case examples that illustrate the key points are offered.

Chapter 4

In this chapter, Lester et al. provide important information about the distinction between researcher-generated and naturally occurring data. Many discursive approaches including conversation analysis and discursive psychology prefer to use naturally occurring data and the rationale for this will be outlined in the chapter. However, it is recognised that collecting naturally occurring data is challenging and therefore the authors provide information about those challenges and pose some potential solutions. This chapter includes guest contributions from active researchers, including PhD students, practitioners, and academics, all of whom utilise naturally occurring data in their work.

Chapter 5

A powerful application of conversation analysis (CA) is to re-examine features of verbal communication diagnostically associated with ASD (e.g., apparent problems with conversation, echolalia, idiosyncratic language). In this data-driven tutorial chapter, Muskett draws on his experiences as an academic psychologist and clinical speech and language therapist to lead the reader through the following questions. First, how do we undertake CA with ASD data, and with what methodological assumptions? Second, what are the broad theoretical implications of the kinds of findings that are generated when CA is used in this way? And finally, how might these findings be applied to underpin real-world practice across a range of clinical, educational, and social care contexts?

Chapter 6

In this chapter, Brownlow et al. seek to explore the positioning of individuals with autism within clinical consultation sessions. They draw upon the previous work of Edley (2001) in applying the principles of critical discursive psychology to a section of data drawn from a clinical consultation session. In doing this, they use the data to illustrate how the method of analysis works in practice. The chapter explores issues of power, dominant repertoires, positioning and ideological dilemmas operating within the therapeutic context. Discussion of the strengths and limitations of the method of data analysis are considered, in addition to implications for researchers using the method.

Chapter 7

In this chapter, Dickerson and Robins outline the way in which examining body movement, gaze and gesture, and their sequential placement can facilitate a better understanding of interactions where a child with an ASD has limited productive language ability. Specifically, the chapter demonstrates the way in which drawing on the principles of conversation analysis in the careful analysis of video recordings can reveal intricacies and competencies that might otherwise be easily missed. The chapter starts by outlining the practical and ethical considerations that should inform data collection and then illustrates the sorts of discoveries that can emerge when careful attention is paid, not simply to spoken communication in isolation—but to embodied communication in context.

Chapter 8

Smart and Denman provide invaluable guidance for research students and early career researchers on how to get the most out of their supervisory experience when developing a discursive project examining ASD. Based on their own experiences as supervisor and supervisee, they draw out how students and supervisors can make the most from the resources they have access to, the types of projects that might be produced, and reveal similarities and differences between the student and supervisor's perspectives. Finally, they draw attention to key 'learning thresholds' that students might experience when using a discursive approach, leading to students feeling lost, particularly around conducting analysis and integrating methodological and applied assumptions. They consider techniques for getting through these moments and achieving successful completion of the research project.

Chapter 9

In this chapter, interactions between four clinicians and a man who has ASD accompanied by an Learning Difficulties (LD), and who is detained on a Forensic Learning Disability ward in a secure psychiatric hospital, are analysed. The peculiar context of engaging patients who have not themselves initiated the rehabilitative process is explored, since this has a bearing on the nature of the interactions. Dobbinson demonstrates how the four clinicians each approach talk with Malcolm, the service user, according to their own styles of working, although all orientate to a variety of common interactional issues. Reflections from two of the clinicians illustrate the variety of perspectives which inform different clinicians' practice. Nevertheless, Dobbinson ultimately stresses the importance of good communication and consistency of approaches within clinical teams when working with ASD patients.

Chapter 10

This study investigates various ways verbally fluent children with autism spectrum disorder (ASD) respond to questions about emotions on the ADOS-II (Autism Diagnostic and Observation Schedule). Specifically, Stickle et al. examine the children's *I don't know* (IDK) utterances as responsive to these emotion questions, questions designed to tap into the children's capacity for abstract thinking. Findings reveal that the children's use of IDK is not haphazard or disorderly but rather reveal four distinct interactional patterns. Stickle et al. also document clinicians' formulations of questions that seem to create difficulty for children diagnosed with ASD to respond and clinicians' practice that work to encourage the production of valid responses from the children. Overall, this research broadens our understanding of the abilities of children given the diagnosis of autism that lie outside of what is officially being tested.

Chapter 11

In this chapter, Mohamed Zain and colleagues provide an account of formulaic and repetitive language produced by a preschool-aged Malay-speaking child with mild ASD. Using conversation analysis, they consider the functions of a repetitive expression, *apa tu* ('what's that'), that was used frequently by the child across two 30-minute dyadic play sessions. By positioning the analyses against existing ASD-relevant findings about interactions involving English-speaking participants, the authors reflect upon the possibilities offered by CA for cross-linguistic research about diagnosed individuals.

Chapter 12

In this chapter, Rendle-Short demonstrates how conversation analysis advances our understanding of the interactional difficulties faced by children who have diagnoses of Asperger's syndrome (DSM-IV). Micro-analyses of individual cases allow the conversation analysis researcher to delve into the detail of interaction, encouraging meticulous explication of central interactional concerns such as action formation, turn taking, sequence organisation, recipient design and repair. The focus of this chapter is on different contexts in which a child might pause or be silent and how such pauses are responded to. The first context is an intra-turn pause that occurs within a turn of talk that is introducing a new topic of conversation. The second context is an inter-turn pause or gap that occurs between turns at talk, following a question. The final context builds on the previous two sections by analysing a small video interaction of two children engaged in a spontaneous activity, with the pause occurring after the other child has fallen down because she has hurt herself. It highlights how conversation analysis can be used as a pedagogic tool for teachers, parents, and children. By teaching children the principles of the methodology, they become their own mini-analysts, empowering them to better understand their interactional contributions and how such contributions might be responded to.

Chapter 13

In this chapter, Bottema-Beutel and colleagues explore the ways in which adolescents with ASD experience self and others through the creation of a fictional storyboard. They describe two main spheres of relating to others: the sphere of character action and the sphere of audience reception. Characters' inner lives are enacted through descriptions of their actions and activities. In addition, they show that the adolescents with ASD in the study take into account the audience of their fictional narrative by relying on genre conventions to ensure that their story will be appreciated as such by an audience. Analyses suggest that it is not the experience of self or other per se that is at risk in individuals with ASD, but the flexibility with which self and other are brought into being. Too rigid adherence to explicit sociocultural conventions can result in enactments of the other that are not aligned with the interlocutors' enactment of similar others. Given these findings, the authors argue that it is not only mental state language into which we should look for insights about a sense of self and relatedness displayed by individuals with ASD. Autistic understanding of self and others is enactive and sociocultural; it is rooted in action and convention.

Understanding the Transcription System

You will note as you go through the chapters in this book that most of the discourse analytic approaches and conversation analysis rely on a specific system of transcription. This is because the transcription system is designed to represent the words and other verbal utterances (e.g., pauses) made by the speakers in the exact way that they were uttered in the original conversational turns. However, for those who are unfamiliar with the details of this transcription system, it can seem quite daunting and confusing, so we introduce the key symbols and debates here in this introduction chapter.

In qualitative research, there have been debates about the role of transcription, but despite that there is some general agreement that transcription is an active process (Lapadat, 2000). We recognise that not all forms of discourse analysis have widely accepted conventions for transcription, but conversation analysis does and some forms of discourse analysis borrow this for their work. For conversation analysis, the Jefferson system was specifically designed to reflect the analytic stance of the approach (Jefferson, 2004). For this approach, transcription is viewed as a core analytic activity and the first step in developing a better understanding of the communicative processes (Roberts & Robinson, 2004). The system used is a highly detailed representative system of symbols and the conventions are designed to intuitively build on familiar forms of literary notation (Hepburn & Bolden, 2013). Many of the authors contributing to this text utilise the Jefferson system.

Important point

! It is important not to underestimate how long it takes to produce a Jefferson transcript. Estimates have suggested that it takes approximately 1 hour to transcribe 1 minute of data (Roberts & Robinson, 2004).

Most of the extracts that you will see throughout the chapters have these different symbols to show *how* things were said by the speakers. To help familiarise you with some of the more common symbols used in this book, we outline the basic Jefferson system in Table 1.3 representing symbols taken from Jefferson (2004) and Hepburn and Bolden (2013).

Table 1.3 Jefferson transcription symbols

Symbol	Explanation
(.)	When a full stop symbol is surrounded by round brackets it shows that a micro pause happened in the conversation.
(0.2)	A number inside brackets denotes a timed pause. This is a pause long enough to time and subsequently show in transcription.
[]	Square brackets denote a point where overlapping speech occurs. This shows the exact point in the turn where the overlap or interruption happened.
> <	Arrows surrounding talk like these show that the pace of the speech has speeded up.
< >	Arrows in this direction show that the pace of the speech has slowed down.
()	When rounded brackets are shown with nothing between them, it shows that the words could not be heard by the analyst.
((note here))	Double brackets are used to present a note to the reader; for example, it may show that the speaker nods their head, or shakes their hand, or other non-verbal behaviour.
Under	If the word or part of a word is underlined, it denotes a raise in volume or emphasis.
↑	An upward arrow means there is a rise in intonation.
↓	A downward arrow means there is a drop in intonation.
→	An arrow like this denotes a particular sentence of interest to the analyst.
CAPITALS	Where capital letters appear it denotes that something was said loudly or even shouted.
=	The equal sign represents latched speech, a continuation of talk.
:::	Colons appear to represent elongated speech, a stretched sound.

Summary

In this chapter, we offered a general overview to this edited volume. In doing so, we provided a very brief introduction to the history of mental illness, as well as the varying ways in which normality and abnormality have been constructed. We also provided a critical discussion of language used to characterize and construct the very meanings of 'mental health' and 'mental illness'. We also included a listing of the chapter abstracts, which are included in this volume. Finally, we provided a discussion of the commonly used transcription system found throughout the book. We summarise the key points from this introduction chapter in the box below.

Summary of practical highlights

1. The history of mental illness makes visible how the very meanings of 'mental illness' and 'mental distress' are culturally and historically specific.
2. What counts as 'normal' is typically understood in comparison to constructions of 'abnormality'.
3. Language used to describe mental health disorders and people experiencing mental distress has often been pejorative, with such language having consequence. Indeed, the language used to describe people is consequential.
4. A specialised transcription system, the Jefferson Method, is used to represent both what is said and how things are said.

References

American Psychiatric Association. (2013). *Diagnostic and statistical manual of mental disorders* (5th ed.). Washington, DC: American Psychiatric Association.

Bailey, A. J. (2008). Autism as a global challenge. *Autism Research, 1*, 145–146.

Baird, G., Cass, H., & Slonims, V. (2003). Diagnosis of autism. *British Medical Journal, 327*(7413), 488–493.

Baker, D. (2011). *The politics of neurodiversity: Why public policy matters*. Boulder, CO: Lynne Rienner.

Bone, C., & Marchant, N. (2016). A critical discursive perspective on psychiatric hospitals. In M. O'Reilly & J. N. Lester (Eds.), *The Palgrave handbook of adult mental health: Discourse and conversation studies* (pp. 459–478). Basingstoke: Palgrave Macmillan.

Brownlow, C. (2010). Presenting the self: Negotiating a label of autism. *Journal of Intellectual and Developmental Disability, 35*(1), 14–21.

Clay, R. M. (1966). *The Mediaeval hospitals of England*. London: Frank Cass.

Davis, L. J. (1995). *Enforcing normalcy: Disability, deafness and the body*. New York: Verso.

Fee, D. (2000). The broken dialogue: Mental illness as discourse and experience. In D. Fee (Ed.), *Pathology and the postmodern: Mental illness as discourse and experience* (pp. 1–17). London: Sage.

Foucault, M. (1965). *Madness and civilization: A history of insanity in an age of reason*. New York: Vintage books.

Frances, A., & Nardo, J. (2013). ICD-11 should not repeat the mistakes made by DSM-5. *The British Journal of Psychiatry, 203*, 1–2.

Georgaca, E. (2012). Discourse analytic research on mental distress: A critical overview. *Journal of Mental Health*. doi:10.3109/09638237.2012.734648

Gilson, S., & DePoy, E. (2015). Child mental health: A discourse community. In M. O'Reilly & J. N. Lester (Eds.), *The Palgrave handbook of child mental health: Discourse and conversation studies* (pp. 117–138). Basingstoke: Palgrave Macmillan.

Griffiths, L. (2001). Categorising to exclude: The discursive construction of cases in community mental health teams. *Sociology of Health and Illness, 23*(5), 678–700.

Grob, G. (1995). The paradox of deinstitutionalisation. *Society, 32*, 51–59.

Grue, J. (2011). Discourse analysis and disability: Some topics and issues. *Discourse and Society, 22*(5), 532–546.

Hepburn, A., & Bolden, G. (2013). The conversation analytic approach to transcription. In J. Sidnell & T. Stivers (Eds.), *The Handbook of conversation analysis* (pp. 57–76). West Sussex: Blackwell Publishing, Ltd.

Horwitz, A. (2002). *Creating mental illness*. Chicago: University of Chicago Press.

Huws, C., & Jones, R. (2008). Diagnosis, disclosure, and having autism: An interpretative phenomenological analysis of the perceptions of young people with autism. *Journal of Intellectual and Developmental Disability, 33*(2), 99–107.

Jefferson, G. (2004). Glossary of transcript symbols with an introduction. In G. Lerner (Ed.), *Conversation analysis: Studies from the first generation*. Amsterdam: John Benjamins Publishing company.

Karim, K., Ali, A., & O'Reilly, M. (2014). *A practical guide to mental health problems in children with autistic spectrum disorder: "It's not just their autism"!* London: Jessica Kingsley Publishers.

Lafrance, M., & McKenzie-Mohr, S. (2013). The DSM and its lure of legitimacy. *Feminism and Psychology, 23*(1), 119–140.

Lester, J., Karim, K., & O'Reilly, M. (2015). "Autism itself actually isn't a disability": The ideological dilemmas of negotiating a 'normal' versus 'abnormal' autistic identity. *Communication & Medicine, 11*(2), 139–152.

Lester, J., & O'Reilly, M. (2016). Repositioning disability in the discourse of our time: A study of the everyday lives of children with autism. In G. Noblit & W. Pink (Eds.), *Education, equity, and economy* (pp. 133–160). New York: Springer.

Lester, J., & Paulus, T. (2012). Performative acts of autism. *Discourse and Society, 23*(3), 259–273.

Mayes, R., & Horwitz, A. (2005). DSM-III and the revolution in the classification of mental illness. *Journal of the History of the Behavioural Sciences, 41*(3), 249–267.

Nadesan, M. H. (2005). *Constructing autism: Unraveling the 'truth' and understanding the social.* New York: Routledge.

Nauert, R. (2011). Viewing autism as difference, not just a disability. Retrieved from PsychCentral http://psychcentral.com/news/2011/11/04/viewing-autism-as-difference-not-just-disability/31091.html

O'Dell, L., & Brownlow, C. (2015). Normative development and the autistic child. In M. O'Reilly & J. N. Lester (Eds.), *The Palgrave handbook of child mental health: Discourse and conversation studies* (pp. 296–310). Basingstoke: Palgrave Macmillan.

O'Reilly, M., Karim, K., & Lester, J. (2015). Should Autism be classified as a mental illness/disability? Evidence from empirical work. In M. O'Reilly & J. Lester (Eds.), *The Palgrave handbook of child mental health: Discourse and conversation studies* (pp. 252–271). Basingstoke: Palgrave Macmillan.

O'Reilly, M., & Lester, J. (2016). Introduction: The social construction of normality and pathology. In M. O'Reilly & J. Lester (Eds.), *The Palgrave handbook of adult mental health: Discourse and conversation studies* (pp. 1–20). Basingstoke: Palgrave Macmillan.

Porter, R. (1997). *The greatest benefit to mankind: A medical history of humanity from antiquity to the present.* London: Harper Collins Publishers.

Porter, R. (2002). *Madness: A brief history.* Oxford: Oxford University Press.

Roberts, F., & Robinson, J. (2004). Interobserver agreement on first-stage conversation analytic transcription. *Health Communication Research, 30*(3), 376–410.

Russell, J. B. (1972). *Witchcraft in the Middle Ages.* Ithaca, NY: Cornell University Press.

Shorter, E. (1997). *A history of psychiatry: From the era of the asylum to the age of Prozac.* New York: John Wiley and Sons.

Sigerist, H. E. (1951). *A history of medicine. Primitive and archaic medicine.* New York: Oxford University Press.

Thomas, P., & Bracken, P. (2004). Critical psychiatry in practice. *Advances in Psychiatric Treatment, 10,* 361–370.

Timimi, S. (2008). Child psychiatry and its relationship to the pharmaceutical industry: Theoretical and practical issues. *Advances in Psychiatric Treatment, 14,* 3–9.

Walker, M. (2006). The social construction of mental illness and its implication for the recovery model. *International Journal of Psychosocial Rehabilitation, 10*(1), 71–87.

Williams, J. G., Higgins, J. P., & Brayne, C. E. (2006). Systematic review of prevalence studies of autism spectrum disorders. *Archives of Disease in Childhood, 91*(1), 8–15.

Wing, L. (1981). Language, social and cognitive impairments in autism and severe mental retardation. *Journal of Autism and Developmental Disorders, 11*(1), 31–44.

Wing, L. (1996). *The autistic spectrum.* London: Constable and Company Ltd.

Wolff, S. (2004). The history of autism. *European Child and Adolescent Psychiatry, 13*(4), 201–208.

World Health Organization (WHO). (2014). International Classification of Diseases (ICD). Retrieved from http://www.who.int/classifications/icd/en/

Wykes, T., & Callard, F. (2010). Diagnosis, diagnosis, diagnosis: Towards DSM-5. *Journal of Mental Health, 19*(4), 301–304.

Recommended Reading

Broderick, A. A., & Ne'eman, A. (2008). Autism as metaphor: Narrative and counter narrative. *International Journal of Inclusive Education, 12*(5–6), 459–476.

Nadesan, M. H. (2005). *Constructing autism: Unraveling the 'truth' and understanding the social.* New York: Routledge.

Michelle O'Reilly is a senior lecturer at the University of Leicester (Greenwood Institute of Child Health) and a Research Consultant with Leicestershire Partnership NHS Trust. Michelle's research interests are broadly in the areas of child mental health, family therapy, and the sociology of health and illness. Furthermore, she is a qualitative methodologist who has written extensively about theory, methods, and ethics. Michelle has published many journal articles and books in her areas of interest, recently co-editing two handbooks (child mental health and adult mental health) for Palgrave, as well as a book for Sage on interviewing children and young people for research. For more details, please consult http://www2.le.ac.uk/departments/psychology/ppl/michelleOReilly/index.

Jessica Nina Lester is an Associate Professor of inquiry methodology at Indiana University, USA. She teaches research methods courses, including discourse analysis, with much of her research focused on the study and development of qualitative methodologies and methods. Her research is situated within discourse studies and disability studies, with a particular focus on education and mental health contexts. She has also published books related to qualitative methodologies and research practices, including *An introduction to educational research: Connecting methods to practice* with Chad Lochmiller. In the area of mental health, Jessica co-edited two handbooks focused on mental health and discourse and conversation analysis. For more details, please consult http://portal.education.indiana.edu/ProfilePlaceHolder/tabid/6210/Default.aspx?u=jnlester and http://www2.le.ac.uk/departments/psychology/research/child-mental-health/cara-1/bio2.

Tom Muskett is a Senior Lecturer in psychology at Leeds Beckett University, the UK. Tom's professional background is in speech and language therapy. He has worked in clinical and educational roles with children with diagnoses of autism and their families and previously led a clinical training programme at the University of Sheffield, the UK. Informed by his experiences in these roles, Tom's teaching and research aims to explore how children's 'development' and 'disorder' can be rethought methodologically, socially, and politically. For more details, please see http://www.leedsbeckett.ac.uk/staff/dr-thomas-muskett/.

Part I

Practical Steps for Doing DA and CA Research in ASD

2

Autism Spectrum Disorder: An Introduction

Khalid Karim

Learning Objectives

By the end of this chapter, you will be able to:

* Recognise why doing research in ASD is useful.
* Describe ASD.
* Identify the history of the condition.
* Differentiate the different terminology to describe ASD.
* Recognise the ways in which ASD is diagnosed and classified.
* Evaluate the aetiology of ASD.
* Describe the core components of ASD and the gender differences.
* Appraise the usefulness of discourse and conversation studies in the field.

K. Karim (✉)
University of Leicester and Leicestershire Partnership Trust, Leicester, UK

© The Author(s) 2017
M. O'Reilly et al. (eds.), *A Practical Guide to Social Interaction Research in Autism Spectrum Disorders*, The Language of Mental Health,
https://doi.org/10.1057/978-1-137-59236-1_2

Introduction

Over the last few years, there has been increasing interest in the condition that is referred to as autism spectrum disorder (henceforth, ASD). Not too long ago this problem was thought to be rare, with literature in the mid-twentieth century claiming it occurred in only 1 in every 10,000 children. We now appreciate that the condition is much more common, occurring in up to 1 in every 100 children. Despite this apparent increase in ASD, there remains considerable controversy around many facets of the disorder. This is particularly regarding the diagnostic criteria and the lack of a definitive test which can categorically confirm its presence in an individual. Consequently, it has been argued that the existence of the condition has been greatly exaggerated (Timimi, 2011), while others claim that it is just an alternative way of viewing the world (Beardon & Worton, 2011).

Against this background, the subsequent increase in research has been dramatic and there are numerous opportunities to explore different aspects of ASD which have not been addressed to any great degree. It should be acknowledged that while this condition can superficially appear quite straightforward, in reality it is a complex collection of problems. The interaction between these problems can cause considerable impairments and affects how an individual functions within the world. Consequently, when working with or researching individuals with ASD, a thorough understanding of the condition is essential. The focus of this chapter is to provide you with some basic knowledge. It is important that you have a good appreciation of the spectrum of the condition, the criteria for diagnosis, and the range of symptoms and behaviours before you begin any research in this area. This chapter is a good starting point.

Why Study ASD?

There has been enormous coverage in the media and substantial literature published on ASD. This condition has gone from relative obscurity to one that dominates many of the discourses on language, behaviour, and learning disabilities, and has generated substantial interest in multiple disciplines. The nature of ASD impacts upon areas as diverse as education, health, social care, the voluntary sector, and even economics. In the UK, this condition has also generated so much momentum that it is the only mental health condition which has its own statute: the Autism Act (2009). This may reflect the experience of individuals and families who struggled to get help.

Important point

! There is a very active research field around ASD internationally
• covering the biological, physiological, psychological, educational, and therapeutic aspects of this condition, but it remains a poorly understood disorder.

While there has been significant research into the biological and psychological components together with diagnostic process, it is acknowledged that research into viable treatments or management options for both adults and children remains fairly limited, resulting in a lack of clarity on how to help these individuals. Even the terminology has undergone revisions, with ASD becoming the latest favoured term. Somewhat problematically, there remains no clear consensus on the exact symptom profile of ASD. The interpretation of certain elements, such as what characterises social impairment, for example, has led to significant diagnostic variability. In addition, this also may partly explain the increase in diagnosis.

While there are many opportunities for research into ASD, the area around social interaction and language provides an interesting platform for new ideas and therefore provides a chance for further research. Added to this, working with individuals with ASD can be rewarding and fascinating. It therefore makes sense to pursue this perspective further. Before you go any further with the chapter, it is worth reflecting upon your own views on this, which is encouraged in the activity in Box 2.1.

Box 2.1 Activity on reflection

Activity

You have elected to read this book for a reason and it is probably because of your interest in ASD and/or the potential of discursive approaches for its study. Before continuing with the chapter, take some time to reflect on why you think undertaking research in the area of ASD is useful and your own motivations for doing so.

What Is ASD?

Before looking at ASD in any depth, it is essential to develop a broader overview. ASD is considered a neurodevelopmental condition which affects approximately 1% of the population (Karim, Ali, & O'Reilly, 2014).

> The term 'neurodevelopmental' disorder, which includes ASD, describes the situation in which the brain has developed and matured in a way that fundamentally changes its reaction to the outside world and therefore affects certain behaviours and emotional responses.

These neurodevelopmental disorders can present from a young age. In addition to ASD, this term also includes other conditions such as attention deficit hyperactivity disorder (ADHD) and tic disorders.

There has been a significant increase in the diagnosis of ASD in recent years although this issue tends to court controversy. As noted earlier in the chapter, in the middle of the twentieth century, this condition was only described in 1 in every 10,000 children, and although it is now generally accepted to be 1 in every 100, some estimates have gone down to 1 in every 60 children. Generally, 1% is the currently accepted prevalence rate (Brugha et al., 2011). Although it is described as a condition primarily of the male gender, ASD is increasingly being recognised in females.

> **Important point**
>
> ! Females with ASD remain poorly recognised and are diagnosed less
> • frequently than would be expected.

While many aspects of ASD affect the thinking and behaviour of an individual, there are some key features which make up the condition. In considering the spectrum of ASD, it is important to recognise that there is a wide range of presentations under the diagnostic label. Some with ASD have associated learning disabilities, while others can be extraordinarily gifted intellectually, but they share some common features:

- Difficulties in social interactions
- Difficulties in communication
- Difficulties in social imagination

The recent DSM-5 has outlined two core domains of ASD: (1) social interaction domain, to include deficits in language and social communication, and (2) behavioural domain, in terms of repetitive or restrictive behaviours (American Psychiatric Association, 2013).

There are several other associated difficulties which occur in ASD but the three core components should be present for diagnosis. When looking at these key features, it may be useful to first appreciate that the diagnosis of ASD covers a wide range of biologically different disorders which present in a similar way. When our understanding of the genetic and physiological processes underpinning the symptoms increases, we may consider the area very differently. However, at present this has little effect on how the individual receives help.

One of the difficulties faced by professionals when deciding whether someone has ASD is the lack of any definitive diagnostic tool. There is no single genetic test or imaging technology that can be used to categorically give the diagnosis, like there is for physical conditions such as diabetes. Instead, a diagnosis for ASD is made through careful elicitation of the individual's problems and their developmental difficulties. Observing the person's interaction is an essential part of the diagnostic process but this adds a significant degree of subjectivity on the part of the observer/diagnosing clinician. In other words, clinicians professionally judge the individual as displaying behavioural impairments across the three core features (Muskett, Body, & Perkins, 2013). There are structured interview schedules such as:

- the ADI (Autism Diagnostic Inventory)
- the DISCO (Diagnostic Interview for Social and Communication Disorders)

These are used together with observational tools such as the ADOS (Autism Diagnostic Observation Schedule).

Important point
> ❗ These schedules and observational tools are still dependent upon the skills of the clinician.

Normality and Pathology

When considering the concept of ASD, it is useful to reflect on what constitutes normality and disorders. Central to this is our conceptualisation of 'impairment'. In practice, the range of difficulties that an individual with ASD experiences can be extremely variable. Therefore, when assessing any of the key features, there must be in some form of internal comparison with our own individual understanding of what is a normal ability for a certain age. Consequently, this will lead to a judgement regarding whether the person involved is affected to such a degree that they can be considered in having an impairment. This can be assessed against many domains of a life: social, emotional, academic, and work. For some children, for example, this is obvious, particularly if they are nonverbal, as the difference between them and their peers is very clear. For others, who may be intellectually very able, this difference may only become apparent in certain circumstances.

For example: A highly regarded academic who is very good in a discrete research area, but when promoted to a position which requires people management, they find this stressful and overwhelming as they struggle to relate to others, due to their limited interpersonal skills.

Before this is discussed further look at the activity in Box 2.2.

Impairments clearly vary depending upon the setting so the tendency is to review how somebody is functioning in a range of contexts, commonly home, school/work, and their social and leisure activities. Even in the general population, people have a range of social and communication abilities without being autistic and some people are better at this than others. Therefore, the boundary between what can be considered normal and not-normal is quite fluid and can be open to interpretation (O'Dell & Brownlow, 2015).

For example: Some individuals may be socially awkward due to intense shyness, but this does not necessarily make them autistic.

Conceptually, this reflects the notion that normality is socially constructed and what is deemed as acceptable in contemporary culture is defined by the language and agreed perceptions of what is viewed as normal. As with all social constructs, this is a fluid concept and can partially explain the increasing prevalence of this condition. This fluidity of the concept is important when conducting research in this area, as the very boundaries related to ASD are blurred, and there are some questions regarding its classification as a mental disorder or disability (Lester, Karim, & O'Reilly, 2015; O'Reilly, Karim, & Lester, 2015). Parents of children with ASD and those with ASD may, however, use the construct as a way of explaining their behaviours, although some position ASD as a gift (Lester & Paulus, 2012). Thus, the very evaluation of normality involves some level of measurement based on socially constructed patterns of normal distribution (Sarangi, 2001).

Box 2.2 Reflecting on normality

Activity

The notion of normality can mean different things, and before you read further into the chapter, try to write down your own definition of normality now.

For example: Some people with ASD resist the notion that they are impaired and argue instead that it is the environment and social situations around them that are problematic. One such group use the term 'Aspies' to describe themselves.

This view is consistent with the idea of neurodiversity. 'Neurodiversity' is itself a controversial term which constructs atypical neurodevelopment, such as ASD, as simply normal human difference (Jaarsma & Welin, 2011). Jaarsma and Welin argued that this movement of neurological diversity arose in the 1990s and advocates argued that the common view of neurological diversity as pathological is inappropriate and such differences should be respected.

History of ASD

Understanding the history of ASD is useful in contextualising the research literature and our current perception of this condition. Clearly, ASD has been prevalent throughout human development, and some writers have described the inherited component of ASD as being essential for human progress. The thinking style commonly seen in ASD can promote a different way of seeing the world and, together with a degree of obsessionality, can be beneficial when pursuing new ideas.

For example: Some writers have argued from an evolutionary perspective that if the ASD gene was eliminated, people would have spent their time socialising and chatting in the cave and the progress we have made would not have been achieved. (Grandin, 2008)

Important point

! Think about all of the original thinkers and how they have
• generated their ideas for progress; how hard was it for them to challenge contemporary thinking and how much work did they have to put into developing these ideas?

Generally, the first descriptions of ASD are attributed to two people:

1. Leo Kanner (1943)
2. Hans Asperger (1944)

Leo Kanner was an Austrian-born child psychiatrist who described a certain pattern of behaviour in 11 children in an early seminal paper. These children were described as displaying a strong need for sameness, aloneness, and obsessive behaviour, and he was keen to distinguish these children from the prevailing concept of schizophrenia which was used to label many individuals at that time.

At approximately the same time, Hans Asperger, a German paediatrician described four boys who displayed certain characteristics, including difficulties in forming friendships, limited empathy skills, absorption in particular special interests, conversations that tended to be one-sided, and clumsy movements. In many ways, these children displayed similar characteristics, but with Asperger's work being published in German, it failed to reach the mainstream literature until its translation and promotion after his death.

While Kanner did attribute some aspects of ASD to parenting, he felt that it could not be fully explained by this factor alone, but there have been other interpretations of children's behaviour which are now generally discredited. During the twentieth century, there was a very strong promotion of the psychodynamic causes of child mental health disorders. Although the effect of parents on their children's development is still acknowledged as critical for normal development, it can also influence the development of certain psychiatric conditions. In 1967, Bettleheim proposed that if a mother's style of parenting was particularly cold and unavailable, it caused the child to emotionally shut down and this was a cause of ASD. He referred to this as the 'refrigerator mother' and a whole generation of mothers felt to blame for their child's problems. This view has now been generally discredited; however, with the development of genetics research, this has the potential to re-invoke these feelings of guilt.

Following a re-examination of the work of Hans Asperger, Lorna Wing (a British child psychiatrist) and Judith Gould (a British clinical psychologist) coined the term 'autistic spectrum disorder' (Wing,

---

Box 2.3 Triad of impairments

Triad of impairments

1. Impairments in reciprocal social interaction. In other words, these individuals have problems in social situations.
2. Qualitative impairments in communication. In other words, these individuals have problems with speech, conversing with others, and in communicating generally.
3. Restricted, repetitive, and stereotyped patterns of behaviour, interests, and activities. In other words, these individuals tend to be rigid in their thinking.

1981a; Wing & Gould, 1979). In this description, Wing (1981a, 1981b) described the classic 'triad of impairments' (described in Box 2.3) which is now so closely associated with ASD, although it should be noted that DSM-5 has reconfigured this into two domains (described earlier). Additionally, as the field continues to undergo development and in the latest diagnostic manual (DSM-5) the name has been changed to 'autism spectrum disorder' (American Psychiatric Association, 2013).

Terminology and Diagnostic Classification of ASD

When making a diagnosis of ASD, the pattern of behaviours and symptoms are expected to meet an internationally agreed set of criteria. In clinical settings, the diagnosis and classification of ASD rests on one of two classification systems, that is, the *International Classification of Diseases* (ICD) and the *Diagnostic and Statistical Manual of Mental Disorders* (DSM) and these are outlined in Table 2.1.

It is clear that the terminology around ASD has evolved as the conceptualisation of the disorder has matured. Understanding the changes in terminology and the changes in diagnostic classification systems is essential when interpreting the available literature. The clearest example of these changes is the use of Asperger's syndrome. This first appeared in diagnostic manuals in the 1990s, but with the latest revision of the DSM

Table 2.1 DSM and ICD

Classification system	Description
ICD	The ICD is the World Health Organization's classification of diseases. The ICD is a standardised diagnostic tool for health management and clinical settings, as well as for epidemiology. Its function is to monitor the general health of different populations and to monitor incidence and prevalence of particular diseases. Like the DSM, ICD has undergone several revisions and overtime the classification of diseases has changed. Its latest revision is currently in process, with an anticipated release date of 2018 for ICD-11. Within the ICD (version 10) there is a subsection which is the classification of mental and behavioural disorders and it is this section that deals with ASD, which is listed under pervasive developmental disorders.
DSM	The DSM is now in its fifth edition (DSM-5) and is a standardised manual of mental disorders that is utilised by mental health professionals in the USA and in many other countries. The purpose of the DSM was to that all mental health disciplines could draw upon this for classifying the full range of mental disorders and each of these is outlined with appropriate criteria for judgement. Thus, the DSM outlines the diagnostic classification, the criteria for categorisation and the descriptive text to illustrate what the disorder is. The DSM has a rich and interesting history and there used to be limited agreement as to what mental disorders were and which ones ought to be included. Over time the DSM has grown and changed, with the initial first version only containing seven disorders.

produced by the American Psychiatric Association (DSM-5), the term has been removed and replaced with autism spectrum disorder.

> **Important point**
>
> ! Note that the new inception is autism spectrum disorder, not the
> • original autis**tic** spectrum disorder.

Interestingly, the diagnostic manuals never included the term 'autistic spectrum disorder', favouring autism, or Asperger's as the appropriate terms, but this usage was commonly cited in the research literature. What has confused the matter somewhat for parents, researchers, and clinicians alike is the range of different terms that have been available to describe ASD and these include:

- ASD;
- Asperger's syndrome;
- pervasive developmental disorder;
- autistic spectrum disorder;
- autism spectrum disorder;
- high-functioning ASD.

While there are some subtle differences between these terms, which tend to reflect the child's development of language and other skills, in reality they all reflect the same core characteristics of a central condition. This has now been synthesised as ASD in the latest version of the diagnostic manual (DSM-5) and Asperger's syndrome has been controversially removed.

Important point

! When reviewing the literature, pay close attention to the varying
• terms used to describe ASD and also the changing criteria (this will be important for your search terms).

Core Elements of ASD

For many years, the core features of ASD were divided up into the classical triad of impairments (refer back to Box 2.3). This arbitrarily separated communication difficulties and social difficulties. However, there is increased recognition that these individual attributes are intertwined, as shown in the latest version of DSM-5. Due to the constant evolution in our understanding of ASD, these elements do undergo revision and differences in the terminology used to explain the impairments.

Box 2.4 Activity on defining the characteristics of ASD

Activity

Have a look at some of the literature that defines ASD and see if you can make a list of the key characteristics of the condition. You can then compare your list to the descriptions provided next.

For simplicity, the core elements of ASD can be divided into specific areas:

1. Difficulties in social interaction
2. Difficulties in communication
3. Difficulties in social imagination
4. Difficulties in thinking
5. Sensory and processing problems

Before the chapter is continued, try the activity suggested in Box 2.4.

Difficulties in Social Interaction

Recognising the difficulties that an individual with ASD can have in understanding and recognising the unwritten social rules which govern our daily interactions is a central feature of this condition. In general, the ways in which we learn how to socially engage with each other is an innate process and while it is guided by parents, carers, and other influential figures, it is something that tends to occur naturally. These social 'rules' can be affected by many factors such as, age, gender and culture, and problematically for someone with ASD they are not applied uniformly. An understanding of how to behave in a particular circumstance or social setting is predominately a subconsious process. It is unclear why those with ASD struggle to learn these rules and for those working or living with these individuals it can be difficult to know how much the person with ASD understands these unwritten social conventions.

Difficulties in social interaction can vary from one person with ASD to another quite considerably. While some do not understand even the basic social rules, others apply them in different ways in different circumstances.

> *For example:* Consider Sacks' (1992) argument that talk is often sequentially organised into adjacency pairs; that is, a question is followed by an answer. A person with ASD may not provide the expected answer as the expectation of a response is a social convention which is innately recognised.

There is considerable variation in the general population in terms of social competencies, with some individuals being clearly more socially able than others. However, for those with ASD, it is the extent of these difficulties and whether it causes an impairment which defines the issue. As would be expected, this can be highly subjective on whether any individual is socially able or not.

> *For example:* An apparently simply unwritten rule is when to hug someone. Some children with ASD may not hug (or even go near) another person even when they are a close relative such as parent or grandparent, others however may hug everyone they meet, even strangers. This is a reflection that some do not know that hugging is a social convention, some are aware that it is, but do not want to do so, while others are unaware of the social boundaries of the action.

> *For example:* The concept of personal space is an indefinable social rule that has considerable variation depending on who we are with. Some individuals with ASD have a particularly large personal space while others struggle to recognise this issue and also the effect it is having on the other person (discomfort).

Recognising our effect on other people and the emotional response from others is a social skill which develops as we mature. This emotional understanding is taken from the way someone acts and looks and also what they can say in response. The unfortunate impact of having difficulties in social interaction is that these individuals may find it challenging to form social relationships with peers. Children with ASD may find it difficult to form or sustain friendships and this can lead to isolation. Additionally, they may behave in ways that are detrimental to social relationships.

For example: Telling the teacher when another child has behaved badly, which in turn may create hostility.

Obviously, this shows connection between social abilities and communication, which is now explored.

Difficulties in Communication

Separating communication from social interaction is entirely artificial but may be useful to consider the different components of communication separately in the context of ASD. There are clear difficulties for individuals with ASD with verbal and nonverbal communication but also in their expressive and receptive abilities:

• Expressive—the way in which they express what they mean through language or gestures
• Receptive—the way in which they take in and understand what is communicated to them.

In older classifications of ASD, there had to be communication difficulties before the age of three years present in the child (except for Asperger's), but in more recent conceptions this is less clearly specified. Some individuals with ASD never develop much of a vocabulary (if any at all), while others are extremely verbal, but use this in a socially awkward way.

For example: An individual with ASD may speak at length fluently on a given topic of their choice, but does not actively listen to any response the recipient may voice and thus the conversation is very one-sided.

The reciprocal nature of communication obviously has a significant social element, and the context of the communication is essential to it being fully understood. In other words, both speakers are constantly engaged in social interaction, which an individual with ASD may find difficult. Subsequently this can lead to misunderstandings and frustrations when they are not being fully understood. The receptive element of communication, and the ability to take meaning from what is being said to the individual with ASD is an element of communication which can cause problems. Understanding linked concepts which are common in natural discourse can be problematic as only a partial meaning may be extracted from the dialogue by those individuals. Sometimes this can be a problem of understanding the actual words spoken, while in others it can be a problem of the time taken to process what has been said.

In typical face-to-face social discourse, it is the nonverbal communication which provides the context in which the verbal communication is delivered. It can also be the sole method of communication in some situations, with facial expressions and eye gaze being particularly important. Many individuals with ASD struggle to understand aspects of nonverbal communication, with difficulties in reading the body language of others. There can be limited use of gestures, and facial expressions such as smiling which can make the interaction feel quite stilted.

For example: Individuals with ASD when speaking to another are unlikely to make eye contact, and may even face in a different direction. This can affect their reading of other's nonverbal communication and in their expression of their own nonverbal communication.

Difficulties in Social Imagination

When using the term 'social imagination', it is important to differentiate this from simply 'imagination'. It is clear that some individuals with ASD have a very limited innate imagination and therefore find any sort of imaginary play or similar activities difficult, while others can have a very vivid and at times fantastical imagination. This compares with the use of social imagination, which is the ability to imagine oneself in a particular situation and can be used by individuals to form the basis with which to predict particular outcomes.

For example: Many individuals with ASD can get anxious about change that may happen in the future. This could be a change of school for children, going on holiday, or even trying a different food. Envisioning how one might manage such a situation while pulling on past experiences is an essential component of social imagination.

Connected to social imagination is an area of thinking, often referred to as 'theory of mind' (Baron-Cohen, 1989). Theory of mind is a useful concept, as it explains how we interact with those around us by our appreciation of a situation from their perspective, that is, 'putting yourself in their shoes'. This element of cognition is an essential part of social development, and difficulties in this area can lead to misunderstandings of the thoughts and behaviours of others.

> *For example:* The ability to lie is partially dependent on theory of mind, as deception requires an understanding of the beliefs of the other person.

Interestingly, this ability to deceive can be variable with some individuals having a total inability to lie, while others just lie very badly. In normal development, this ability develops throughout childhood and this may explain why some children with ASD have developed it to a greater or lesser degree.

> *For example:* A child with chocolate all around his or her face claiming he or she did not eat the chocolate bar demonstrates an inability to deceive in a convincing way.

Difficulties in Thinking

In addition to the theory of mind, which is a well-established aspect of ASD, there are other typical features commonly found in these individuals. They tend to have a quite rigid thinking style, often struggling to see the nuances and subtleties within situations and ideas. This style of thinking can also lead to situations being seen as either 'black or white' with little understanding that most areas of life are more ambiguous or abstract. Together with this type of thinking, can be an associated inflexibility in actions and behaviour, *and a rigid* adherence to routines. This can give additional difficulties with any type of change as individuals with ASD tend to want to follow the same patterns of daily activities. Interestingly, in some people with ASD, they can manage major changes such as going on holiday, but find minor changes such as a different morning cereal more distressing. This reaction can be difficult for those around the individual to understand, which can lead to further distress. Furthermore, there is considerable variation between individuals. A further difficulty in thinking style is the tendency to become obsessed with a certain idea or activity. This can lead to the development of 'special interests' in which the individual becomes fixated on one particularly narrow area, but this interest can often become overwhelming. This obsessive thinking can dominate the individual's world and lead to greater difficulties and additional mental health problems (Karim et al., 2014).

> *For example:* An adult diagnosed with ASD who is high functioning goes to work every day by the exact same route. On a day when there is a road block and the road is impassable, this creates a high level of anxiety for that individual.

Sensory and Processing Problems

It should be appreciated that our brain is constantly receiving information to all of our senses. It then takes this information and processes it to a form which we then use on a daily basis. We are unaware of most of this information as it is processed subconsciously, but if reminded can be perceived by the conscious mind.

> *For example:* A clock may be ticking in your room all day, but you only notice it if someone points it out to you.

In many people with ASD, their brain can struggle to process this information in the same way. As a consequence, they can become hypersensitive, but also hyposensitive to different sensations (defined in Table 2.2). They may become, for example, very sensitive to certain smells, tastes, certain noises, or under-sensitive to sensations.

This effect on the senses can occur in all the different sensory modalities:

- Smell
- Sight
- Taste

Table 2.2 Definitions of hypersensitivity and hyposensitivity

Sensitivity type	Description
Hypersensitivity	Hypersensitive refers to an increased or oversensitivity to the sensory environment. *For example:* Not tolerating cooking smells or gagging over certain tastes or textures of food.
Hyposensitivity	Hyposensitivity refers to a reduced or under-sensitivity to the sensory environment. *For example:* Poor sensations to pain or always feeling hungry.

- Touch
- Auditory
- Vestibular (balance)
- Proprioception (embodiment—awareness of the body)

To understand vestibular sensory processing, it may be useful to think about the sensation felt when coming off a fair ground or play park ride that spins. Those with vestibular hypersensitivity will feel extremely nauseous and may vomit, while those with hyposensitivity may come off completely unaffected, while others look dizzy. When considering proprioception, hyposensitivity is commonly seen in individuals with ASD. These individuals can struggle when they are unable to see their hand, for example, when brushing their hair or cleaning themselves on going to the toilet, as they are relying on their proprioception to tell them where their hand is.

These sensory difficulties can be further exacerbated by anxiety, but also the person coping with these problems can become anxious due to the stress of trying to filter out the sensory input. This problem can often go unrecognised and may be one of the central features in the eating problems these individuals commonly encounter.

For example: Many autistic children dislike sudden loud noises, such as fireworks, and this may be a consequence of the noise being unanticipated but also their ability to process the noise when it occurs. (Karim et al., 2014)

Interaction Between the Elements

Clearly there is a close interaction between these different elements within the interactions of those with ASD with others. When considering a specific area of impairment as so referred to by DSM-5, it can be problematic to separate the issue into component parts, and it may be better to consider these links. When considering issues such as an understanding of humour or certain uses of language, such as metaphors, this becomes particularly evident. Humour has a significant social element to its understanding, but it also can rely on language and thinking style. Some individuals with ASD for this reason find visual humour easier to understand than verbal jokes or sarcasm.

> *For example:* Consider the metaphor 'pull your socks up', intended as an encouragement. To an individual with ASD, they may take this literally and look at their socks. This is because it is verbally delivered with an intended meaning, beyond its literal meaning and is abstract.

Other Significant Influences

While the core elements of ASD are fundamental to describing individuals with these difficulties, it needs to be appreciated that there are other aspects of ASD which are also fairly common. Many of these individuals will have problems with coordination, sleep, and many have restricted eating patterns or a limited diet. Physical problems including epilepsy or bowel difficulties are quite common in this group and co-morbid mental health difficulties including attention deficit hyperactivity disorder (ADHD), anxiety disorder, or obsessive compulsive disorder (OCD) are increased in number. The prevalence of co-existing intellectual disabilities is also a significant factor in a number of individuals diagnosed with ASD. These factors complicate the diagnosis, treatment pathways, and potential research with these groups as the variation between individuals with ASD can be fairly extensive.

There is an increasing body of literature on the difficulties that individuals with neurodevelopmental problems, including ASD, have with executive functioning. Executive functioning refers to a group of cognitive processes which are involved in organising and directing other aspects of thinking and behaviour. These include working memory, mental flexibility, organisation and planning abilities, attention, problem solving, impulse control, verbal reasoning, multi-tasking, and inhibition (Chan, Shum, Toulopoulou, & Chen, 2008). In many young people with ASD, these difficulties become more apparent as they mature and they are expected to undertake tasks independently. These impairments can have a negative impact on all the other difficulties, but they can be easily missed by those working with both the adults and children.

Gender Differences

As noted earlier in the chapter, many more boys than girls are diagnosed with ASD. Consequently, the diagnostic criteria have reflected the typical male presentation of this problem, but it is increasingly recognised that there are many girls who could be diagnosed as having ASD. With a greater understanding of the diagnostic criteria, there is a recognition that girls can present with a different profile of symptoms (Nichols, 2008). In some cases, the presentation can be the same as in boys, but in others there can be important differences. They tend to be less rigid in their thinking style, less routine driven, and their interests can be more socially appropriate.

> *For example:* Girls tend to share interests that their typically developing peers have, such as a music band or television programme.

Girls also often have a best friend whose presence can mask the girl's deficits in the social arena. It is only when they become older that the ASD may become more obvious as they are having to cope with increasingly complex social environments. It is essential when working with or doing research with individuals diagnosed with ASD that girls are compared to other age-appropriate girls as this will facilitate an accurate account of the problem.

Support and Care

There is no clear treatment for those with ASD despite some of the claims made by various individuals and organisations. The problem in knowing if a treatment itself has been effective is complicated by the interplay between all of the different components of this condition but also that in young people development can be an unpredictable process.

> *For example:* Some children do not speak until much later than the developmental norm, but it is difficult to say if an intervention on an individual level has promoted language development if they start speaking or whether it would have occurred naturally.

This may be one of the reasons that there has been a relative dearth in the literature surrounding positive interventions. The main stay of helping individuals and families is a development in their understanding of the condition and dealing with particular problems that increase stress and anxiety. For most individuals with ASD, anxiety is something that is easily raised and then this can affect how they manage in their daily lives. With the increased recognition of co-existing problems (see Karim et al., 2014) in ASD, this provides another opportunity to ameliorate some problems. However, there is no single consistent way in which to help someone with ASD and any intervention needs to be tailored to their individual needs. There are a range of different interventions used with ASD, which are indicated in Table 2.3. I recommend you follow up with some additional reading around these as some of these have very limited evidence bases and some are more accepted and popular than others.

Discourse and Conversation Studies of ASD

Research into ASD is a rapidly expanding field, with all the facets of this condition being explored from multiple angles. There is extensive literature on the biological and psychological conceptualisation of this disorder, with a focus on the genetic, neurochemical, and neurophysiological aspects. The language component of ASD has been described and exam-

Table 2.3 Interventions for ASD

Intervention	Description
Speech and language therapy	Addressing language and communication difficulties commonly associated with ASD
Applied behaviour analysis (ABA)	Intensive behavioural programme (Lovaas, 1987)
Early Start Denver Model	This is a structure approach which is relationship approach using play as a tool for learning (Rogers, 2013)
Relationship development intervention (RDI)	Interaction based intervention which is a family-based behavioural treatment (Gutstein, Burgess, & Montford, 2007)
TEACCH	Treatment and Education of Autistic and Communication-Handicapped Children—a school-based intervention (Penerai, Ferrante, & Zingale, 2002).
Complementary and alternative medicines/therapies	A number of non-evidence-based alternative approaches for different aspects of ASD.
Sensory integration training	Works on the sensory processing difficulties experienced by those diagnosed with ASD.
Pharmacological interventions	This includes a range of medicines targeting particular symptoms.

ined quite extensively over the years, but there remain many nuances which have had limited research such as those around social interaction. An important contemporary focus that has begun to emerge in the field is on the social interaction between those diagnosed with ASD and their families, peers, professionals and others.

Discourse and conversation studies therefore are fairly new to the area of ASD but there is a growing body of work. Considering that communication and social interaction are core elements of this disorder, a greater understanding would be beneficial. Assumptions are often quickly made around the behaviour of those with ASD and this is often given using a neuro-typical perspective. Although we know that these individuals perceive and think about the world differently, our interpretation of their actions can often originate from the thinking style consistent with the non-autistic mind. Therefore, in-depth analysis of the interactions becomes important to either challenge or confirm these pre-existing assumptions to further understand the autistic perspective.

Considering that this type of research approach has only recently impacted upon the mainstream ASD literature (see O'Reilly, Lester, & Muskett, 2016; Sterponi & de Kirkby, 2016), there are considerable opportunities to explore new avenues of research, particularly with our changing understanding of ASD. Therefore, this provides an opportunity for those interested in this research area to make a significant contribution to a new field.

Unfortunately, I have only been able to touch on a very small part of the condition which we call ASD, and for anyone undertaking any research in this field, I would suggest reading about ASD from the different disciplinary approaches such as sociological, anthropological, psychological, medical, and so on. While at times this may seem a little turgid and impenetrable, it is nonetheless important to view ASD from different perspectives. However, one of the best ways of learning about any condition is to spend some time with the people who have this as a diagnosis. It would provide a richness which can otherwise be missing.

Summary

Undertaking research with either adults or children on the ASD spectrum using a discourse or conversation analysis approach provides a unique way to understand this complex condition. In recent years, ASD has received growing recognition and the rates of diagnosis have increased dramatically. It remains, however, a condition which has a number of controversies, particularly around what constitutes valid and reliable diagnostic criteria and there remains no single diagnostic tool. The key features of ASD remain difficult to consistently define; however, it is clear that many individuals are considerably affected by the condition. Understanding ASD requires an appreciation of the different facets that interact and other difficulties which can influence an individual on a day-to-day basis. The history of ASD has been shaped by both positive and negative influences and will continue to evolve in the future.

This chapter has been designed to help you learn about ASD and its core features. This has been done in a practical way, and a summary of the practical highlights is presented in Box 2.5.

Box 2.5 Practical highlights summary

Summary of practical highlights

1. Do not cut time when reading the literature. It is important to spend lots of time reading around the different aspects of the condition from different disciplinary perspectives. It is important to understand the controversies.
2. With ASD being such a broad spectrum of presentations and problems, it may be useful to focus the study on a narrower area of study.
3. A strong understanding of ASD is essential to inform the analysis.
4. Spend time with individuals on the ASD spectrum before undertaking any research.

References

American Psychiatric Association. (2013). *Diagnostic and statistical manual of mental disorders* (5th ed.). Washington, DC: Author.

Asperger, H. (1944). Die Autistischen Psychopathen, in Kindesalter (Autistic psychopaths in childhood. *Archiv für Psychiatrie und Nervenkrankheiten* (in German), *117*, 76–136.

Autism Act. (2009). Retrieved from http://www.legislation.gov.uk/ukpga/2009/15

Baron-Cohen, S. (1989). The autistic child's theory of mind: A case of specific developmental delay. *Journal of Child Psychology and Psychiatry, 30*(2), 285–297.

Beardon, L., & Worton, D. (Eds.). (2011). *Aspies on mental health: Speaking for ourselves.* London: JKP.

Bettelheim, B. (1967). *The empty fortress: Infantile ASD and the birth of the self.* New York: The Free Press.

Brugha, T., McManus, S., Bankart, J., Scott, F., Purdon, S., Smith, J., et al. (2011). Epidemiology of autism spectrum disorders in adults in the community in England. *Archives of General Psychiatry, 68*(5), 459–465.

Chan, R. C. K., Shum, D., Toulopoulou, T., & Chen, E. Y. H. (2008). Assessment of executive functions: Review of instruments and identification of critical issues. *Archives of Clinical Neuropsychology, 23*(2), 201–216.

Grandin, T. (2008). *The way I see it: A personal look at ASD & Asperger's.* Arlington, TX: Future Horizons.

Gutstein, S., Burgess, A., & Montfort, K. (2007). Evaluation of the Relationship Development Intervention program. *Autism, 11*(5), 397–411.

Jaarsma, P., & Welin, J. (2011). Autism as a natural human variation: Reflections on the claims of the neurodiversity movement. *Health Care Analysis, 20*(*1*), 20–30.

Kanner, L. (1943). Autistic disturbances of affective contact. *Nervous Child, 2*, 217–250.

Kanner, L. (1968). Reprint. *Acta Paedopsychiatr, 35*(4), 100–136.

Karim, K., Ali, A., & O'Reilly, M. (2014). *A practical guide to mental health problems in children with Autistic Spectrum Disorder: "It's not just their ASD"!* London: Jessica Kingsley Publishers.

Lester, J., Karim, K., & O'Reilly, M. (2015). "ASD itself actually isn't a disability": The ideological dilemmas of negotiating a 'normal' versus 'abnormal' autistic identity. *Communication & Medicine, 11*(2), 139–152.

Lester, J., & Paulus, T. (2012). Performative acts of autism. *Discourse & Society, 23*(3), 259–273.

Lovaas, I. (1987). Behavioural treatment and abnormal educational and intellectual functioning in young autistic children. *Journal of Consulting and Clinical Psychology, 5*, 3–9.

Muskett, T., Body, R., & Perkins, M. (2013). A discursive psychology critique of semantic verbal fluency assessment and its interpretation. *Theory and Psychology, 23*(2), *205–226.*

Nichols, S. (2008). *Girls growing up on the Autistic Spectrum*. London: Jessica Kingsley Publishers.

O'Dell, L., & Brownlow, C. (2015). Normative development and the autistic child. In M. O'Reilly & J. Lester (Eds.), *The Palgrave handbook of child mental health* (pp. 296–310). Basingstoke: Palgrave Macmillan.

O'Reilly, M., Karim, K., & Lester, J. (2015). Should ASD be classified as a mental illness/disability? Evidence from empirical work. In M. O'Reilly & J. Lester (Eds.), *The Palgrave handbook of child mental health* (pp. 252–271). Basingstoke: Palgrave Macmillan.

O'Reilly, M., Lester, J., & Muskett, T. (2016). Special section editorial: Discourse/conversation analysis and ASD Spectrum Disorder. *Journal of Autism and Developmental Disorders, 46*(2), 355–359.

Penerai, S., Ferrante, L., & Zingale, M. (2002). Benefits of the Treatment and Education of Autistic and Communication Handicapped Children (TEACCH) programme as compared with a non-specific approach. *Journal of Intellectual Disability Research, 46*(4), 318–327.

Rogers, S. J. (2013). Early start Denver Model. Encyclopaedia of Autism Spectrum Disorders, pp. 1034–1042. Retrieved March 20, 2017, from http://link.springer.com/referenceworkentry/10.1007%2F978-1-4419-1698-3_1821

Sacks, H. (1992). *Lectures on conversation* (Vols. I & II, edited by G. Jefferson). Oxford: Basil Blackwell

Sarangi, S. (2001). Expert and lay formulation of 'normality' in genetic counselling. *Bulletin Suisse de Linguistique Appliquee, 74*, 109–127.

Sterponi, L., & de Kirby, K. (2016). A multidimensional reappraisal of language in autism: Insights from a discourse analytic study. *Journal of Autism and Developmental Disorders, 46*(2), 394–405.

Timimi, S. (2011). (Letters) Autism is not a scientifically valid or clinically useful diagnosis. *British Medical Journal, 343*, d5105. doi:10.1136/bmj.d5105

Wing, L. (1981a). Asperger's syndrome: A clinical account. *Psychological Medicine, 11*(1), 115–129.

Wing, L. (1981b). Language, social and cognitive impairments in ASD and severe mental retardation. *Journal of Autism and Developmental Disorders, 11*(1), 31–44.

Wing, L., & Gould, J. (1979). Severe impairments of social interaction and associated abnormalities in children: Epidemiology and classification. *Journal of Autism and Developmental Disorders, 9*(1), 11–29.

Recommended Reading

Karim, K., Ali, A., & O'Reilly, M. (2014). *A practical guide to mental health problems in children with autistic spectrum disorder: "It's not just their ASD"!* London: Jessica Kingsley Publishers.

Lester, J., Karim, K., & O'Reilly, M. (2015). "ASD itself actually isn't a disability": The ideological dilemmas of negotiating a 'normal' versus 'abnormal' autistic identity. *Communication & Medicine, 11*(2), 139–152.

Nichols, S. (2008). *Girls growing up on the Autistic Spectrum*. London: Jessica Kingsley Publishers.

Wing, L., & Gould, J. (1979). Severe impairments of social interaction and associated abnormalities in children: Epidemiology and classification. *Journal of Autism and Developmental Disorders, 9*(1), 11–29.

Khalid Karim works as a consultant child and adolescent psychiatrist for Leicestershire Partnership NHS Trust and as a clinical academic at the University of Leicester in the School of Psychology. Khalid specialises in neurodevelopmental disorders and has a particular interest in autism spectrum disorder (ASD) and has recently co-authored the book *A practical guide to mental health problems in children with autistic spectrum disorder: It's not just their autism!* with Alvina Ali and Michelle O'Reilly.

3

Social Constructionism, Autism Spectrum Disorder, and the Discursive Approaches

Michelle O'Reilly and Jessica Nina Lester

Learning Objectives

By the end of this chapter, you will be able to:

- Describe the core tenets of social constructionism.
- Appreciate the value of a social constructionist approach.
- Critically appraise the usefulness of social constructionism in the study of ASD.
- Recognise some of the common different types of discursive approaches to the study of ASD.
- Evaluate the benefits and limitations of the different discursive approaches in the study of ASD.

M. O'Reilly (✉)
University of Leicester, Greenwood Institute of Child Health, Leicester, UK

J.N. Lester
Indiana University, Bloomington, IN, USA

© The Author(s) 2017
M. O'Reilly et al. (eds.), *A Practical Guide to Social Interaction Research in Autism Spectrum Disorders*, The Language of Mental Health,
https://doi.org/10.1057/978-1-137-59236-1_3

Introduction

This chapter highlights the practical ways that a social constructionist perspective shapes the way in which analysts might employ discourse analysis for the study of autism spectrum disorder (ASD). We focus on discourse analysis in this chapter, and conversation analysis is dealt with in Chap. 5 by Muskett. Specifically, we divide this chapter into three sections, each building upon the other. First, we offer a general overview of social constructionism, highlighting how the linguistic turn shaped how scholars have come to view and ultimately study language. We point to some of the essential principles that undergird a social constructionist research agenda. Our discussion of social constructionism lays the foundation for a more applied consideration of the usefulness of discourse analysis approaches to the study of language, and more specifically ASD. Then, second, we highlight the usefulness of approaching the study of mental health, specifically autism, from a variety of discursive perspectives. We provide a general description of key approaches to discourse analysis, offering examples of how these approaches are used in practice. Finally, we discuss how social constructionist and discourse analysis perspectives inform the study of ASD. In doing so, we point to the varied ways in which autism, as a construct, might be defined, as well as how various interactions can and have been studied from these particular epistemological and analytical lenses. Throughout, we provide exemplar cases.

Before you begin reading this chapter, there are some concepts and terms that we will be using that are important for your understanding of the chapter. We present these in Table 3.1 as an overview to support the reading of this chapter.

We also recommend you read Chap. 1 of O'Reilly and Kiyimba (2015), as it provides a comprehensive overview of theoretical concepts in qualitative research:

O'Reilly, M., & Kiyimba, N. (2015). *Advanced qualitative research: A guide to contemporary theoretical debates*. London: Sage.

Table 3.1 Commonly used concepts and terms in the chapter

Term/concept	Description
Ontology	Ontology refers to the ways in which reality is conceptualised and understood. Thus, ontological questions are those which have a concern with whether a social reality can exist independently from human interpretation (Ormston, Spencer, Barnard, & Snape, 2014).
Epistemology	Epistemology is concerned with knowledge. Thus, epistemology relates to the relationship between the knower and what can be known (Guba & Lincoln, 2004). Put simply, epistemology refers to theories of knowledge (Harding, 1987).
Social constructionism	Social constructionism is a general term that refers to a range of approaches with a focus on language. Broadly speaking, it is an epistemological position that challenges the conventional assumptions about individuals and society. Simply put, this position argues that knowledge is social constructed through language use.
Language as action	Viewing language as action means taking the position that speech is not composed simply of assertions but actually creates a situation; language encourages action. Put simply, words 'do' things. Some theorists propose that language is performative, and indeed most linguists argue this to be the case and hence will often use the phrase 'language as action'.
Theoretical framework	It is necessary for research to be organised in relation to a conceptual framework and this involves a process of decision making that expects the researcher to reflect on their own ontological and epistemological positions. Thus research is underpinned by a theoretical framework which in essence refers to the philosophical foundation of the work.
Discourse analysis	This is a broad umbrella term for several approaches to the analysis of talk and text. In sum, while there are different types of discourse analysis, they share the view that language performs a social action in interaction (i.e., that language is performative and not simply a reflection of mental processes).

Overview of Social Constructionism

It is important to recognise that there exists a broad range of different theoretical and epistemological frameworks to guide researchers in their work (see O'Reilly & Kiyimba, 2015, for an overview). Within these frameworks, there are many positions that focus on *language as action*. Research on ASD that utilises discourse analysis (henceforth DA) can operate from a range of theoretical positions. However, social constructionism is a common and broad theoretical framework that is frequently subscribed to by researchers working within this tradition. While the various approaches to DA work from a variety of positions, it has been argued that they generally share a broader commitment to a social constructionist viewpoint in the sense that they all see language as functional, constructive, and context-bound (Wetherell, Taylor, & Yates, 2001).

Important point

! While most take a constructionist position, we recognise that not *all* discourse analysts would describe themselves as social constructionists. Some, for instance, may claim to be social constructivists or post-structuralists.

Describing Social Constructionism

It is important to recognise that there is no single perspective of social constructionism. Rather, social constructionism is thought to be a loose assembly of a range of approaches that have been argued by Burr (2003) to include:

- Deconstructionism: A critical position in relation to the relationship between text and meaning and one that questions traditional assumptions about 'truth'
- Post-structuralism: A perspective that argues that for individuals to understand objects, it is important that one studies the object, as well as the systems of knowledge that produced the object
- Critical psychology: A psychological perspective drawing upon critical theory, which challenges the central tenets of psychology
- Discourse analysis: A contemporary approach to analysis that covers a range of sociolinguistic approaches and focuses on language

Broadly speaking, there are three types of social constructionism that have emerged in the literature, each having slightly different foci, and these Brown (1995) described and are summarised briefly in Table 3.2.

What we seek to highlight here is that 'social constructionism' is a broad and general term to describe a cluster of approaches that focus on language and that these have varied meanings. Accordingly, social constructionism cannot be considered a unified framework (Brown, 1995). In broad terms, social constructionism is an epistemological position that challenges the conventional view of fixed, measurable characteristics within people, groups, and society. This position considers social and psychological phenomena to be constituted through social and interpersonal processes (Georgaca, 2012). Although there are differences between social constructionists, there are some key assumptions of social constructionism, which Gergen (2009) outlined and are summarised in Table 3.3.

What these assumptions demonstrate is that social constructionism takes a critical position towards taken-for-granted knowledge and emphasises cultural and historical specificity (Burr, 2003). Social constructionists, then, see the human experience (including perceptions) as not being fixed or predetermined aspects of an individual but

Table 3.2 Types of social constructionism (Brown, 1995)

Type	Description
Spector and Kitsuse perspective	Spector and Kitsuse (1977) offered an American view that was concerned with a focus on a social definition of health conditions, rather than one focused on whether a health condition is 'truly' real or not.
European perspective	The European perspective on social constructionism was grounded in European postmodern theory and originated with the earlier work of Foucault. This social constructionist perspective focused on social actors, groups, and institutions, and maintained a primary concern with issues of power.
The SSK view	The Sociology of Scientific Knowledge's (SSK) perspective on social constructionism grew out of the work of Latour (1987), who advocated that the production of scientific 'fact' was indeed the result of mutually conceived actions by scientists.

Table 3.3 Assumptions of social constructionism (Gergen, 2009)

Assumption	Description
The taken-for-granted world is challenged	Social constructionism presents radical doubt about the taken-for-granted world. In other words, this perspective challenges the reality of what we often take for granted.
Knowledge is specific	It is argued that knowledge is historically, culturally, and socially specific.
Knowledge is sustained by social process	It is argued that knowledge is not fundamentally dependent upon empirical validity; rather, it is sustained by social process.
Explanations are social actions	Explanations and descriptions of phenomena are not viewed as 'neutral'; rather, they are thought to constitute social actions, and these social actions function to sustain certain patterns to the exclusion of others.

instead as mediated linguistically, culturally, and historically (O'Reilly & Kiyimba, 2015). As such, social constructionism can be viewed as an orientation to a range of research positions with similar methodological perspectives, theoretical foundations, and implications (Gubrium & Holstein, 2008).

Comparing Macro- and Micro-Social Constructionism

Typically, in the literature, macro- and micro-social constructionism have been differentiated. Gubrium and Holstein (2008) distinguished these two forms. Macro-social constructionism is broadly concerned with the role that social and linguistic structures play in shaping the social world. Researchers employing a macro-social constructionist approach tend to focus on the broader (thus more macro) discourses that circulate in society and function to generate and sustain inequality. Thus, macro-social constructionists have a broader concern with power. Micro-social constructionism is focused on the micro-structures of language, and researchers who employ this perspective tend to focus on talk, situated interaction, and local culture. Those employing a micro-social constructionist approach argue that knowledge is not static, but is instead co-constructed in the detail of the mundane interactions of everyday life. We would encourage you to reflect on your personal perspective by engaging with the activity in Box 3.1.

Box 3.1 Reflecting on the macro/micro distinction

Activity

Different approaches to DA are typically underpinned by either macro- or micro-social constructionism. It is therefore important to consider which perspective sits most comfortably with your own worldview, as this will ultimately shape the type of research you do and the approach to DA that is most suited to your own research project. Take a few moments to reflect on this and write down which position suits your research.

Box 3.2 Activity on concepts

Activity

Using a range of terms, we have introduced you to some complex terminology. We encourage you to take a moment to assemble a short glossary of the key terms. There is a glossary at the back of this book to help, and Table 3.1 presented at the beginning of the chapter. However, prior to turning to these resources, we would encourage you to create your own definitions and develop a comprehensive list of definitions of terms.

So far in this chapter, we have introduced you to many different complex terms and it can take a little while to process this information. However, these concepts are central to discursive work in ASD and so we would encourage you to take some time to reflect and think about the meaning of those terms. Try the activity in Box 3.2.

Discursive Approaches to the Study of Language

There are several approaches that you might take to carrying out a DA project. It is thus most appropriate to think about 'discourse analysis' as an umbrella term that encompasses a range of methodological perspectives aimed at studying the ways in which language produces the world. Broadly, the various approaches to DA assume that talk and text do not neutrally reflect the world; rather, language produces social realities (Jørgensen & Phillips, 2002). Discourse analysts are therefore committed to the study of talk and text and examine it in varying ways and at varying levels.

> *For example:* Attending to everyday talk versus considering abstract notions of discourse.

For the purposes of this chapter, we offer an abbreviated introduction to the most common three approaches to DA. While our description of these approaches to DA is not comprehensive, we aim to offer the 'basics' in hopes that you will then further explore the approach (or approaches) of greatest interest to you. We discuss the following approaches:

1. Traditional DA
2. Discursive psychology
3. Critical DA

In considering these three different approaches to DA, it is important to recognise that many of these approaches are closely related and that there are many other DA approaches that could be considered (Lester & O'Reilly, 2016).

Traditional DA

Grounded in the traditions of ethnomethodology and social constructionist perspectives (Potter & Wetherell, 1987), a traditional approach to DA is centred on three core concepts:

1. Interpretative repertoires
2. Subject positions
3. Ideological dilemmas

First, interpretative repertoires refer to the common sense yet contradictory ways that people talk about the world (Potter & Wetherell, 1987).

This concept has been conceived of as being a coherent way of describing something, which includes a certain set of words and expressions. Second, subject positions are often referenced when analytically considering the discursive process whereby the identity of oneself or another is positioned (Edley, 2001). Using adjectives or categories, it is assumed that a speaker positions herself and others. For instance, you may position someone as a 'single woman', thereby constructing the identity of that person in a very particular way. Third, an ideological dilemma (Billig et al., 1988) refers to the idea that everyday common knowledge is full of contradictions, with expressed beliefs and values never fully fixed.

> *For example:* A 'good mother' may evoke an ideological dilemma when talking about her life as both a 'good mother' and a 'successful professional', describing both her career goals and the significant amount of time she spends with her children.

Discursive Psychology

Discursive psychology is an approach that is informed by ethnomethodology, social constructionism and Wittgenstein's perspective on language (Edwards & Potter, 1992). Broadly, this approach to DA has historically focused on examining how psychologized constructs, such as memory or cognition, 'are produced, dealt with and made relevant by participants in and through interaction' (Hepburn & Wiggins, 2005, p. 595). More recently, researchers using discursive psychology have begun to draw upon conversation analysis, as they focus more specifically on the sequential organisation of talk.

Critical DA

Informed by the traditions of linguistics, semiotics, and other forms of DA, critical DA gives primary focus to the role of discourse in the production of power within social structures. Typically, analysts drawing upon critical DA attend to how language serves to produce, sustain, and legitimise inequities (Wooffitt, 2005). Broadly, critical DA takes up a critical orientation to the analysis and the social world and maintains a commitment to examining and critiquing dominant ideologies. Ultimately, this approach to DA seeks to incite social change (Morgan, 2010). Indeed, there are various ways in which one might carry out a critical DA project.

Important point

! Fairclough, van Dijk, and Wodak are key scholars who each offer
• unique perspectives regarding discourse and the study of power.

Using DA in Research

In selecting a DA-type approach for your study, you need to think about which one most suits your theoretical position and approach to ASD. You need to think carefully about which DA approach you plan to use for your own work and whichever one you do choose will require you to engage in much more reading beyond this chapter. We provide you with some practical tips in Box 3.3 to think about in the planning stage of your work.

Box 3.3 Research tips for a DA and ASD project

Research tips

1. As you begin thinking about and developing your DA study, it is important to keep in mind the DA is an umbrella term that encompasses a variety of perspectives to the study of language. Thus, you need to think carefully about the DA approach you plan to take and explicate the reasons for your decision.
2. Carefully describing the DA perspective, you will employ in your project is crucial, as each perspective brings with it very particular perspectives on discourse and the analysis process. Spending ample time reading about a particular DA approach is essential and well worth the effort.
3. Designing a DA research study includes the careful consideration of how you will generate a corpus of data. As you consider your phenomenon of interest, it is helpful to think about the ways in which you might build your data set in logistically reasonable and ethical ways.
4. While it is not required, it is often useful to consider using a computer-assisted qualitative data analysis software package to support you in managing your research project and analysing your data (see Lester, 2015a; Paulus & Lester, 2016, for examples).

Box 3.4 Activity to reflect on your own project

Activity

As you reflect upon your own research interests related to ASD, take a moment to consider how you might come to make sense of this diagnosis differently by orienting to it from a discursive perspective. As you do so, answer the following questions:
- What is your research topic of interest related to ASD?
- How might studying this topic from a discursive perspective shape your understanding of ASD?
- Which approach(es) to DA might you find useful for your research topic? Why?
- What type of data might you collect in such a discourse study?

It is important that you think about the research tips you have been given in Box 3.3 and consider some of the practical issues that may arise in your own work. To help you with this planning stage further, we encourage you to reflect on your study and provide you with an activity in Box 3.4.

Applications of Discursive Approaches to Mental Health

Although this chapter focuses on individuals diagnosed with ASD specifically, it is helpful to have a broader appreciation of how DA approaches have been employed to better understand mental health more generally. Although it is recognised that there are tensions around describing ASD as a disability or mental disorder (O'Reilly, Karim, & Lester, 2015), it is a condition that is classified as a mental condition medically. Traditionally, ASD has been described as a neurodevelopmental disorder whereby the individual presents with a number of difficulties in a range of areas of daily functioning and indicates impairments in some aspect of the brain/nervous system originating from a developmental cause (Karim, this volume; Karim, Ali, & O'Reilly, 2014). Notably, within the medical literature, ASD has been conceptualised as a mental disorder and is featured in the *Diagnostic and Statistical Manual of Mental Disorders*—version 5, now framed as 'autism spectrum disorder' (American Psychiatric

Association, 2013), and in the *International Classification of Diseases of mental and behavioural disorders*, version 10 (Word Health Organization, 1992). It is therefore helpful to conceptualise a broader understanding of social constructionism, language and mental health to appreciate the relevance for ASD and to consider a more critical perspective on the nature of the condition.

Social Constructionism and Mental Health

There is a great deal of research focused on mental health that has been underpinned by social constructionism (e.g., Harper, 2006; O'Reilly & Lester, 2015; O'Reilly & Lester, 2016). It is generally recognised that social constructionist work in relation to mental health began in the 1960s whereby researchers sought to examine both psychiatric and community understandings of mental illness, and predominantly focused on the impact of mental health labels (Mulvany, 2000). Arguably, social constructionism is an approach well suited to the study of mental health. The core tenet of this perspective in relation to mental health is that professional practices of diagnosis, treatment, and service provision are not based on an objective implementation of scientific practices, but instead are actually constructions that are linked to the context by social, institutional, and practical considerations (Georgaca, 2012).

Thus, the social constructionist position has been actualised through research utilising different types of DA, reflected in the turn to language in mental health. This has led to a greater recognition of the importance of language and a call for further attention regarding how language creates reality. For mental health, this means that clinicians no longer need to view mental illness as a discovered truth, but instead see it as something that is socially constructed (Walker, 2006).

Important point

❗ Discourse analysis has a lot to offer to the study of mental health and illness and is particularly useful for appreciating how the turn to language can offer a new perspective on clinical practice.

Understanding ASD from a Discursive Perspective

The everyday ways of talking about ASD have typically been situated within and informed by medical discourses, wherein autism is positioned within a deficit perspective and assumed to be an internal trait. Historically, much of the talk surrounding ASD has been grounded in cultural beliefs and assumptions related to notions of abnormality and normality (Ashby, 2010; Broderick & Ne'eman, 2008; Davis, 1995; Lester & Paulus, 2014). The medical and scientific literature focused on ASD has typically described it as a biological fact, with positivistic methodologies (e.g., experimental designs) most often used to study autism (Nadesan, 2005).

Some scholars have noted that conducting qualitative research, including DA, within a field as medicalised as ASD is quite difficult given that 'most of the language of the field assumes a shared, normative perspective' (Biklen et al., 2005, p. 14). Perhaps it is unsurprising then that much research focused on ASD has either predated or simply not taken into account the discursive turn; rather, much of this research has worked from a realist position. Consequently, scholars, such as Nadesan (2005), have argued that because research focused on ASD has drawn heavily upon the 'assumptions of the natural sciences' (p. 2), the sociocultural and political conditions that have shaped the very meaning(s) and existence of ASD have often been overlooked and/or minimised. Fundamentally, then, ASD has been understood as a 'natural' entity that exists apart from the discourses and everyday political and social conditions that have made it possible.

In contrast to medicalised perspectives, understanding ASD from a discursive perspective fundamentally shifts how the very notion of ASD is conceptualised, particularly when one commits to carrying out a social constructionist project. Rather than orienting to ASD as an ahistorical entity that exists outside of discourse, a discursive perspective results in acknowledging that it is always already negotiated and produced in everyday talk. It follows then that a researcher who views ASD from a discursive perspective can fairly assume that 'autism is a concept developed and applied, not discovered' (Biklen et al., 2005, p. 12). In making such an assumption, the researcher orients to meanings as never being guaranteed or given, but rather acknowledges that '… things [including autism] can acquire different meanings and functions in different historical contexts and situations' (Glynos & Howarth, 2008, p. 167). Thus, understanding ASD from a discursive perspective reframes the condition as being situated within a broader social history of specific disciplinary knowledge (e.g., psychiatry and many other 'helping' professions) and institutional histories that have contributed (and continue to contribute) to the very making of ASD (Rocque, 2007).

Important point

! There are many challenges to viewing ASD as a disability or as a mental disorder and there are some disability activists who construct this condition in alternative ways (for a discussion see, O'Reilly et al., 2015).

Further, taking up a discursive perspective to ASD allows you to consider the ways in which talk produced in the everyday (e.g., conversations at the market) and institutional activities (e.g., when making diagnostic assessments) function to position people and social activities in particular ways.

For example: Lester (2014) completed a discursive psychology study that illustrated how an occupational therapist's talk positioned a child's non-verbal communication as functional and indexed the child's competence. This stood in stark contrast to other social actors who discursively constructed the 'non-verbal' child's lack of verbal ability as signalling her incompetence.

Indeed, much of the discourse-related research on ASD highlights how the very notions of normal, abnormal, autistic, and non-autistic are contingent upon the everyday discourses and practices that make them possible.

As was noted above, there are many approaches to DA, which result in making sense of talk and the very meaning of discourse in varying ways. Thus, understanding ASD from a discursive perspective does not result in a single way of thinking about it; rather, it is inextricably linked to the

---

Box 3.5 Reflecting on your ASD project

Activity

As you consider your own research interests related to ASD, take a moment to consider how you might come to make sense of autism differently by orienting to it from a discursive perspective. As you do so, reflect upon the following questions:
- How might understanding autism from a discursive perspective change the way you talk about and conceptualise ASD?
- What do you view as the benefits and challenges of orienting to ASD from a discursive perspective?

---

epistemological and ontological claims that a researcher takes up when employing a certain approach to DA.

> *For example:* A researcher may carry out a critical DA project as they are particularly committed to exploring issues of power related to the diagnostic process, as well as the broader historical discourses that have shaped the meaning(s) of ASD.
>
> *For example:* In contrast to this, another researcher may be interested in examining how disabled identities are produced in everyday interactions, drawing upon discursive psychology.

Thus, it is critical to recognise that understanding ASD from a discursive perspective whilst indeed results in deconstructing the condition as a 'natural' entity, does include varying perspectives and often leads to unique research studies. To exemplify this further, we next provide examples of several discourse studies of autism but encourage you to reflect upon the following activity in Box 3.5 first.

Studying ASD from a Discursive Perspective

There is an ever-growing body of qualitative research focused on ASD (e.g., Ashby, 2010; Ashby & Causton-Theoharis, 2009; Bagatell, 2007), as well as conversation analysis research (e.g., Dobbinson, 2016;

Maynard, 2005; Stribling, Rae, & Dickerson, 2007)—some of which is showcased in this book. There is also a body of research, albeit somewhat small, that has drawn upon discursive approaches to research. Indeed, as just one example, the editors of this volume have recently published a special issue on discourse and conversation analysis in the mainstream journal *Journal of Autism and Developmental Disorders* (O'Reilly, Lester, & Muskett, 2016).

To illustrate the value and practical application of DA approaches in the study of ASD, we provide five empirical examples of discursive work in this area in Boxes 3.6, 3.7, 3.8, 3.9, and 3.10., which employ various

---

Box 3.6 Case example 1

Case example 1

For a full version of this study, please read:
- Lester, J. N. (2015). Presuming communicative competence with children with autism: A discourse analysis of the rhetoric of communication privilege. In M. O'Reilly & J. N. Lester (2015) (Eds.), *The Palgrave handbook of child mental health: Discourse and conversation studies* (pp. 441–458). Basingstoke: Palgrave Macmillan.

A good example of how DA research can provide us with a better understanding of ASD is research into communication in children diagnosed with the condition. In a recent study by Lester (2015b), research explored how parents and therapists negotiated the meaning of communication with children diagnosed with ASD who had minimal communication skills or who were non-verbal. The study examined the interactions of these children with their parents and therapists and was situated within a discursive psychology framework, informed by critical theories of disability. The research took place in a paediatric clinic in the USA, which served children with disabilities in the area. A total of 8 therapists participated as well as 12 families, which reflected 12 children aged 3–11 years, 6 fathers and 11 mothers. The data consisted of 175 hours of audio and video recordings of therapy sessions, 8 interviews with therapists and 14 with parents along with 654 pages of handwritten field notes. The findings indicated that there were two key discursive patterns which were: (1) positioning of non-verbal behaviour as explainable, and (2) the co-construction of legitimate communication. The study concluded that verbal skills are privileged in society and that this is conflated with the notion of human competence.

Box 3.7 Case example 2

Case example 2

For a full version of this study, please read:
• O'Dell, L. & Brownlow, C. (2015). Normative development and the
  autistic child. In M. O'Reilly & J. N. Lester (2015) (Eds). *The Palgrave
  handbook of child mental health: Discourse and conversation studies*
  (pp. 296–309). Basingstoke: Palgrave Macmillan.

A good example of discursive social constructionist research that has
examined the use of language is work that has explored how
language constructs normality and pathology. In a recent study,
O'Dell and Brownlow (2015) examined how children with autism are
typically put in a position of deficit. In their research, they argued
that the construction of 'normal development' operates discursively
to position some children as deviating from a norm. They explored
how ideas of the 'normal' child functions to shape our
understandings of children with autism and they interrogated the
discursive practices that construct 'normal development' to see how
children with ASD are viewed as different. In their study, O'Dell and
Brownlow argued that the very concept of 'normality' and its
measurement is framed mostly within a mental health frame and it is
through the powerful mechanism of psychiatric criteria that this is
actualised. To explore this further, the authors examined online
discussion lists over a three-month period and used critical DA to
examine the data. This identified two core themes for analysis which
were the issues surrounding definitions of abnormality and the goal
of achieving normalisation through therapy. They concluded that the
constructions of abnormal behaviour and assumptions about
normality were evidenced in the online discussion groups and they
argued that this is a reflection of the power of these discourses in the
public sphere and one that is based on a neuro-typical perspective.

---

perspectives to DA and ground their interpretations on social constructionist perspectives. In showcasing these five examples, we aim to illustrate how DA affords you the opportunity to approach your research
interest from varying perspectives while taking up the assumption that
language is performative.

Box 3.8 Case example 3

Case example 3

For a full version of this study, please read:
- Avdi, E., Griffin, C., & Brough, S. (2000). Parents' constructions of the 'problem' during assessment and diagnosis of their child for an autistic spectrum disorder. *Journal of Health Psychology, 5*(2), 241–254.

Avdi, Griffin, and Brough (2000) conducted a DA study of 11 semi-structured interviews of parents with a child with ASD, drawing upon a Foucauldian perspective. They also followed a version of Billig's (1996) approach, eventually developing thematic understandings of the broad discourses used when parents talked about their child's 'problem' (i.e., ASD). Overall, the parents primarily drew upon the discourses of normal development, medicine, and dis/ability. As parents shifted their constructions of their child from being normal to disabled, they drew upon the discourse of normal development, often comparing their child with 'abstract notions of universal developmental stages' (p. 246). They also deployed a medical discourse when talking about autism as a 'reified, clearly delineated condition' with some parents displaying ambivalence towards the notion of a 'real' diagnosis. The researchers suggested that when the parents constructed their child as an 'other', they tended to draw upon discourses of dis/ability. Interestingly, once a child was diagnosed as autistic, many parents no longer constructed their child as 'normal' as the two categories (autistic versus normal) were viewed as mutually exclusive. The researchers concluded that the parents held ambivalent and at times conflicting meanings of ASD, with deficit models of dis/ability dominating the ways in which the parents oriented to their child following his/her diagnosis.

Box 3.9 Case example 4

Case example 4

For a full version of this study, please read:
• Jones, S., & Harwood, V. (2009). Representations of autism in Australian print media. *Disability and Society, 24*(1), 5–18.
This paper is a good example of utilising Foucauldian DA (and a content analysis) to explore representations of autism in the media. Specifically, the authors illustrated how the portrayal of ASD in the Australian media was problematic, as ASD was often constructed as being dangerous, debilitating, and a tragedy. The authors noted how the media powerfully effects the way in which this condition is viewed, pointing to the Wakefield study, which reduced the publics' trust in the safety of the MMR vaccine. Specifically, the authors conducted an analysis of 1228 print media articles that were published over a three-year time frame. They coded these articles as either positive or negative. They noted that between 1999 and 2003, positive article outnumbered negative articles; however, from 2004 to 2005, the opposite was true. These more negative articles were described as focuses on the challenges of living with a child diagnosed with autism. The researchers also noted that there was relatively little helpful information related to educational resources. More particularly, the researchers argued that the media coverage of children with ASD pointed to a dual stereotype, as children with ASD were constructed as either being 'uncontrollable and aggressive' or an 'autistic savant'. They suggested that their research points to the dominance of normative medical perspective on autism and the problematic nature of such orientations.

Box 3.10 Case example 5

Case example 5

For a full version of this study, please read:
• Davidson, J. (2010). 'It cuts both ways': A relational approach to access and accommodation for autism. *Social Science & Medicine*, *70*, 305–312.
In this study, the researcher carried out a critical DA to analyse 45 autobiographies of individuals who identified as autistic. Specifically, the researcher sought to consider how the authors of the autobiographies made sense of and talked about their experience of being excluded due to socio-spatial realities. Within this study, the author took a relational approach to ASD wherein she assumed that while people who identify as autistic may want to participate in the social environment, the 'non-spectrum world' (p. 306) must do their part in understanding those who identify as autistic and facilitating their inclusion. Davidson concluded that people with ASD had heightened senses and therefore struggled with processing and navigating environments with particular sensory stimuli. She interpreted these sensory differences as leading to the unjust exclusion of people with ASD from community spaces, particularly as people within autism labels failed to make environmental accommodations. The researcher argued that many of the autobiographical accounts countered the stereotypes and medical discourses that surround autism, and offered counter-discourses that challenge dominant assumptions about ASD and the very notion of inclusion.

Summary

In this chapter, we have sought to introduce you to social constructionism. In doing so, we pointed to how which social constructionist perspectives have resulted in reconceptualising the way in which mental health disorders, such as ASD, can be theorised and studied. We also noted that social constructionism epistemologically and ontologically grounds DA approaches to research. Thus, we also provided a brief overview of seven discursive approaches to the study of language, noting also the application of such approaches to mental health and ASD more specifically. We concluded by providing you with several examples of ASD-related research conducted from varying DA perspectives.

Summary of practical highlights

1. There are many different discursive approaches to the study of ASD and the approach adopted will influence the nature of the findings of a study.
2. There have been tensions regarding classifying autism as a mental disorder and thus a social constructionist approach can help to unpack some of the rhetoric of ASD.
3. There have been a range of DA studies on ASD and practical recommendations are made for those working with people who are diagnosed the condition.
4. It is important in the study of DA that the authors of any such studies provide some indication of the implications of their work and show how the findings might be applied in practice.

References

American Psychiatric Association. (2013). *Diagnostic and statistical manual of mental disorders* (5th ed.). Washington, DC: American Psychiatric Association.

Ashby, C. E. (2010). The trouble with normal: The struggle for meaningful access for middle school students with developmental disability lab. *Disability & Society, 23*(3), 345–358.

Ashby, C. E., & Causton-Theoharis, J. N. (2009). Disqualified in the human race: A close reading of the autobiographies of individuals identified as autistic. *International Journal of Inclusive Education, 13*(5), 501–516.

Avdi, E., Griffin, C., & Brough, S. (2000). Parents' constructions of the 'problem' during assessment and diagnosis of their child for an autistic spectrum disorder. *Journal of Health Psychology, 5*(2), 241–254.

Bagatell, N. (2007). Orchestrating voices: Autism, identity and the power of discourse. *Disability & Society, 22*(4), 413–426.

Biklen, D., Attfield, R., Bissonnette, L., Blackman, L., Burke, J., Frugone, A., et al. (2005). *Autism and the myth of the person alone*. New York: New York University Press.

Billig, M. (1996). *Arguing and thinking: A rhetorical approach to social psychology*. Cambridge: Cambridge University Press.

Billig, M., Condor, S., Edwards, D., Gane, M., Middleton, D., & Radley, A. R. (1988). *Ideological dilemmas*. London: Sage.

Broderick, A. A., & Ne'eman, A. (2008). Autism as metaphor: Narrative and counter narrative. *International Journal of Inclusive Education, 12*(5-6), 459–476.

Brown, P. (1995). Naming and framing: The social construction of diagnosis and illness. *Journal of Health and Social Behavior* (Extra issue), 34–52.

Burr, V. (2003). *Social constructionism* (2nd ed.). London: Routledge.

Davidson, J. (2010). 'It cuts both ways': A relational approach to access and accommodation for autism. *Social Science & Medicine, 70*, 305–312.

Davis, L. J. (1995). *Enforcing normalcy: Disability, deafness and the body.* New York: Verso.

Dobbinson, S. (2016). Conversation with an adult with features of Autism Spectrum Disorder in Secure Forensic Care. In M. O'Reilly & J. N. Lester (Eds.), *The Palgrave handbook of adult mental health: Discourse and conversation studies* (pp. 441–458). Basingstoke: Palgrave.

Edley, N. (2001). Analysing masculinity: Interpretative repertoires, ideological dilemmas and subject positions. In M. Wetherell, S. Taylor, & S. J. Yates (Eds.), *Discourse as data: A guide for analysis* (pp. 189–228). London: Sage.

Edwards, D., & Potter, J. (1992). *Discursive psychology.* London: Sage.

Georgaca, E. (2012). Discourse analytic research on mental distress: A critical overview. *Journal of Mental Health.* doi:10.3109/09638237.2012.734648

Gergen, K. (2009). *An invitation to social constructionism* (2nd ed.). Thousand Oaks, CA: Sage.

Glynos, J., & Howarth, D. (2008). Structure, agency and power in political analysis: Beyond contextualised self-interpretations. *Political Studies Review, 6*, 155–169.

Guba, E., & Lincoln, Y. (2004). Competing paradigms in qualitative research: Theories and issues. In S. N. Hesse-Biber & P. Leavy (Eds.), *Approaches to qualitative research: A reader on theory and practice* (pp. 17–38). Oxford: Oxford University Press.

Gubrium, J., & Holstein, J. (2008). The constructionist mosaic. In J. Holstein & J. Gubrium (Eds.), *Handbook of constructionist research* (pp. 3–12). New York: Guildford.

Harding, S. (1987). Introduction: Is there a feminist method? In S. Harding (Ed.), *Feminism and methodology: Social science issues* (pp. 1–14). Bloomington: Indiana University Press.

Harper, D. (2006). Discourse analysis. In M. Slade & S. Priebe (Eds.), *Choosing methods in mental health research: Mental health research from theory to practice* (pp. 47–67). Hove: Routledge.

Hepburn, A., & Wiggins, S. (2005). Developments in discursive psychology. *Discourse & Society, 16*(5), 595–601.

Jones, S., & Harwood, V. (2009). Representations of autism in Australian print media. *Disability & Society, 24*(1), 5–18.

Jørgensen, M. W., & Phillips, L. J. (2002). *Discourse analysis as theory and method*. London: Sage.

Karim, K., Ali, A., & O'Reilly, M. (2014). *A practical guide to mental health problems in children with Autistic Spectrum Disorder: "It's not just their autism!"*. London: Jessica Kingsley Publishers.

Latour, B. (1987). *Science in action: How to follow scientists and engineers through society*. Cambridge, MA: Harvard University Press.

Lester, J., & O'Reilly, M. (2016). The history and landscape of DA and CA. In M. O'Reilly & J. Lester (Eds.), *The Palgrave handbook of adult mental health: Discourse and conversation studies* (pp. 23–44). Basingstoke: Palgrave Macmillan.

Lester, J. N. (2014). Negotiating the abnormality/normality binary: A discursive psychological approach to the study of therapeutic interactions and children with autism. *Qualitative Psychology, 1*(2), 178–193.

Lester, J. N. (2015a). Leveraging two computer-assisted qualitative data analysis software packages to support discourse analysis. In S. Hai-Jew (Ed.), *Enhancing qualitative and mixed methods research with technology* (pp. 194–209). Hershey, PA: IGI Global.

Lester, J. N. (2015b). Presuming communicative competence with children with autism: A discourse analysis of the rhetoric of communication privilege. In M. O'Reilly & J. N. Lester (Eds.), *The Palgrave handbook of child mental health: Discourse and conversation studies* (pp. 441–458). Basingstoke: Palgrave Macmillan.

Lester, J. N., & Paulus, T. M. (2014). "That teacher takes everything badly": Discursively reframing non-normative behaviors in therapy sessions. *International Journal of Qualitative Studies in Education, 27*(5), 641–666.

Maynard, D. (2005). Social actions, gestalt coherence, and designations of disability: Lessons from and about Autism. *Social Problems, 52*, 499–524.

Morgan, A. (2010, May). Discourse analysis: An overview for the neophyte researcher. *Journal of Health and Social Care Improvement, 1*, 1–7.

Mulvany, J. (2000). Disability, impairment or illness? The relevance of the social model of disability to the study of mental disorder. *Sociology of Health and Illness, 22*(5), 582–601.

Nadesan, M. H. (2005). *Constructing autism: Unraveling the 'truth' and understanding the social*. New York: Routledge.

O'Dell, L., & Brownlow, C. (2015). Normative development and the autistic child. In M. O'Reilly & J. N. Lester (Eds.), *The Palgrave handbook of child mental health: Discourse and conversation studies* (pp. 296–309). Basingstoke: Palgrave Macmillan.

O'Reilly, M., Karim, K., & Lester, J. (2015). Should Autism be classified as a mental illness/disability? Evidence from empirical work. In M. O'Reilly & J. N. Lester (Eds.), *The Palgrave handbook of child mental health: Discourse and conversation studies* (pp. 252–271). Basingstoke: Palgrave Macmillan.

O'Reilly, M., & Kiyimba, N. (2015). *Advanced qualitative research: A guide to contemporary theoretical debates.* London: Sage.

O'Reilly, M., Lester, J., & Muskett, T. (2016). Special section editorial: Discourse/conversation analysis and Autism Spectrum Disorder. *Journal of Autism and Developmental Disorders, 46*(2), 355–359.

O'Reilly, M., & Lester, J. N. (Eds.). (2015). *The Palgrave handbook of child mental health: Discourse and conversation studies.* London: Palgrave Macmillan.

O'Reilly, M., & Lester, J. N. (Eds.). (2016). *The Palgrave handbook of adult mental health: Discourse and conversation studies.* London: Palgrave Macmillan.

Ormston, R., Spencer, L., Barnard, M., & Snape, D. (2014). The foundations of qualitative research. In J. Ritchie, J. Lewis, C. McNaughton-Nicholls, & R. Ormston (Eds.), *Qualitative research practice: A guide for social science students and researchers* (pp. 1–26). London: Sage.

Paulus, T. M., & Lester, J. N. (2016). ATLAS.Ti for conversation and discourse analysis studies. *International Journal of Social Research Methodology, 19*(4), 405–428.

Potter, J., & Wetherell, M. (1987). *Discourse and social psychology.* London: Sage.

Rocque, B. (2007). *Producing personhood in children with autism.* Unpublished doctoral dissertation, University of Colorado.

Spector, M., & Kitsuse, J. (1977). *Constructing social problems.* Menlo Park, CA: Cummings.

Stribling, P., Rae, J., & Dickerson, P. (2007). Two forms of spoken repetition in a girl with autism. *International Journal of Language & Communication Disorders, 42*(4), 427–444.

Walker, M. (2006). The social construction of mental illness and its implication for the recovery model. *International Journal of Psychosocial Rehabilitation, 10*(1), 71–87.

Wetherell, M., Taylor, S., & Yates, S. (Eds.). (2001). *Discourse theory and practice: A reader*. London: Sage.

Wooffitt, R. (2005). *Conversation analysis and discourse analysis: A comparative and critical introduction*. London: Sage.

World Health Organization. (1992). *The ICD-10 classification of mental and behavioural disorders: Clinical descriptions and diagnostic guidelines*. Geneva: WHO.

Recommended Reading

Gee, J. P. (2010). *How to do discourse analysis: A tool kit*. New York: Routledge.

Jørgensen, M. W., & Phillips, L. J. (2002). *Discourse analysis as theory and method*. London: Sage.

O'Reilly, M., Lester, J., & Muskett, T. (2016). Special section editorial: Discourse/conversation analysis and Autism Spectrum Disorder. *Journal of Autism and Developmental Disorders, 46*(2), 355–359.

O'Reilly, M., & Lester, J. N. (Eds.). (2015). *The Palgrave handbook of child mental health: Discourse and conversation studies*. London: Palgrave Macmillan.

Wood, L. A., & Kroger, R. O. (2000). *Doing discourse analysis: Methods for studying action in talk and text*. Thousand Oaks, CA: Sage.

Woofit, R. (2005). *Conversation analysis and discourse analysis: A comparative and critical introduction*. London: Sage.

Michelle O'Reilly is a Senior Lecturer at the University of Leicester (Greenwood Institute of Child Health) and a research consultant with Leicestershire Partnership NHS Trust. Michelle's research interests are broadly in the areas of child mental health, family therapy, and the sociology of health and illness. Furthermore, she is a qualitative methodologist who has written extensively about theory, methods, and ethics. Michelle has published many journal articles and books in her areas of interest, recently co-editing two handbooks (*The Palgrave Handbook of Child Mental Health* and *The Palgrave Handbook of Adult Mental Health*) for Palgrave, as well as a book for Sage on interviewing children and young people for research. For more details, please consult http://www2.le.ac.uk/departments/psychology/ppl/michelleOReilly/index.

Jessica Nina Lester is an associate professor of inquiry methodology at Indiana University, the USA. She teaches research methods courses, including discourse analysis, with much of her research focused on the study and development of qualitative methodologies and methods. Her research is situated within discourse studies and disability studies, with a particular focus on education and mental health contexts. She has also published books related to qualitative methodologies and research practices, including *An introduction to educational research: Connecting methods to practice* with Chad Lochmiller. In the area of mental health, Jessica co-edited two handbooks focused on mental health and discourse and conversation analysis. For more details, please consult http://portal.education.indiana.edu/ProfilePlaceHolder/tabid/6210/Default.aspx?u=jnlester and http://www2.le.ac.uk/departments/psychology/research/child-mental-health/cara-1/bio2.

4

Naturally Occurring Data Versus Researcher-Generated Data

Jessica Nina Lester, Tom Muskett,
and Michelle O'Reilly

Learning Objectives

By the end of this chapter, you will be able to:

- Describe what naturally occurring data is and why it is used.
- Critically appraise the value of using naturally occurring data.
- Recognise the challenges of acquiring naturally occurring data in the field of ASD.
- Appreciate the ethical challenges of doing this type of research.

J.N. Lester (✉)
Indiana University, Bloomington, IN, USA

T. Muskett
Leeds Beckett University, Leeds, UK

M. O'Reilly
University of Leicester, Greenwood Institute of Child Health, Leicester, UK

© The Author(s) 2017
M. O'Reilly et al. (eds.), *A Practical Guide to Social Interaction Research in Autism Spectrum Disorders*, The Language of Mental Health,
https://doi.org/10.1057/978-1-137-59236-1_4

Introduction

This chapter highlights some of the important differences between what is referred to as naturally occurring data and researcher-generated data. In this chapter, we introduce important information about the distinction between these two different types of data and consider why some approaches, such as conversation analysis and discursive psychology, tend to favour data that is naturally occurring. Throughout the chapter, we provide a practical approach to this debate and illustrate some of the real-world applications and ethical challenges of using naturally occurring data for the study of autism spectrum disorder (ASD). For context, the latter part of the chapter includes some 'interview boxes' where guest scholars answer important questions about using naturally occurring data in their own research in relation to ASD.

Naturally Occurring Versus Researcher-Generated Data

It is important to recognise that the function of qualitative research generally is to gain an appreciation of how people's experiences are shaped by their subjective and sociocultural perspectives (Wilkinson, Joffe, & Yardley, 2004). However, whilst there is great diversity in qualitative approaches to research, there is a general consensus that there should be congruence between the theoretical level of research and the pragmatic level (O'Reilly & Kiyimba, 2015; Wimpenny & Gass, 2000). Different methodological approaches are informed by different epistemological and ontological foundations and this fundamentally influences how the research is conducted and the nature of the data collected. This is indeed the case for the choice between naturally occurring data and researcher-generated data. The choice around data type is associated with the methodological and theoretical choices that a researcher makes.

Naturally Occurring Data

Put simply, naturally occurring data are those data that would have occurred regardless of the role of the researcher. In other words, these are data that would have occurred even if the researcher had not been born, or if the researcher was not able to go along and record it (Potter, 1996). Thus, this type of data does *not* require the researcher to structure the environment in hopes of generating data sources.

> *For example:* In a recent study by Solomon, Heritage, Yin, Maynard, and Bauman (2016),* the authors utilised naturally occurring data to examine medical problem presentation in paediatric care. The health care visits involved children with ASD and the authors examined how children's epistemic capabilities and opportunities were socialised into a competent patient role and how this was achieved through the interaction. The naturally occurring data were the interactions that took place within the paediatric care site and those interactions were not dependent upon the presence or existence of Solomon et al.
>
> * This article was part of a collection for a special issue on discourse and conversation analysis studies in the *Journal of Autism and Developmental Disorders.*

Important point

!   Naturally occurring data is a useful way for examining what actually happens in the real world, as it does not rely on retrospective accounts or opinions.

Researcher-Generated Data

One of the best ways to understand naturally occurring data is by its contrast, researcher-generated data. Historically, in qualitative research there has been a preference for researcher-generated data, with interviews being the most common method of data collection. Researcher-generated data are those data which are deliberately 'set up' to address a certain research question or in response to a specific research protocol. In other words, these are data that exist only because a researcher was interested in collecting such data, and most often include data collection methods, such as interviews, focus groups, questionnaires, and so on. In other words, researcher-generated data depend upon the existence of the researcher, as this type of data exists only because of the actions of the researcher.

For example: In a study by Ludlow, Skelly, and Rohleder (2011), the authors used semi-structured interviews to explore parents' subjective experiences of having a child diagnosed with ASD to identify the stressors they felt and the factors that helped them to cope. These interviews would not exist apart from the interests and research practices of the researchers.

Important point

! Researcher-generated data are useful to gain the opinions and
• perspectives of different individuals or groups. However, it relies on the belief that you can reliably access people's thoughts and opinions through targeted questioning.

At this point, we encourage you to reflect on what you have learned so far in the chapter and try undertaking the activity in Box 4.1.

In the aforementioned activity, it should be clear that those data points that are naturally occurring are (a), (c), and (d), and those that are naturally occurring are (b), (e), and (f). While item (a) is technically an interview, it is one that occurs naturally through the media, without any interference from the researcher in the planning or setting up of that interview. However, items (b) and (f), while both interviews, depend on the researcher to collect the data and to ask the interview questions and are therefore researcher generated, as the questions and process are both determined by the researcher. Items (c) and (d) are both events that happen naturally without the researcher needing to set them up (although a video recording of a classroom may need some intervention from the researcher for the recording to happen, the actual classroom event would go ahead regardless). Item

Box 4.1 Activity differentiating naturally occurring and researcher generated

Activity
Thus far in the chapter, we have differentiated between naturally occurring data and researcher-generated data. We now invite you to think about different types of data. Look at the following list and decide which are naturally occurring and which are researcher generated: (a) A televised news interview between a news interviewer and a celebrity talking about disability (b) A semi-structured interview between young men with ASD and a researcher (c) A video recording of a classroom with children who have a range of different disorders (d) A newspaper article reporting on the rise of diagnosis of ASD (e) A focus group with teachers reflecting on their teaching experiences of having a child with ASD in the classroom (f) An instant messenger interview over Skype between a researcher and a parent of a child diagnosed with ASD

(e) is clearly a researcher-generated method as a focus group requires the researcher to plan it, set it up, turn up and ask the questions, and so on.

Critique and Debate

Although it may seem as if a dichotomy exists between naturally occurring and researcher-generated data, the arguments about these two data types are complex. Problematically, sometimes in the literature, a polarised position is ostensibly set up, positioning one type of data as superior to the other, with some arguing that naturally occurring data is of benefit and others defending the use of researcher-generated data.

In the study of ASD, it is important to recognise that a range of different data collection approaches can be beneficial. Thus, what matters is the ways in which claims are made about data and what the data are intended to represent. It is not particularly useful to take up a defensive position; rather, it is important to keep in mind that there are indeed overlaps between naturally occurring and researcher-generated data. In fact, some scholars have cautioned against going too far when distinguishing these data types (Silverman, 2011), as no data source is fully devoid of being influenced by a researcher. Indeed, some labels for researcher-generated data (for instance, 'artificial', 'contrived') do in and of themselves appear negative. Yet, we argue for the value of research in ASD including a range of data collection methods, and recognize that what matters most is congruence between research questions/interests, epistemological assumptions, methodology, methods of data collection, and implementation.

Important point

! Notably, the choice of data depends on how a researcher intends to study a given phenomenon (ten Have, 2002).

Nevertheless, there are arguments that suggest that researchers should consider carefully their data collection method and not simply take-for-granted the value of an interview or focus group (Potter & Hepburn, 2005). Furthermore, one does need to consider carefully how methods, such as interviews, are viewed. The social constructionist conception of an interview assumes that the interview itself is a social setting and the data are co-constructed between the interviewer and the interviewee (Roulston, 2006). Thus the interview is not necessarily a way of obtaining psychologically and linguistically interesting participant responses; rather, it is an interaction in its own right and both parties' talk is of important analytic value (Potter, 2004).

The Value and Benefit of Naturally Occurring Data

Those practicing conversation analysis and those practicing some forms of discourse analysis favour naturally occurring data because of its proposed benefits, which include:

- It removes (at least in part) the researcher's own categories from the data, which tend to get embedded in interview or focus group questions (Potter, 2004).
- There is less researcher interference in the data collection process (Potter, 2002), which can result in generating data that offers useful insights related to a naturalistic environment.
- It opens up novel concerns and issues that may not be expected or allowed for in researcher-generated data (Potter, 2004).
- It provides the actual recording of people living their everyday lives (Potter, 2004).
- It helps researchers to see what happens in real-world interactions, which ultimately can assist them in making recommendations based on real-world practices.
- It supports a researcher in crafting a representation of what actually happened at a research site. While it is possible and common to summarize (from the researcher's memory) interactions that took place at a research site, it is not logistically possible to remember the nuances of an observed interaction (Silverman, 2006). For instance, it is quite difficult to recount the pauses or overlaps in speech, without some type of audio- or video-recorded data. Further, a researcher cannot and perhaps should not attempt to invent conversational sequences (Sacks, 1992).

Challenges of Using Naturally Occurring Data

While there are indeed benefits when collecting naturally occurring data, there are also several challenges that must be considered. It is particularly important to reflect upon the practical limitations of using naturally occurring data in research so that these limitations can be accounted for within the research process. We highlight here an abbreviated list of some of the key challenges and encourage the reader to identify others that might be specific to their research site and interest.

- Gaining access to an appropriate research site can be challenging, particularly when the researcher is requesting to record everyday interactional events. Such a request demands a willingness on the part of the research site to allow for their everyday interactions to become subject to analysis. This can be particularly challenging when working with so-called vulnerable populations. People with ASD and/or educational or clinical sites wherein people with ASD learn or work, are often viewed as vulnerable. As such, it can be quite challenging to gain access to collect naturally occurring data. Thus, a clear rationale regarding the purpose and need for collecting naturally occurring data must be conveyed by the researcher to key stakeholders.
- Naturally occurring data is inevitably 'messy', as the researcher does not structure the nature of the interactions; rather, the researcher considers whatever was happening in a given research site. As such, organising and making sense of the data may feel a bit challenging, particularly as the researcher begins to mull over a seemingly large and amorphous data set.
- The very notion of 'natural' is arguably limiting—and perhaps even an illusion. This is specifically relevant when considering that a researcher will ultimately introduce a recording device, which may impact (even in a limited way) the research participants/interlocutors (Potter, 2004). Therefore, such data are called naturally occurring data rather than natural data.
- The recording devices shape what is ultimately collected and thus depending upon the nature of the devices there could potentially be limitations in what ultimately becomes part of the data set. For instance, if a researcher is collecting video-recorded data at a therapy clinic and the video-recording device was unknowingly positioned in a way in which only the therapist's facial nonverbal interactions were recorded, what the researcher is capable of doing with the data may be limited. Thus, it is critical to carefully consider the nature of the recording devices and how they ultimately shape the nature of the data collected and thus what might ultimately be understood (Heath, Hindmarsh, & Luff, 2010). Notably, it has been argued (e.g., Schegloff,

1987) that if contextual information is important to the interactants, it will be displayed in features of their talk, such as altered forms of turn-taking, or word choices, or in other ways.

- The data may seem incomplete, particularly if 'all' that a researcher has is a set of audio- or video-recordings of a series of interactions. Some scholars could argue that the researcher is missing contextual information (perhaps gained via ongoing observational notes). Some may also argue that audio-recorded data, for instance, results in not having access to important facial expressions and thus the naturally occurring data are limiting and even incomplete.

While these critiques are perhaps fair and accurate, it is important to recognize that no data sources could ever be described as 'complete'. Rather, what is collected, whether it be naturally occurring or researcher generated, is always partial and not fully equivalent to the actual event (Silverman, 2006).

Naturally Occurring Data and Common Ethical Dilemmas

In recent years, the level of scrutiny placed upon research ethics has exponentially increased. Worldwide, many universities now operate according to a *governance-based* approach to ethics, where projects must be reviewed and approved by ethical committees prior to implementation, and researchers are then held accountable for upholding appropriate processes and standards across the life of the project. Much of the driving force for these increasing levels of governance has been from medical science, where several high-profile scandals relating to the unauthorised misuse of patient data and/or body tissues, plus increasing levels of commercial pressures in relation to the evaluation of treatments, have contributed to increasing regulation of research work (Shaw, Boynton, & Greenhalgh, 2005). These cultural shifts that began in medical science have resulted in a proliferation of policies, protocols, and governance frameworks, resulting in similarly high levels of scrutiny now being placed on all disciplines that collect data from human (and non-human) participants. Studies that use naturally occurring data are no exception, and moreover can generate some specific ethical dilemmas that must be attended to by researchers.

To explore these issues further, it is helpful to separate out two different sets of principles that are typically expected to be upheld in the design of research studies: *universal ethical principles* and *information governance*. These will be considered in turn.

Universal ethical principles, which are formalised across a myriad of national and also institution-, profession- and subject-specific policy frameworks, are built upon fundamental contemporary philosophies of ethical practices in biomedical contexts. These key principles are:

- *Beneficence* (doing good);
- *Non-maleficence* (causing no harm);
- *Justice* (treating others equitably); and
- *Respect for autonomy* (acknowledging a person's right to hold beliefs and act upon these beliefs) (see Beauchamp & Childress, 2001).

The application of these broad principles, even across very different research contexts, tends to result in similar practical concerns being highlighted regarding research ethics. For instance, key universal ethical concerns tend to be around promoting researcher integrity, avoiding participant deception, striving for informed consent from participants, and upholding participant rights to withdraw freely from any research without penalty. Specific disciplines or professions then typically produce guidance, directly relevant to their field, which structures how researchers should respond to these challenges.

We have provided you with quite a lot of information at this point, and it would be beneficial now to try the activity in Box 4.2.

This activity helpfully demonstrates the way in which universal ethical issues practically play out in studies that draw upon naturally occurring data. In terms of the kinds of participants involved in a study such as Solomon et al. (2016), there are (at least) three distinct groups that would need to be formally recruited to enable data collection:

Box 4.2 Activity on ethical principles

Activity

Earlier in the chapter, we provided an example of a study conducted by Solomon et al. (2016) where the authors utilised naturally occurring data to examine medical problem presentation in paediatric care clinics. Thinking carefully about such a setting, consider the following questions in relation to universal ethical principles:

(a) What kinds of participants might be involved in a study such as this? What issues of consent might be generated by such participants?
(b) Would any deception be required to undertake this study?
(c) What possible benefits or risks might participation in this study entail?

- The professionals who work in the clinic where data is collected;
- Adult family members of the children who attend the clinic; and
- The children themselves.

Multiple participant groups such as this are common when using naturally occurring data due to the high likelihood that any otherwise-occurring activity will involve a range of individuals. While from a research perspective, each group fundamentally participates in the study on the same footing (i.e., they are recorded and their verbal/nonverbal behaviours are transcribed/analysed), each may present different concerns or anxieties about participation. In a study, such as the above, for example, the professionals may be concerned about their practice being scrutinised or undermined, whilst the family members may be more concerned about confidential information about their children being disclosed as a result of recording (an issue discussed further below). Typically, different information sheets are tailored for each group in a study such as this.

The involvement of children in a study such as the one Solomon et al. (2016) carried out creates additional consent issues for the researcher. Children are typically not considered to possess legal authority to provide consent to participate in studies. Internationally accepted practice suggests that, to ensure that their autonomy remains respected, children should be required to provide informed *assent* (that being a non-binding agreement) to participate in addition to a guardian's formal consent, and moreover maintain personal and instrumental rights to withdraw from the study throughout any recording and its subsequent analysis. A number of practical approaches and protocols for gaining assent have been proposed, such as use of narrative approaches (Mayne, Howitt, & Rennie, 2016) and picture books (Pyle & Danniels, 2015), which may be particularly useful for children with ASD. However, there does remain controversy in this area. For example, current assent approaches have been criticised as undermining the autonomy of children who may be entirely competent to consent, albeit not strictly according to the law (see Baines, 2011).

Although the use of naturally occurring data may increase the requirement for a range of (potentially vulnerable) participants to provide consent, it is important to acknowledge that the aforementioned concerns are by no means specific to this kind of research. Moreover, as the aforementioned activity indicates, there is no need for deception when using naturally occurring data, and whilst it is unlikely that direct benefits would be provided through participation, risks to participants tend to be very low. Fundamentally, this is because the collection of naturally occurring data relies upon capturing otherwise-occurring activities, and hence researchers typically aim to influence or intervene upon these events as little as possible. However, one area where higher ethical risk could be identified relates to the use of audio or video recordings, which is an unavoidable prerequisite of any study collecting naturally occurring data. This risk emerges in relation to the second set of principles that typically underpin the design of research studies, that being information governance.

Information governance relates to the management of data in a manner that is lawful, fair, safe, and upholds the universal principles outlined above, particularly with regard to the confidentiality of data. Many countries have developed specific laws to cover public and private sector handling of personal data, and research projects and institutions must adhere to these laws. Some institutions maintain statutory responsibilities about protecting and safeguarding their service users, particularly if they are deemed vulnerable and/or minors. All of these factors must be considered carefully when designing a project that involves making recordings of participants. In some cases, researchers may need to consider national, legal, and local procedures and regulations simultaneously against their data collection requirements in order to ensure they are fully compliant with all relevant protocols and legislation (Holloway & Wheeler, 2010). Researchers must also remain aware that, given that video and audio recordings are highly person-identifiable data, there may be significant scrutiny of their plans for storing and processing recordings, and the steps that they will take to promote anonymity and confidentiality to the fullest extent possible.

Important point

❗• Typically, schools require prior consent to be provided by each and every student who is captured on a video or audio recording during the process of research. This may cause complexities when, for instance, examining social practices in the classroom.

There are some solutions to potential information governance issues generated by naturally occurring data. Most ethical review committees will expect to see recordings stored securely, ideally in an encrypted format, which is now easier than ever given the wide availability of hardware for this purpose. Pseudonyms can be used throughout written records, and readily available software enables editing of person-identifying audio (such as names), and digital obfuscation of potentially person-identifying features such as logos on clothes, backgrounds, or even participants' faces. Along similar lines, some institutions are more comfortable with use of audio only rather than audio and video, or with recordings being stored and used only on site. However, it is important to acknowledge that decisions such as these will impact upon the analysis process.

Perhaps the most common issue faced by researchers who seek to use naturally occurring data is that participants, professionals, and gatekeepers in institutions may be unfamiliar with the necessity to create and use extensive recordings as part of a research project. This may particularly be the case if they are more acquainted with participation in more traditional forms of research. Reasonably, the prospect of being 'on film' may generate anxiety as to researchers' intentions and future use of data. Here, transparency and understanding on behalf of the researcher is crucial. In some cases, offering debrief follow-ups or dissemination sessions for participants following analysis can help allay fears by clearly demonstrating the outputs of any analysis and use of participants' personal data. The 'Research Tips' box (Box 4.3) offers some practical issues to bear in mind if you are collecting naturally occurring data.

Box 4.3 Research tips

Research tips

1. Remember that to collect naturally occurring data, you will need to comply with ethical standards.
2. You will need a good-quality recording device to capture the data. Sometimes more than one recording device is helpful, particularly when there is background noise or multiple people are in the interaction.
3. If you do not plan to be at the research site, it is important to consider the efforts required on the part of the research participants in recording the everyday interactions. At times, you can set up the devices in a way that makes remembering to 'press record' a simple task. Your aim should be to make it a straightforward process for the research participants and increase the chances that the naturally occurring data will be collected.
4. Where possible video recordings provide more detail of what is going on than audio.
5. You will need to make sure that the participants understand what you are doing and why.
6. When working in sensitive environments, such as a clinical environment, it is critical to carefully consider the implications of recording the naturally occurring data and comply by the protections that may be unique to the research site. For instance, in Lester's (2014) study, which occurred at a paediatric therapy clinic, she was required to comply with the US-based health regulations in addition to the expectations and requirements of her ethics review board.

Benefits of Naturally Occurring Data in ASD Research

As discussed earlier in this volume and elsewhere (e.g., Timimi, Gardner, & McCabe, 2010; Nadesan, 2005), research into ASD is typified by hypothesis-driven, quantitative, and increasingly biological approaches. More recently, there has been acknowledgement of the importance of qualitative research in the area (Bőlte, 2014), reflecting the emergence of an increasingly dense body of work based around analyses of ASD-themed interviews, focus group, and open-ended questionnaire data (e.g., Ludlow et al., 2011). A smaller, but growing thread of typically qualitative work on ASD uses naturally occurring data. Despite the relatively low volume of research in this area, it is already becoming clear that such studies can make a unique contribution to knowledge about ASD, which—depending on researcher orientation—can augment, triangulate, or, in some cases, challenge existing knowledge and theory (O'Reilly, Lester, & Muskett, 2016).

First, some researchers use naturally occurring data to examine directly the manifestation of behaviours (verbal and nonverbal) that are associated with a diagnosis of ASD. Whilst there is a very large research literature focusing on ASD's 'symptomatology', the majority of studies in this area use data derived from controlled observations of structured or semi-structured tasks. Conversely, the benefit of naturally occurring data when examining behaviours of ASD is its high level of ecological validity and its enabling of the consideration of ASD in spontaneous and socially situated contexts.

> *For example*: Stribling, Rae, and Dickerson (2007) conducted a study on echoed talk, which is discussed further in the following section.

Second, naturally occurring data enable a more distributed research focus on communication and interaction; rather than solely examining the individual diagnosed with ASD, the possibility emerges to also consider their interlocutors and the structures of the interactions in which they participate in more broadly. Such a distributed research focus is evident in the chapters in the second half of this volume, where it is demonstrated how such data can provide an ecologically valid source of findings about how participants *respond* when in interactions involving people with ASD. Such findings have direct practical relevance for considering how best to support people with the diagnosis, and in addition enable identification of participants' *tacit understandings* of ASD, as demonstrated through their real-time responses during social interaction. Such findings augment the kinds of explicit understandings of ASD that might be probed through semi-structured interview or focus group designs.

Finally, naturally occurring data enable the examination of topics of relevance to understanding ASD that hitherto have received little research attention.

> *For example:* Comparatively little work has set out to understand the social and institutional contexts experienced by people with ASD across their daily lives.

Conversely, studies drawing on naturally occurring data have presented highly ecologically valid findings on the social organisation and structure of a variety of relevant contexts in which people with ASD participate, including home life, schools, therapeutic interactions, psychological tests, and clinics. In the following section, illustrative examples of such studies will be provided.

Examples of Naturally Occurring Data in ASD Research

There is a growing body of research around ASD that is drawing upon naturally occurring data, particularly when completing conversation analysis- or discourse analysis-related studies. We highlight here three examples to provide you with a greater appreciation for the possibilities that naturally occurring data affords those engaged in the study of ASD.

First, Elinor Ochs, a linguistic anthropologist, directed an ethnographic study of the everyday lives of children, aged 8-12 years, with Asperger's disorder and high-functioning autism (Ochs & Solomon, 2004). Broadly, the study attended to the social worlds of 16 participating families. The research team gave attention to the children's conversational interactions with family members during dinner time, with peers and teachers during the school day, and in transit to and from school. As such, it is fair to describe their data as naturally occurring, as the interactions they collected would have occurred regardless of the researchers' involvement. Specifically, their corpus of data included 320 hours of video and 60 hours of audio-recorded naturalistic data, and was analysed using conversation analysis. A full issue of *Discourse Studies* (2004) was devoted to the work of Ochs and her research team (Ochs & Solomon, 2004). The research team's analysis of this data corpus resulted in a variety of analyses. For example, Kremer-Sadlik (2004) reported on how participating children with ASD answered 75% of all question-answer sequences appropriately, especially as their family members modelled acceptable interactions and corrected the child's speech to match normative expectations. As another example, Sterponi (2004) reported that the participating children displayed an understanding of social rules, initiating conversations with peers in which they called upon others to negotiate moral positions. Ultimately, Ochs concluded that her research team's intentional shift away from researching autism in 'laboratory settings' made possible new insights about autism 'against the backdrop of everyday social behavior' (p. 143). In this way, Ochs explicitly highlighted the great benefits to the study of ASD.

Second, Stribling, Rae, and Dickerson (2007) conducted a conversation analysis on the talk of an adolescent girl with ASD. These researchers analysed six hours of video recordings of the participant within the context of her special education classroom. The researchers provided a detailed interactional analysis showing the interactions of the participant with ASD and the school staff. It was noted that the participant displayed two forms of verbal repetitions:

1. An immediate repeating of the prior speaker's utterance, or
2. A delayed repeating of her own prior talk.

The authors suggested that the participant's repetitions constituted an adaptation to interaction that allowed her to display pragmatic competence despite her limited lexicon. In this way, the naturally occurring data created opportunities for the researchers to closely analyse the happenings of everyday life in a special education classroom. Through their analysis, they generated important insights related to the micro-features of the participant's talk.

Third, Fasulo and Fiore (2007) examined ASD from an ethnomethod-ologically oriented analytical perspective and described their work as drawing upon discursive psychology (one approach to discourse analysis). The researchers recorded and analysed conversations that occurred during 10 therapeutic sessions. These conversations included a therapist and two boys with 'high functioning autism' (p. 226). The researchers described the goal of their study as being 'to show that therapeutic intervention could be strengthened if it was founded on a better awareness of the nature of talk-in-interaction' (p. 225). Drawing upon the work of Ochs and Solomon (2004) and others, Fasulo and Fiore (2007) drew upon conversation analysis and oriented to the unique talk of the participants with ASD as doing something functional within the interactions, and suggested that perhaps the therapist had an unrealistic model of conversational sequences. Their findings suggested that the educational objectives of the therapeutic program conflicted with the way in which the therapist discursively carried out the therapy session.

> *For example:* One goal was to improve the children's 'correctness of speech', yet the researchers indicated that many of the therapist's 'corrective' conversational turns stifled another goal of improving social interaction (p. 240), as the children often stopped speaking upon being 'corrected' by the therapist.

Additionally, the therapist engaged in continual questioning of the children, assuming that this approach would elicit appropriate language. However, the researcher showed how such questioning shifted the 'dialogue' to an 'interrogation' session (p. 240). The researchers concluded that therapists needed to learn how to make sense of the unique conversational patterns of children with ASD and to resist the desire to privilege normative or expected patterns of speech.

Now we recommend you try the activity in Box 4.4, which invites some personal reflection.

We conclude this chapter with some useful information from scholars in the field. We conducted three text-based interviews with people undertaking research using naturally occurring data to illustrate some of the important and practical aspects of this kind of work. These are presented in Boxes 4.5, 4.6, and 4.7.

Box 4.4 Activity on reflection

Activity

Take a moment to reflect upon your own research interests in the field of ASD. As you do so, consider the following:
1. Make a list of potential research sites and describe the nature of the naturally occurring data that you might collect at this site.
2. Considering the research site(s) you noted above, what might be some of the challenges in gaining access to the site and ultimately recording the data?
3. What types of questions might you potentially explore at the research site(s) noted above?

Box 4.5 Interview 1: Rachael Gabriel, Associate Professor (University of Connecticut, USA)

What was the project about?
The goal of this project was to investigate how teachers use language to mediate student understanding during reading comprehension instruction and to examine how students identified as 'at risk' for or having reading difficulties interact with instruction. There is consensus in the fields of literacy education and teacher education surrounding the importance of explicit comprehension strategy instruction and teacher modelling. However, there are few research-based guidelines for coaching teachers to provide more effective models or explanations for their students, especially when it comes to complex and invisible constructs like comprehension of text. This study was aimed at building upon existing research on the role of teacher language in mediating student understanding to identify features of language use that effectively support comprehension growth, especially for students with reading difficulties.

Can you describe your data sources?
We used four data sources for this study. First, we collected naturally occurring teacher talk during reading comprehension lessons by videotaping ten 80–90-minute English/Language Arts lessons over a four-month period of a single school year. Videotaping was scheduled to occur on two consecutive days once per month in order to capture lessons that do not finish within a single period and to capture samples from across several months. The videos were recorded by the researchers, who also generated field notes and created post-observation memos after each video capture. These notes constituted a second source of data.

In addition to classroom videos and field notes, we conducted interviews with each teacher (n = 8) and three or four students from each classroom who had been identified as having reading difficulty by their teacher (n = 30). Interviews were conducted both at the beginning and end of the study. After interviewing the students, we administered a small battery of reading motivation, comprehension, and fluency assessments, which served as pre- and post-study assessments of reading motivation and proficiency.

What were the ethical procedures and access involved?
In order to secure university Institutional Review Board approval for this study, we generated four sets of consent forms: one for teachers, one for parents of all students, one for parents of students who would be assessed and interviewed, and an assent form for all students involved in videotaping. We began recruitment by contacting school administrators and lead teachers informally via email. When our contacts expressed initial interest, we followed up with a formal letter of invitation that requested an official letter of support from an authorized representative of the school district. Our research plan, consent/assent forms and letters of support from participating schools were submitted to the IRB at each of our universities for approval before participants were recruited. The proposal and consent forms outlined how data would be secured and later destroyed, when and how confidentiality would be maintained (e.g., through the use of pseudonyms and participant identification numbers), and what participation involved for each participant. Upon IRB approval, we emailed teachers invitations to participate and held info sessions to answer questions about the study. Once teachers signed consent forms, they agreed to distribute and collect consent and assent forms to the teachers and students in their classes so that we would have permission to videotape, take notes, interview, and collect assessment data.

What were the benefits and challenges of using this kind of data in the field of ASD?
Technology for recording classroom talk has changed dramatically even over the last three years both in terms of the quality of equipment and the pricing and accessibility of better quality tools for capturing the complexity and detail of classrooms where a range of interactions take place simultaneously. As technology improves, however, increased possibilities for data collection often generate complexities for data analysis. This project was both supported and limited (framed) by the talk we could and could not capture. Specifically, though we set out to investigate teaching and learning interactions, we were best able to capture teacher talk, with student contributions and peer-to-peer discussions muted, muffled, or too often overlapping to understand and transcribe. This study turned into a study of teacher talk, rather than classroom discourse, by default, rather than by design, when our attempts to use individual microphones or directional microphones failed to capture group work, partner work, or other instances of overlapping speech. If the study were conducted tomorrow or two years from tomorrow, there would be options for capturing and layering individual voices and multiple views of the classroom. Still, I have come to view recording as a layer of analysis in itself in that there is always a decision about what parts of the classroom are in view, in focus, and in range for audio. There will always be aspects of classroom life and interaction that are not captured, and these may include the silences, absences, and nuances that disappear in transcripts but carry meaning for the participants.

Box 4.6 Interview 2: Sushie Dobbinson, forensic speech and language therapist, Humber Mental Health NHS Trust

What was the project about?
In fact, there were two projects. The first was on storytelling in patients on a forensic learning disability ward in the medium secure psychiatric hospital where I work. In all, six patients contributed (useful) data, which were naturally occurring conversations between them and staff members, mainly forensic nurses with specialism in learning disability, nursing assistants (who have no clinical qualifications but who carry out much of the work with the patients), an occupational therapist, a psychologist, and two speech and language therapists, one of whom was me. I was interested in how the patients included deception, sometimes fantastical, sometimes evasive, in their stories and wondered how this arose in interactions, what sort of a function it served for the patients, if any, and how it was responded to by staff. Up to this point, clinical staff had routinely cited deception, particularly when it was overt or flamboyant, as a barrier to the wider objective of reducing risk in the patients' behavioural repertoires.

The second project was to identify patients with ASD across all of the wards in the forensic hospital and examine how different practitioners accommodated to their needs. For this project, I first undertook awareness raising amongst the staff about ASD, then asked them to identify patients who might fit the criteria for ASD diagnosis. This included completing AQ10 screens. I consulted with MDTs to decide which of the patients may benefit from a full diagnostic assessment using ADI-R and ADOS 2. Patients who might have ASD but for whom no clinical benefit could be ascertained from a diagnosis were discounted from the process at this stage; for example, a patient who displayed ASD traits across the three areas of dysfunction had made positive, albeit slow, progress through a long forensic history. Since his discharge was imminent, it was considered a diagnosis may 'set him back', would add nothing to his risk reduction profile and capacity to function well in the community, and therefore would not be appropriate at this stage.

In all, three previously undiagnosed patients in the forensic hospital were found to have ASD, two of whom were on the LD ward and also part of the previous project.

Can you describe your data sources?

Data were gathered from forensic LD patients in naturalistic conversation with the practitioners mentioned above. Participants were asked to just talk as they usually would during a scheduled therapy session. The patients who took part all had a verbal age of at least 7 (measured using BPVS II) and had given their consent to take part, and again, prior to all recorded conversations. Conversations were audio-recorded for the second project, audio- and videorecorded for the first. For the first project, prompt questions were used, but these were not always successful, and in the end, data that occurred following these prompts were not used. The usual process of anonymization of names, dates, and places took place, and any talk about offences was closed down or omitted from transcripts so as not to compromise the security of the patients or hospital. I transcribed the data myself. Both projects are ongoing.

Summary

In this chapter, we have introduced you to the concepts of naturally occurring data, data which occurs naturally without interference from researchers, and researcher-generated data, data which relies on the researcher to be collected. We have highlighted how naturally occurring

What were the ethical procedures and access involved?
Neither project received funding, since I did not apply for any, seeing the studies as the basis for future work for which I did intend to apply for funding. However, Humber NHS Foundation Trust allow me one day a week and the use of Trust resources to work on both projects. They have been continually supportive, although not a particularly research-focused Trust, being small and beleaguered by financial constraints. The first project was accepted by the Research Ethics Committee for Yorkshire. I was given permission for the second by the Clinical Governance committees of the Trust, and the hospital and ward multidisciplinary teams (MDTs), who act as overseers of clinical governance at hospital and ward levels. Each patient gave consent to take part in the studies, after receiving information in accessible formats. As lead forensic SALT, I had access to all of the patients in the hospital, where there are wards for people who have a mental illness (usually schizophrenia), treatment-resistant mental illness, personality disorder, and learning disability.

What were the benefits and challenges of using this kind of data in the field of ASD?
A major benefit was that patients who had been considered difficult because of the nature of their interactions with staff began to be seen as interesting by the staff. Whether the shift in perspective was purely due to the studies is unlikely, but in any case, there was a shift in response to circular topics, exhaustive repetition, and infelicitous recollection of information. Practitioners who knew about my work, at least on the LD ward, instead of becoming frustrated or irritated by these interactions, began to work more collaboratively with them, rather than closing them down. Meanwhile, awareness of ASD has increased across the hospital, such that now I receive unsolicited referrals from right across the hospital, wherever there is suspicion of undiagnosed ASD. The LD ward where I do most of my work has changed practice with their ASD patients, while the rest of the hospital is beginning to.

data can be beneficial for the study of ASD, noting also what some of the challenges of collecting such data might be. This included a discussion of the particular ethical challenges that can occur when using data of this kind. To help your understanding, we have provided you with examples of research that used naturally occurring data as well as interviews with scholars in the field. We offer some final practical highlights from the chapter in Box 4.8.

Challenges were numerous. Perhaps one of the most difficult is that CA traditionally makes use of short data extracts and gives primary focus to sequential turns. The kind of use I wanted to make of CA necessitated a broader perspective. Repetition, infelicitous storytelling and other features of ASD talk tend to extend over many turns and become woven both within the fabric of and between conversations. One of my most prolific informants carried on themes between practitioners, layering past conversations on present ones, continually recalling and reconstructing things previously said. At any one time it was difficult to pick out what was happening without reference to something that had gone before. It was as if, while talking to him, in the forms, responses, and trajectory of the talk, all previous conversations with staff on the ward were present. While dealing with this was essential in terms of working with the patient to reduce his risk and was relatively straightforward to address as a clinician, it was very difficult to demonstrate how this was done in a chapter or a paper. Long data extracts are neither easily accessible nor interesting for readers. Similarly, I had to invent ways of demonstrating topic movement to readers that could be more or less understood. In short, clinical and academic requirements do not always easily overlap, and, for me at least, it seems that combining the two can only be accomplished with some compromise of either clarity or completeness.

Box 4.7 Interview 3: Helen Cameron, PhD student (University of Sheffield, the UK)

What was the project about?
This project examined institutional talk featuring young children with language and communication impairments, specifically interactions in speech and language therapy sessions, and compared and contrasted this with the everyday talk of the same children interacting with their families at home. The project came about from my work as a speech and language therapist where I worked with parents to develop strategies to support their child's language and communication development through everyday interaction and routines outside of the clinic setting. Parents would anecdotally comment that the interaction between the child and the therapist during a therapy session looked or felt different than when they as parents tried to replicate the therapeutic goals or activities at home, despite employing the same communication-supporting strategies. My project thus explored this perceived difference, using conversation analysis to examine the interactional strategies used to support children's language and communication in both therapy sessions with a therapist, and in everyday life at home with parents/caregivers. While this project was not focused exclusively on children with ASD, a number of the child participants had a diagnosis of ASD.

Can you describe your data sources?
The institutional/ clinical data were obtained by videoing speech and
language therapy sessions taking place in a University clinic. The
children were either attending therapy sessions with qualified speech
and language therapist, or a student speech and language therapist
being supervised by a qualified clinician. A block of four weekly
sessions were recorded per child using fixed recording equipment
available in the clinic. These same families were also provided with
portable recording equipment to make video recordings of everyday
routines in their home during the weeks in between therapy sessions. I
provided families with guidance on how to operate the recording
equipment, and some general direction on what type of activities to
record and how much to record, but I was not present during the
filming at home. A variety of participant-produced recordings were
ultimately collected from families, including recordings of meal times,
shared book reading and free play both within the home and in
outside play areas.
What were the ethical procedures and access involved?
The project was ethically approved via the Department of Human
Communication Sciences Research Ethics Review Panel within the
University of Sheffield. Prospective children and families were
identified through their attendance at the University clinic, and all
participants had previously consented to be contacted regarding
research projects taking place in the department. Therapists and
student therapists were identified through their voluntary work in the
university clinic. Prospective participants were contacted by email sent
via administrators who acted as gatekeepers. All participants were
provided with information outlining the scope of the project, how the
data would be used and the secure storage of the recordings. All
participants were required to consent to the research team accessing
the video recordings and the use of the anonymous data to be used in
written reports, whereas the showing of videos at research meetings or
other such activities was optional. Given the children's age and level of
communication ability, parents provided consent for their children to
participate. Parents were advised that if they felt their child was upset
or distressed by being recorded that they should stop filming, as this
would be interpreted as a child not assenting. Families, therapists, and
student therapists all self-selected to participate in the project and
recruitment ceased once the maximum number of families had been
reached.

What were the benefits and challenges of using this kind of data in the field of ASD?

The use of naturally occurring data allowed for collection of interactions involving children with ASD that are representative of their everyday lives. By collecting data across two contexts, it was possible to compare and contrast children's interactions at home with their families, and with speech and language therapists in the clinic. The method of participants recording their own data at home without a researcher present allowed for access to elements of family life that may not have been possible otherwise, such as bed-time stories and family meal times. This method also aimed to reduce participant reactivity to the camera, although analysis did show participants remained aware of being on film, suggesting that although 'naturally occurring', we cannot make assumption that recorded data is entirely 'natural'. A further benefit was that families played a more collaborative role in the research process by having control over what was recorded and submitted as data.

The use of participant-produced data did incur some challenges. There was large variability in the amount of data produced by the different families. Some families reported it was difficult to find the time to film or to remember to start recording; although this in itself is perhaps reflective of the real family life that was aiming to be captured by the research! The usability of some of the data in terms of transcription was also a challenge, as some segments were compromised by background noise and the positioning of the camera. On balance though, these difficulties were outweighed by the benefits of capturing the real-life examples of everyday talk and interaction featuring young children with ASD.

Box 4.8 Practical highlights summary

Summary of Practical Highlights

1. Naturally occurring data collection can be a useful way of doing research in the field of ASD.
2. Collecting data from children or adults who have a diagnosis of ASD and their families or professionals working with them, has great potential to reveal an understanding about their lives.
3. There are ethical issues that are important in collecting naturally occurring data and this is particularly important if researching sensitive areas.
4. It is important that you are familiar with the governance guidelines and ethical principles when doing work of this kind.

References

Baines, P. (2011). Assent for children's participation in research is incoherent and wrong. *Archives of Disease in Childhood, 96(10)*, 960–962.

Beauchamp, T. L., & Childress, J. F. (2001). *Principles of biomedical ethics* (5th ed.). Oxford: Oxford University Press.

Bőlte, S. (2014). The power of words: Is qualitative research as important as quantitative research in the study of Autism? *Autism, 18(2)*, 67–68.

Fasulo, A., & Fiore, F. (2007). A valid person: Non-competence as a conversational outcome. In A. Hepburn & S. Wiggins (Eds.), *Discursive research in practice: New approaches to psychology and interaction* (pp. 224–246). Cambridge: Cambridge University Press.

Heath, C., Hindmarsh, J., & Luff, P. (2010). *Video in qualitative research*. London: Sage.

Holloway, I., & Wheeler, S. (2010). *Qualitative research in nursing and healthcare* (3rd ed.). Oxford: Wiley-Blackwell.

Nadesan, M. (2005). *Constructing Autism: Unravelling the 'truth' and understanding the social*. New York: Routledge.

Kremer-Sadlik, T. (2004). How children with autism and Asperger syndrome respond to questions: A 'naturalistic' theory of mind task. *Discourse Studies, 6(2)*, 185–206.

Ludlow, A., Skelly, C., & Rohleder, P. (2011). Challenges faced by parents of children diagnosed with autism spectrum disorder. *Journal of Health Psychology, 17(5)*, 702–711.

Mayne, F., Howitt, C., & Rennie, L. (2016). Meaningful informed consent with young children: Looking forward through an interactive narrative approach. *Early Child Development and Care, 186(5)*, 673–687.

Ochs, E., & Solomon, O. (2004). Introduction: Discourse and autism. *Discourse Studies, 6(2)*, 139–146.

O'Reilly, M., & Kiyimba, N. (2015). *Advanced qualitative research: A guide to contemporary theoretical debates*. London: Sage.

O'Reilly, M., Lester, J. N., & Muskett, T. (2016). Discourse/conversation analysis and autism spectrum disorder. *Journal of Autism and Developmental Disorders, 46(2)*, 355–359.

Potter, J. (1996). *Representing reality: Discourse, rhetoric, and social construction*. London: Sage.

Potter, J. (2002). Two kinds of natural. *Discourse Studies., 4(4)*, 539–542.

Potter, J. (2004). Discourse analysis as a way of analysing naturally occurring talk. In D. Silverman (Ed.), *Qualitative research: Theory, method and practice* (2nd ed., pp. 200–221). London: Sage.

Potter, J., & Hepburn, A. (2005). Qualitative interviews in psychology: Problems and possibilities. *Qualitative Research in Psychology, 2*, 1–27.

Pyle, A., & Danniels, E. (2015). Using a picture book to gain assent in research with young children. *Early Child Development and Care, 186*(9), 1438–1452.

Roulston, K. (2006). Close encounters of the 'CA' kind: A review of literature analysing talk in research interviews. *Qualitative Research, 6*(4), 515–534.

Sacks, H. (1992). *Lectures on conversation*. Oxford: Blackwell.

Schegloff, E. (1987). Between macro and micro: Contexts and other connections. In J. Alexander, R. Munch, B. Giesen, & N. Smelser (Eds.), *The micro-macro link* (pp. 207–234). Berkeley: University of California Press.

Shaw, S., Boynton, P. M., & Greenhalgh, T. (2005). Research governance: Where did it come from, what does it mean? *Journal of the Royal Society of Medicine, 98*(11), 496–502.

Silverman, D. (2006). *Interpreting qualitative data* (3rd ed.). London: Sage.

Silverman, D. (2011). *Interpreting qualitative data: A guide to the principles of qualitative research* (4th ed.). London: Sage.

Solomon, O., Heritage, J., Yin, L., Maynard, D., & Bauman, M. (2016). 'What brings him here today? Medical problem presentation involving children with Autism Spectrum Disorders and typically developing children. *Journal of Autism and Developmental Disorders, 46*(2), 378–393.

Sterponi, L. (2004). Construction of rules, accountability and moral identity by high-functioning children with autism. *Discourse Studies, 6*(2), 207–228.

Stribling, P., Rae, J., & Dickerson, P. (2007). Two forms of spoken repetition in a girl with autism. *International Journal of Language & Communication Disorders, 42*(4), 427–444.

ten Have, P. (2002). Ontology or methodology? Comments on Speer's 'natural' and 'contrived' data: a sustainable distinction? *Discourse Studies, 4*(4), 527–530.

Timimi, S., Gardner, N., & McCabe, B. (2010). *The myth of autism: Medicalizing men's and boys' social and emotional competence*. Basingstoke: Palgrave Macmillan.

Wilkinson, S., Joffe, H., & Yardley, L. (2004). Qualitative data collection: Interviews and focus groups. In D. Marks & L. Yardley (Eds.), *Research methods for clinical and health psychology* (pp. 38–55). London: Sage.

Wimpenny, P., & Gass, J. (2000). Interviewing in phenomenology and grounded theory: Is there a difference? *Methodological Issues in Nursing Research, 31*(6), 1485–1492.

Recommended Reading

Bőlte, S. (2014). The power of words: Is qualitative research as important as quantitative research in the study of autism? *Autism, 18*(2), 67–68.

O'Reilly, M., Lester, J. N., & Muskett, T. (2016). Discourse/conversation analysis and autism spectrum disorder. *Journal of Autism and Developmental Disorders, 46*(2), 355–359.

Stribling, P., Rae, J., & Dickerson, P. (2007). Two forms of spoken repetition in a girl with autism. *International Journal of Language & Communication Disorders, 42*(4), 427–444.

Timimi, S., Gardner, N., & McCabe, B. (2010). *The myth of autism: Medicalizing men's and boys' social and emotional competence*. Basingstoke: Palgrave Macmillan.

Jessica Nina Lester is an associate professor of inquiry methodology at Indiana University, the USA. She teaches research methods courses, including discourse analysis, with much of her research focused on the study and development of qualitative methodologies and methods. Her research is situated within discourse studies and disability studies, with a particular focus on education and mental health contexts. She has also published books related to qualitative methodologies and research practices, including *An introduction to educational research: Connecting methods to practice* with Chad Lochmiller. In the area of mental health, Jessica co-edited two handbooks focused on mental health and discourse and conversation analysis. For more details, please consult http://portal.education.indiana.edu/ProfilePlaceHolder/tabid/6210/Default.aspx?u=jnlester   and   http://www2.le.ac.uk/departments/psychology/research/child-mental-health/cara-1/bio2.

Tom Muskett is a senior lecturer in psychology at Leeds Beckett University, the UK. Tom's professional background is in speech and language therapy. He has worked in clinical and educational roles with children with diagnoses of autism and their families and previously led a clinical training programme at the University of Sheffield, the UK. Informed by his experiences in these roles, Tom's current teaching and research aims to explore how children's 'development' and 'disorder' can be rethought methodologically, socially, and politically. For more details, please see http://www.leedsbeckett.ac.uk/staff/dr-tom-muskett/.

Michelle O'Reilly is a senior lecturer at the University of Leicester (Greenwood Institute of Child Health) and a research consultant with Leicestershire Partnership NHS Trust. Michelle's research interests are broadly in the areas of child mental health, family therapy, and the sociology of health and illness. Furthermore, she is a qualitative methodologist who has written extensively about theory, methods, and ethics. Michelle has published many journal articles and books in her areas of interest, recently co-editing two handbooks (child mental health and adult mental health) for Palgrave, as well as a book for Sage on interviewing children and young people for research. For more details, please consult http://www2.le.ac.uk/departments/psychology/ppl/michelleOReilly/index.

5

Using Conversation Analysis to Assess the Language and Communication of People on the Autism Spectrum: A Case-Based Tutorial

Tom Muskett

Learning Objectives

By the end of this chapter, you will be able to:

- Critically compare traditional perspectives on assessment of language and communication in autism spectrum disorder (ASD) to practical approaches grounded in conversation analysis (CA).
- Apply CA to reinterpret apparently unusual language produced by a child with a diagnosis of ASD.
- Evaluate the strengths, limitations, and opportunities associated with use of CA as a communication assessment approach.

T. Muskett (✉)
Leeds Beckett University, Leeds, UK

© The Author(s) 2017

M. O'Reilly et al. (eds.), *A Practical Guide to Social Interaction Research in Autism Spectrum Disorders*, The Language of Mental Health,
https://doi.org/10.1057/978-1-137-59236-1_5

Introduction

A diagnosis of ASD implies that experiences of social interaction, both for the diagnosed individual and for their interlocutors, may be different from what is typical. During my work as a speech and language therapist (SALT) with children with a diagnosis of ASD, I would often reflect upon interactions in which I participated and wonder: *what just happened then?* Sometimes, what *had* just happened was a difficult experience, such as a child becoming distressed or behaving in a way that I found to be challenging. At other times, it may have been less emotionally raw but equally troubling; perhaps a misunderstanding had emerged yet passed unresolved, or I had been confronted with my own inability to make sense of a child's communication.

These feelings were a theme of my practice experiences. However, I felt unequipped to resolve them. During my clinical training, I had been taught to recognise and describe certain language and communication behaviours, and to use these observations to differentiate between clinical presentations. I had studied mainstream psychological and linguistic theories of what might cause these behaviours, and had been trained to use standardised, published assessments of aspects of communication. Yet none of these skills were proving to be helpful in resolving some of the real-life interactional issues that I encountered through my work. Whilst my clinical training had endowed me with an ability to answer questions such as 'why, generally, do children with ASD do X?', I was much more interested in ascertaining 'why did *this* child *just* do X, and what did it mean *for them?*' For this more personalised and contextualised concern, a different approach to language, communication, and interaction was required.

In this chapter, I will introduce an approach to assessment grounded in use of conversation analysis (CA). I aim to demonstrate that this approach generates a novel *interactional* perspective on language and communication in ASD that directly addresses the aforementioned concerns. Later in the chapter, I will present a case example of an 11-year-old with ASD and will support you to conduct analysis to reconceptualise aspects of this child's communication through this interactional lens.

First, I will consider in more detail the rationale for a new approach to assessment.

Assessing Language and Communication in ASD

All traditions of practice have complex social histories. In the case of assessing language and communication (in ASD or otherwise), the contemporary status quo relating to how we 'measure' aspects of an individual's language is grounded in a historically specific perspective on what language and communication *are*. This basic understanding, endemic across the social and behavioural sciences, constructs 'language', 'communication' and 'interaction' as being domains of psychological ability or competence that are located within the individual (Potter & te Molder, 2005). Hence, from this perspective, language, its sub-elements (e.g., vocabulary, syntax), and the act of communication itself become constructed as if indexing stable psychological skills and attributes. As with all psychological constructs (see also intelligence quotient, personality attributes, and so forth), these are then frequently presented as analogous to physical body parts in their measurability (see Danforth, 2002).

Psychological measurement is now so pervasive that it is typically interpreted as synonymous with, rather than analogous to, physical assessment. However, it is important to acknowledge that the legitimacy of so-called psychometrics is a historically specific phenomenon, itself located in the development and naturalisation of psychology as a set of 'scientific' practices (Rose, 1989). Therefore, treating language and communication as psychologised, individually residing and measurable systems is ultimately a philosophical choice, and moreover, has inevitable consequences for the outcomes of assessment. These are discussed elsewhere in depth (e.g., Muskett, Body, & Perkins, 2012), but, briefly, the issues are twofold.

- First, if we assume language and communication to be stable psychological constructs, then any assessments we undertake will adopt these same assumptions whereby findings are interpreted as reflecting unchanging and consistent individual competencies. In other words, a child's scores on an individualised vocabulary assessment or a checklist of social communication becomes *their* 'vocabulary ability' or 'pragmatic competence' respectively, rather than a reflection of what they did at a certain moment in time within specific parameters.

• Second, assessments are built to tell us about the individual alone, outside of any social context. Indeed, most assessment approaches are designed to mitigate the effects of socially contextual factors (including assessor effects) on the outcomes.

Whilst taken-for-granted, these assumptions may be problematic because they do not reflect what happens in social interaction. When interacting with a child with ASD, my experience has been that (just like in all interactions) my interlocutor has been far from 'unchanging' and 'consistent' in their communication behaviours, and that social context (e.g., who is speaking, to do what, and where) had an immeasurable role in what actually happened (cf. Muskett, 2016). This is where CA comes in. CA models language and communication (and other behaviours) as fundamentally *social* rather than individual phenomena. Without denying that *individuals* do ultimately perform behaviours, CA (as with other discursive methods) begins from the position that such behaviours must be understood within a social context. This orientation opens opportunities for new forms of socially leaning assessment.

Principles of Assessment Using CA

There are two basic tenets of CA. First, analytic focus falls on the *sequential organisation* of interaction. In other words, a turn's design or function is considered both in relation to what has just occurred, and as opening a slot for a certain kind of following turn. Every turn in an interaction is both a *hearing* and a *doing* (Bilmes, 1992): an indication of a speaker's understanding of what has just been said, and an action that is similarly revealed through the following speaker's turn.

Through the above principle, CA work has demonstrated forms of sequences associated with specific kinds of interactional settings. Such sequences can be understood in terms of how participants collaboratively and in real time produce utterances that 'fit' their immediate context of speaking, which in turn has been shaped by the previous utterance.

> *For example:* A classroom interaction is characterised by a three-part sequence comprised of an initiation (typically a question) turn by the teacher/instructor, a response by the pupil/student, and a subsequent evaluation/feedback turn by the teacher/instructor (an IRF sequence; see Mehan, 1979). From a moment-by-moment perspective, the teacher's initiation turn opens a subsequent space in time for a student response. By producing a fitted answer, the student can be seen to 'hear' that the first turn as necessitating such a response. In turn, this opens a position for the teacher to provide the sequence-closing evaluation turn.

Thus, speakers are not rigidly bound to the contexts projected by previous turns, and hypothetically could do anything at any point in interaction. However, if turns are absent or fail to indicate awareness of the moment in time (the *sequential context*) in which they are produced, co-speakers typically respond to them as socially problematic (Sacks, Schegloff, & Jefferson, 1974).

> *For example:* A missing R-turn in a classroom IRF sequence would lead to the teacher demonstrating its absence by, for instance, asking the question again.

The second basic tenet of CA is related to this: sequential analysis is grounded in the responses of the participants *in* the interaction itself. In other words, a turn uttered by a speaker can be analytically regarded as being a 'question' if another participant in the interaction treats it as such by providing an answer. In turn, the answer can be regarded as fitted if the asker of the question accepts it.

Important point

! There is an *order* to how interaction unfolds in that participants
• can be seen to organise the unfolding talk, resolve misunderstandings, and so forth.

These principles offer opportunities for rethinking interactions involving people with communication difficulties, including ASD. First, by focusing on participant responses, the *real social consequences* of communication behaviours within an unfolding interaction can be examined. This provides a different view of communication difficulties than, for instance, applying professional knowledge of 'typical' behaviour and development to identify apparently problematic behaviours. From a CA perspective, just as a turn can be considered a question if treated as such by co-speakers, a contribution may be considered problematic when responded to as if a problem. This simple principle enables understanding of what constitutes *interactional* difficulties for speakers across different contexts, and the examination of roles played by co-speakers in the emergence and resolution of such difficulties. Second, variation in the manifestation of ostensibly problematic turns/behaviours can be identified and examined in relation to their sequential context. This raises particular questions that require some reflection:

- Do certain language and communication behaviours emerge following specific forms of prior turns, or in particular kinds of sequence?
- Moreover, what *actions* do these behaviours perform in the unfolding interactions?

Important point

! Psychologized approaches to assessment generate representations of assessed individuals that tacitly construct communication difficulties as static, individually located disorders. Conversely, CA approaches to assessment can focus on variation in communicative phenomena, the functions of certain behaviours, and the role played by co-speakers in their manifestation.

A Process for CA-Based Assessment

As a research approach, CA requires collection of naturally occurring recordings and detailed transcription of data, followed by iterative data-driven analysis to identify phenomena of interest (Psathas, 1995). Evidently, therefore, it is labour and time intensive. However, elements of the methodology can be applied in an assessment context in a manner that does not necessitate such intensive work. I outline next a pragmatic implementation of CA for assessment purposes:

1. Consider, impressionistically, your phenomena of interest:

   a. Does the subject of your assessment echo language?
   b. Not always answer questions?
   c. Disengage in conversations or activities?
   d. Apparently shift topic in a way that is hard to follow?

   All such behavioural phenomena must occur in a sequential context, and therefore are suitable for examination using a CA approach (and in fact have been before; for a review, see Garcia, 2012). Your behaviour(s) of interest will then direct the subsequent focus of analysis.

Important point

! It should be noted that this approach deviates from sampling in 'pure' CA research (I discuss this further below)

---

2. Video record your subject in interaction with others. Remember that interaction differs depending on broader context. For example: *in a classroom versus chatting with friends versus intergenerational family interaction, and so on.*
3. It is important therefore that you choose your setting and co-speakers to reflect your practical needs. For example: *If you are working at a whole-family level, you may wish to invite family members to participate in the recording.*
4. Watch the video and identify instances of your phenomena of interest. It is important that you watch the video on several occasions to familiarise yourself with the data.
5. Create short transcriptions of illustrative instances of these phenomena to enable their consideration in sequential context. Your aim at this point should be to generate enough transcribed material to

examine what was happening prior to your target phenomena, and the sequence that occurred afterwards. Try to collect examples that differ from one another, including when the target phenomena are *not* occurring, to mark out the boundaries in variation around the inter-actional issues that you are examining.

6. Examine the extracts turn-by-turn, building on the principle that each speakers' contribution is both a hearing and a doing (Bilmes, 1992). Compare extracts to identify emergent themes in:

   a. variation in the phenomena of interest,
   b. their sequential positioning,
   c. the role of co-speakers in their manifestation.

As noted previously, the aforementioned process does deviate from purist approaches to CA. These are characterised by so-called unmotivated analysis, where research questions emerge from the data itself (see Psathas, 1995). In contrast, the above process requires an assessor to make assumptions about what might be of interest *prior* to examining recordings. As will be demonstrated below, this may lead to the finding that the phenomena of interest to the assessor did not appear to be of interest to the participants during the interaction itself. From a CA perspective, this would be seen to represent a problematic imposition (Schegloff, Jefferson, & Sacks, 1977). However, notwithstanding academic debates about whether it is truly possible to undertake unmotivated analysis (see Billig, 1999), from a practice perspective a lack of participant response to what could be *assumed* to be problematic communication behaviour is an important finding. This will be explored below.

Let us now move on to a case example, where the above approach is used to assess an aspect of communication presented by a child with ASD. Throughout this example, activities have been provided to enable you to work through the data. If it is your first time engaging with a CA approach, you may find it useful to lay a blank piece of paper over each extract and then expose it line-by-line to consider each turn in sequence. With practice, this sequential reading approach will become second nature.

Case Example

This case example is based around Aled (pseudonym assigned for this analysis), a boy aged 11 years 6 months at the time of the recording. Aled had been recruited into a research project about interactions involving children with ASD. As part of this project, Aled was recorded twice in undirected play-based interaction with unknown adult interlocutors, for an hour in total. Aled had been diagnosed with ASD six years earlier, and experienced co-existing moderate difficulties with language and learning. He was educated in a special school principally for children with ASD and related difficulties.

In this case example, I will use one of Aled's recordings to demonstrate the assessment possibilities offered by CA. Prior to Aled's inclusion in the project, his teachers and family had completed a questionnaire about his communication. Through this, they highlighted that Aled often used impressionistically unusual or apparently self-generated (*neologistic*) language, and could sometimes reportedly be difficult to understand because of this. Such behaviours are closely related to ASD: 'idiosyncratic and/or repetitive language' (including neologism) is included in diagnostic criteria and therefore is commonly produced by diagnosed individuals (Volden & Lord, 1991). Within psychologised approaches to research and practice with ASD, it is typically assumed that such language reflects underlying disorder in an individual's representational or semantic system. Accordingly, research has indirectly examined language meaning in ASD via individual assessments such as picture and category sorting (Tager-Flusberg, 1991) and so-called verbal fluency paradigms, where participants list as many items from a given semantic category as possible (Dunn, Gomes, & Sebastian, 1996; for a CA-based critique of verbal fluency, see Muskett, Body, & Perkins, 2013).

Whilst the findings of this body of work remain equivocal, it remains the case that a 'semantic deficit' is still offered as a plausible factor in, or even explanation of, aspects of ASD's language and cognitive profile (e.g., Moseley et al., 2013). This psychological approach, where 'idiosyncratic language' is constructed as emergent from static, individually residing, and measurable representational deficits, can be contrasted against a CA account where 'idiosyncratic language' can straightforwardly be rethought in terms of its *sequential properties*. A CA approach raises the following questions:

- In what circumstances did Aled use unusual language, and with what consequence?
- How did his co-speaker respond, and to what extent do these responses indicate interactional problems?
- Finally, to what extent did misunderstandings following unusual language reflect actions on behalf of both speakers?

Such questions imply a less deficit-focused account of Aled's behaviour, with more emphasis on understanding its social rather than individual significance.

I will now explore these issues by examining illustrative extracts that demonstrate the variation in Aled's language use across the 30-minute recording. The CA-based assessment process outlined earlier was followed and its findings indicated overlapping themes. Aled's unusual language ranged from subtle instances of unusual word combinations to striking stretches of unusual and/or neologistic talk. However, across almost all instances, Aled's adult interlocutor Suzie (a 19-year-old female SALT student—pseudonym assigned for analysis) did not explicitly respond to what had preceded as if problematic. In some cases, this was unsurprising: sequential analysis of much of Aled's impressionistically unusual language indicated that it would have been unlikely to have been problematic in terms of shared meaning. However, in other instances, the unusualness of Aled's talk appeared far more significant, yet there was typically no clear orientation by Suzie to any emergent problems. Indeed, there was only one instance in the recording where Suzie explicitly attempted to clarify aspects of Aled's talk.

To examine these phenomena, let us first analyse instances of subtly unusual language in order to build a coherent, non-judgemental picture of Aled's language use; to begin with more clearly problematic stretches of talk would result in aspects of his communicative competence potentially being overlooked.

Consider extract 1 below. Here, Suzie (S) and Aled (A) are playing with toys, including characters from *Transformers* and the *Toy Story* films, and have just been discussing a robot in relation to when it appeared on television (line 1). In line 5, A produces impressionistically slightly unusual language: the phrase 'big walking legs'. Whilst from a common-sense

---

Box 5.1 Activity

Activity 1

Starting with line 5 of Extract 1:
(a) Look at what has just happened in prior turns, and consider the broader context. Collocation error or not—does A's turn fit here?
(b) What happens immediately after A's turn? Is there anything in that A's turn projects for in the next position? What would we be looking for in this position as evidence of 'interactional problems'?
(c) What actually happens? What does this tell us about S's understanding of line 5?

---

perspective this makes semantic sense, the phrase is linguistically idiosyncratic because it combines words that do not typically directly co-occur (a so-called collocation error). Given that collocation '*is not explicitly seen as a component of contextual meaning*' (Tognini-Bonelli, 2001, p. 163), it might be predicted that this turn would not cause particular interactional issues in terms of shared understanding. Let us now examine the extract to see what happened. Turn to Box 5.1:

Extract 1

```
00:14:54
   1  S     was it a long time ago
   2        (...) (A and S manipulate the robots)
   3  A     >°yes:°<
   4        (..) ↑°(bee::>ye<)°
 →5        (..) °it° (.) ↑it (.) has .hhh ↑big (.) walking legs
   6        (...)        (A sniffs, puts down robot
   7              and reaches for Buzz Lightyear)
   8        and >th[is is]<=
   9  S            [yeah?]
  10  A     = Buzz Lightyear (.)↓s:::aying
```

Through completing activity 1, you will have built a sequential picture of this relatively minor example of unusual language. You should have noted that A's 'big walking legs' turn clearly addresses the current focus of talk at that moment, and therefore is fitted into the unfolding context of the interaction. There is a pause following line 5 where either party could have spoken. This is appropriate, as A's turn does not project for any particular kind of subsequent response. However, S *could* have in this position acted to indicate problems in A's prior talk, but she does not. When A does speak again, it is to mark appropriately a shift to a new focus of discussion (note the 'and'-prefacing of line 8), to which S demonstrates positive receipt in overlap just following the 'and' part of A's new turn. Therefore, in this short extract, S does not explicitly query what appears to be impressionistically unusual language, and moreover ratifies the topical shift away from the toy with 'big walking legs'. This provides evidence that A's collocation error is not of interactional significance for S as a participant.

Recall that Aled's family and teachers reported unusual language to be a significant part of his communication needs. However, on close scrutiny, minor word combination 'errors' such as that in extract 1 in fact formed the majority of Aled's impressionistically idiosyncratic talk. Whilst these unusual phrases varied in terms of the context in which they emerged, they were consistently not responded to as problematic by S. Consider extract 2, which illustrates a similar but contextually different instance in Box 5.2.

Box 5.2 Activity

Activity 2

In extract 2, Aled is playing with *Thomas the Tank Engine* toys when he produces another unusual combination of words ('thirsty water') in line 6. From a linguistics perspective, this combination violates selection-restriction rules (Chomsky, 1965) regarding which lexemes are semantically permitted to co-occur within a grammatical context. But does this 'linguistic error' have real-life consequences?

(a) Between lines 3 and 13, what *activity* does Aled appear to be doing? How, sequentially, does this interaction differ from extract 1?

(b) In what way is the *sequential context* of the pause following line 6 different from that following 'walking legs'? As a hint, in extract 2, Aled is taking a very long turn.

(c) Imagine being in S's shoes in these interactions. Would it have felt easier to speak in the pause after 'walking legs' or 'thirsty water'?

Extract 2

```
00:06:03
   1  S    what did they do?
   2       (..)
   3  A    .hhhh (.) well (..) they had a drink
   4       (..) at the water tower (..) °shh::°
   5       (..) Bill (..) was- (..) wa:s
 →6       (..) having lots of thirsty water.
   7       (..) Peter Sam (.) and Mavis waited for Bill
   8       .hhhh Bill said (.) ↑goodbye
   9       (..) and it was Mavis's turn
  10           (A makes slurping sound on inbreath)
  11       (..) she had lots of fuel-
  12       (..) she went back to >the engine< shed
  13       (...) and Peter Sam .hhh had lots of fuel
  14           (A makes two slurping sounds on inbreath)
  15  S    [heheh
  16  A    [and he said (.) ↑goodbye
  17       (..) then (..) Bill >revved<
```

Comparing extracts 1 and 2, it appears that in the latter Aled is telling a story with his toys. This is reflected by the sequential organisation of this interaction, as A appears positioned as storyteller and S the 'uninformed' listener (see Goodwin, 1987). Differential interactional rights to extract 1 visibly apply, with A's turns being considerably longer and S not speaking during the many pauses that punctuate A's talk. Note that, in this context, S does not respond at all to either line 6 (including the idiosyncratic noun phrase 'thirsty water') or indeed most of the rest of Aled's talk, despite these pauses. Her next turn is, in fact, a minimal burst of laughter in line 15 following A's 'slurping' sounds.

S's responses, or lack of, in the above must be considered in relation to the sequential context of an unfolding story. In extract 2, we can perhaps assume that the phrase 'thirsty water' provides S with no issues as a co-conversant. However, given her role of listener, she would not have been well positioned to do anything about it regardless, as to do so would have required an interjection into A's storytelling. In this way, extract 1 differs from the above in that there, S *could* have taken the floor

---

Box 5.3 Activity

Activity 3

Here, as part of his story, A 'voices' a character between lines 14 and 23. In this stretch of interaction, there is significant and ongoing use of unusual (and arguably neologistic) language.
(a) Reading this section of the interaction, do you predict that S would have understood what A was talking about?
(b) What does she do sequentially following this stretch of talk? Does she demonstrate understanding, misunderstanding, or neither?
(c) Look carefully at lines 24 and 25. Reading back over the extract, where does the content of this line come from?

---

following 'big walking legs' had she wanted to. This is an important point when we consider extract 3, which leads directly on from the above, see Box 5.3:

Extract 3

```
00:07:29
  1  A    (..) the driver jumped from Bill
  2       (..) and fruit (...) and (..) sour >juice<
  3       .hhh (...) spla::ttered
  4       (..) ↑all over Bill
  5       (..) f::oosh::::::
  6       (..) splat (.) splat (.) ↓spla::t .hhh
  7  S    [what did he] crash in[to that]=
  8  A    [and they]            [guh:::]
  9  S                                    =made fruit juice
 10       go all over hi(hehe)m?
 11       (.)
 12  A    .hhh the truck
 13       (..) and then (..) the fat controller (.) came up
→14       (..) **Bill** (...) **you are** (.) **attes::ted**
→15       .hhh **something** .hhh **that'choo:: m::ade**
→16       . **no aggressive agreement**
 17       .hhh ↑**yes sir** (..) **no sir**
→18       .hhh ↓**you are** (.) **inclu:ding:**
```

```
→19          .hhh a- hhh jam factor:y
 20          (..) ↑yes sir (..) no sir
 21          (.)↓well (.) go back (.) to the engine shed .hhh and
 22          (..) >get 'im to< come out (..) <until you're clean>
 23          (..) (A searches through bag of toys)
 24   S      so he crashed into a load of fruit
 25          and it all turned into jam?
 26          (..)
 27   A      ye::s::
 28          (...)
 29   S      ↑ah:: (.) dear:: ↓heh
 30          (..) what- (.) what flavour jam did he make?
```

Here, Aled uses unusual language between lines 14 and 19. From the recording and transcript, the gist of these turns is unclear. There are many pauses throughout A's talk but, as in extract 2, S upholds her role of listener by not speaking until A appears to have finished this episode of his story (line 24). What S then does is striking: rather than querying the unusual language explicitly, she glosses over it by building a turn that combines previously agreed earlier details of the story (lines 7–10) with one of the few elements of lines 14–19 ('jam factory') that appears to fit. S's turn therefore seeks clarification of a simplified version of the story minus the idiosyncratic parts (a 'so'-prefaced turn-type known as a *formulation*: Garfinkel & Sacks, 1970). A's response in line 27 accepts this glossing as adequate, which enables the interaction to progress despite use of language such as 'attested', 'aggressive agreement', and 'including a jam factory' remaining unresolved.

To summarise the extracts so far, it appears that

- a uses a range of unremarkable, subtly unusual and strikingly unusual language.
- unusual language is by no means clearly interactionally problematic according to his co-speaker.
- the sequential consequences of such language depends upon the larger context in which he is using it.
- even markedly unusual language is not necessarily explicitly addressed by his co-speakers.

Box 5.4 Activity

Activity 4

In extract 4, A and S are playing with a Buzz Lightyear toy. Note lines 7 and 8: here, A uses an apparently self-generated phrase ('super equipment technical device') which is not usually associated with Buzz Lightyear.

(a) Why would we analytically suggest that S does not understand the meaning of 'super equipment technical device'? To ascertain this, look at what happens after his first use of this phrase.

(b) How does A then respond in his following turn? What does S do next, and what does this indicate about whether repair has 'worked'?

(c) Do you feel that repair is ultimately achieved below?

The final point has some consistencies with speakers' everyday tendency to avoid correcting one another during interaction (in CA terms, *repair*: see Schegloff, Jefferson, & Sacks, 1977). It is striking, however, that even highly unusual language is not directly addressed in these instances.

Important point

! Why might people *avoid* repairing one another? Think about your own experiences of not understanding people, or not being understood. How did you feel in these situations? Moreover, are there any 'special factors' at play in the above extracts which might contribute to S's lack of repair attempts?

Given these discussions, it now makes sense to examine the single instance where S did attempt to repair A's unusual talk. Let us examine this episode in sequence, look at Box 5.4.

Extract 4

```
00:26:58
  1  S    [woo:::]
  2  A    [I'm gonna] help (.) ↓him
  3       (...)              (A moves Buzz close to robot toy,
```

```
  4                        knocking it over)
  5    A     now I can't get (.) close enough (.) to ↓him
  6          (..) >this is a job<
 →7          .hhh for s:::uper .hhh equipment
 →8          .hhh technical .hhh de↑vice
  9          (..) Buzz Lightyear (..) to the res::↓cue.
 10          (...)          (A continues to hold Buzz, before S
 11                         reaches forward towards a different
 12                         toy)
→13    S     Aled?
→14          (.) what ↑is the s:uper equipment
→15          (.) technical device.
 16          (..)       (A, holding Buzz in his right
 17                         hand, moves the toy to his right,
 18                         continuing to look at it)
 19    A     well (..) he's s:::uper (.) equipment (.)
 20          technical de↑vice .hhh re↑porting for duty
 21                      (during the above turn, A reaches with
 22                         his left hand for two different
 23                         toys, picking up the second)
 24          (..)
→25    S     what- (.) what is it?
→26          (.) what's the super equipment technical device:
→27          what does it do?
 28          (..)       (A puts down the second toy and picks up
 29                         the Batman Flyer, flapping its
 30                         wings for half the following turn
 31                         before putting the Flyer down)
 32    A     erm:::
 33          (...)
 34    A     help (..) s:::omebody (..) out (..) in
 35          (..) s:::ix s:econds
 36          (.)
→37    S     in six seconds? (.) that's quick?
 38          (.)            (A puts down Buzz)
 39    A     I'm- (..)
 40          ↑let's have another play with this (.) trains .hhh
```

Here, S attempts to clarify the meaning of 'super equipment technical device' following its use in lines 7–9. Her turn is prefaced with Aled's name, and therefore strongly projects for an answer from A. However, his response

---

Box 5.5 Activity

Activity 5

In extract 5, A uses 'super equipment technical device' for the first time. Examine S's responses after the two instances of this phrase during this extract. How do these differ?

(lines 19–20) is tautological (note the 'well' at turn beginning, which marks it in advance as not being fitted to the question; see Schiffrin, 1987, p. 125). S provides no explicit evaluation of A's turn, instead producing three clarification-seeking questions which end with the original clarification attempt ('what is [it]') being reformulated to the somewhat different 'what does it do'. As is typical in interaction (Sacks, 1987), A's (positively received) answer in lines 32–35 addresses the final turn of the prior sequence (line 27) rather than either lines 25 or 26. Hence, by modifying her initial question to support A's engagement in her clarification sequence, S arguably did not ultimately clarify the meaning of 'super equipment technical device'.

The aforementioned extract demonstrates the only explicit attempt by S to clarify A's prior talk. However, it in fact illustrates the *final* usage of 'super equipment technical device' by Aled in this recording: beforehand, he had used this chunk of language some 19 times over 10 minutes without S seeking clarification on any occasion. This again implies some reticence on S's behalf to problematize A's unusual language. What, therefore, happened on the *first* occasion of his use of this term? Have a look at Box 5.5.

Extract 5

```
00:16:30
   1            and >th[is is]<=
   2   S              [yeah]
   3   A                        =Buzz Lightyear (.) ↓s:::aying
 →4            .hhh s::uper equipment .hhh technical device .hhh
 →5            re↑porting for duty
   6            (..)          (by the end of A's turn, S has
   7                           put her robot down)
   8   S        heh ha ha ha .hhh=(S sniffs)
   9            (.) was that from Toy Story one or Toy Story two
```

```
10          (.)
11  A       er:::m (.) I don't ↑kn:ow
12          (.) I can't remember
13          .hhh he (..) you just open his head up
14          (...)        (A sniffs and S touches Buzz Lightyear
15                          with her left hand)
16  S       yea::        [:h?
17  A            [I'm Buzz Lightyear for
→18         (.) s:::uper equipment .hhh technical device (..)
→19         re↑porting fer (.) duty
20          (.)
21  S       yeah?=heh ha ha ha ha
22          (..)         (during S's turn, A reaches forward
23                          with Buzz Lightyear before putting
24                          the toy down directly in front of S;
25                          when on the floor, S lays her hand on
26                          Buzz)
27  A       'ey Suze
```

Immediately following the first deployment of 'super equipment technical device' in lines 5 and 6, there is a relatively long pause, arguably indicating some problem with the prior turn, before S produces a turn of laughter (line 8). S then asks: 'Was that from *Toy Story* one or *Toy Story* two?'. The 'that' to which she refers appears to be the *phrase* 'super equipment technical device' (compare against, for example, 'Was *he* from *Toy Story* one or *Toy Story* two?' which would tie to Buzz Lightyear). S's turn therefore initiates a clarification of sorts, but not regarding the actual meaning of the phrase: instead, it projects for A to locate his current talk within wider shared understandings about the *Toy Story* films. Unfortunately for S however, the 'shared' knowledge offered in her turn is seemingly irrelevant since 'super equipment technical device' is not derived from *Toy Story*. A's non-clarifying response in lines 11 and 12 is therefore contextually appropriate.

A again then deploys a turn containing 'super equipment technical device'. This time, S's response consists of a minimal 'yeah?' followed by another burst of laughter (line 21), which merely projects for further talk from A. From this point on, S provides only minimal responses to A's repetition of 'super equipment technical device' until extract 4. Hence, her subtle demonstration of lack of understanding in line 9 passes unnoticed, meaning that the opportunity for shared meaning around this language is potentially lost.

Discussion

In this chapter, a CA-based process for assessing the communication behaviours of people diagnosed with ASD has been presented and illustrated through a case example of a child who was described to use unusual language. Whilst such language use could, from a psychological perspective, be interpreted as either indexing ASD or reflecting underlying cognitive difficulties, the CA approach argued for in this chapter recasts it as a phenomenon inevitably emergent through the structures of social interaction. Findings from this socially leaning assessment included:

- The extent to which the child's talk was impressionistically unusual varied significantly.
- Regardless of the level of idiosyncrasy, the child's talk could be seen to fit the immediate interactional context.
- The child's co-speaker typically glossed over unusual language, even when it was likely to have caused barriers in shared meaning.
- The child demonstrated some ability to self-repair, but required some interactional support and clear prompts to do so.

In professional work, assessment should always have the capacity to direct intervention. The approach offered in this chapter has utility in this regard. Whilst psychologised approaches to assessment imply interventions on or around the individual, the CA-based process outlined above can directly inform professional work addressing *interactional* issues via training interlocutors to modify aspects of their communication behaviour. Whilst this is a relatively new area in relation to ASD, extensive work on comparable approaches has been carried out around aphasia (acquired language difficulties following brain damage). Here, there is strong emerging evidence that CA-informed changes to interlocutor behaviour can reduce the incidence both of problems with shared understanding and, given the inherently mediating role played by co-speaker, of the manifestation of language difficulties in the first place (e.g., see Beeke et al., 2014). Applying this to the above, S (or other speakers) could be worked with to avoid glossing over repair in instances where they have failed to understand, or ensuring that A is provided with scaffolded opportunities to self-repair.

In addition to facilitating shared meaning, these strategies may well have a consequential effect around A's overall responsivity and/or levels of repetition, as both of these features of communication have been demonstrated in other CA work to be directly mediated by co-speakers (see Muskett, 2016). Finally, but equally important, findings could be used to re-adjust others' perceptions of the assessed individual; recall that unusual language had been reported to be A's main communication problem, yet this observation was not upheld when A's use of such language was examined in real time. In short, 'idiosyncratic language' is clearly not always an interactional problem, and it may be of practical benefit to work sensitively with those around A to facilitate their understanding of this.

The opportunities offered by the approach outlined in this chapter are broad. For instance, as demonstrated elsewhere in this volume, CA can be powerfully applied to interactions involving speakers who do not use verbal means to communicate. Here, CA-based assessment could be used in exactly the same way as above, but to identify sequential aspects of physical and non-verbal communication that may have otherwise been overlooked. The approach outlined above may have significant application for work with individuals adjudged to behave in a challenging manner, providing a nuanced perspective on issues such as escalation, de-escalation, and crisis incidents. Whilst the case example examined only one dyad, use of recordings of multiple co-speakers or, alternatively, feeding back findings from one co-speaker to a range of relevant parties can lead to a rigorous, holistic, and valid assessment.

To conclude, it is important to highlight two potential barriers in relation to CA-based assessment approaches.

- First, as discussed in Chap. 4, the requirement to make recordings must be considered in relation to any local information governance requirements and with the express permissions of all captured on the video. It should be acknowledged that, in some environments, such recording may therefore not be possible.
- Second, producing transcription of recordings is a relatively resource-intensive activity, which may preclude many professionals from undertaking a 'full' analysis such as that presented above.

In saying this, however, transcription does not need to be anywhere near at the level of detail presented above to enable a meaningful sequential analysis. Moreover, in my experience, observers quickly become attuned to interpreting real-time interactions sequentially in real time. Hence, it may be possible for an experienced and practised professional to implement aspects of the above process without making transcriptions, or even recordings. This represents an interesting area for further development of this approach.

Summary

In this chapter, I have discussed forms of professional assessment, enabling you to critically compare practical approaches grounded in CA to traditional perspectives on assessment. In so doing, I have worked through a tutorial-based single case example, enabling readers to apply CA to reinterpret the unusual language of a child with a diagnosis of ASD. Furthermore, I have discussed potential applications of assessment findings in relation to intervention and considered different applications of the approach described in this chapter. This has supported readers to evaluate the strengths, limitations, and opportunities associated with use of CA in assessment. In summary, therefore, I present the key practical messages in Box 5.6.

Box 5.6 Summary of practical highlights

Summary of Practical Highlights

1. Most existing approaches to the assessment of language and communication in ASD are underpinned by a construction of communication as if reflecting an individual, static competency.
2. Assessment approaches grounded in socially oriented perspectives on language and communication can generate alternative representations of speakers with ASD.
3. Conversation analysis provides a workable framework for such interactional assessment.
4. Assessment findings can directly inform interventions that aim to target interactional systems and environments rather than remediate individuals.

References

Beeke, S., Johnson, F., Beckley, F., Heilemann, C., Edwards, S., Maxim, J., et al. (2014). Enabling better conversations between a man with aphasia and his conversation partner: Incorporating writing into turn taking. *Research on Language and Social Interaction, 47*(3), 292–305.

Billig, M. (1999). Conversation analysis and claims of naivety. *Discourse and Society, 10*, 572–576.

Bilmes, J. (1992). Mishearings. In G. Watson & R. M. Seiler (Eds.), *Text in context: Contributions to ethnomethodology*. London: Sage.

Danforth, S. (2002). New words for new purposes: A challenge for the AAMR. *Mental Retardation, 40*, 21–24.

Dunn, M., Gomes, H., & Sebastian, M. (1996). Prototypicality of responses of autistic, language disordered, and normal children in a word fluency task. *Child Neuropsychology, 2*, 99–108.

Garcia, A. C. (2012). Medical problems where talk is the problem: Current trends in conversation analytic research on aphasia, autism spectrum disorder, intellectual disability, and Alzheimer's. *Sociology Compass, 6*(4), 351–364.

Garfinkel, H., & Sacks, H. (1970). On formal structures of practical actions. In J. C. McKinney & E. A. Tiryakian (Eds.), *Theoretical sociology: Perspectives and developments* (pp. 338–360). New York: Appleton-Century-Crofts.

Goodwin, C. (1987). Forgetfulness as an interactive resource. *Social Psychology Quarterly, 50*, 115–131.

Mehan, H. (1979). *Learning lesson*. Cambridge, MA: Harvard University Press.

Moseley, R., Mohr, B., Lombardo, M. V., Baron-Cohen, S., Hauk, O., & Pulvermuller, F. (2013). Brain and behavioral correlates of action semantic deficits in autism. *Frontiers in Human Neuroscience, 7*, 725.

Muskett, T. (2016). Examining language and communication in autism spectrum disorder—In context. In K. Runswick-Cole, R. Mallett, & S. Timimi (Eds.), *Re-thinking autism: Diagnosis, identity and equality* (pp. 300–316). London: Jessica Kingsley.

Muskett, T., Body, R., & Perkins, M. (2012). Uncovering the dynamic in static assessment interaction. *Child Language Teaching Therapy, 28*, 87–99.

Muskett, T., Body, R., & Perkins, M. (2013). A discursive psychology critique of semantic verbal fluency assessment and its interpretation. *Theory & Psychology, 23*(2), 205–226.

Potter, J., & te Molder, H. (2005). Talking cognition: Mapping and making the terrain. In H. te Molder & J. Potter (Eds.), *Conversation and cognition* (pp. 1–54). Cambridge: Cambridge University Press.

Psathas, G. (1995). *Conversation analysis: The study of talk-in-interaction.* Thousand Oaks, CA: Sage.

Rose, N. (1989). *Governing the soul: The shaping of the private self.* London: Routledge.

Sacks, H. (1987). On the preferences for agreement and contiguity in sequences in conversation. In G. Button & J. R. E. Lee (Eds.), *Talk and social organisation.* Clevedon: Multilingual Matters.

Sacks, H., Schegloff, E. A., & Jefferson, G. (1974). A simplest systematics for the organization of turn-taking in conversation. *Language, 50,* 696–735.

Schegloff, E. A., Jefferson, G., & Sacks, H. (1977). The preference for self-correction in the organisation of repair in conversation. *Language, 53,* 361–382.

Schiffrin, D. (1987). *Discourse markers.* Cambridge: Cambridge University Press.

Tager-Flusberg, H. (1991). Semantic processing in the free recall of autistic children: Further evidence for a cognitive deficit. *British Journal of Developmental Psychology, 9,* 417–430.

Tognini-Bonelli, E. (2001). *Corpus linguistics at work: Studies in corpus linguistics.* Philadelphia: John Benjamins.

Volden, J., & Lord, C. (1991). Neologisms and idiosyncratic language in autistic speakers. *Journal of Autism and Developmental Disorders, 21,* 109–130.

Recommended Reading

Psathas, G. (1995). *Conversation analysis: The study of talk-in-interaction.* Thousand Oaks, CA: Sage.

Taylor, C., & White, S. (2000). *Practising reflexivity in health and welfare.* Buckingham: Open University Press.

Tom Muskett is a Senior Lecturer in psychology at Leeds Beckett University, the UK. Tom's professional background is in speech and language therapy. He has worked in clinical and educational roles with children with diagnoses of autism and their families and previously led a clinical training programme at the University of Sheffield, the UK. Informed by his experiences in these roles, Tom's teaching and research aims to explore how children's 'development' and 'disorder' can be rethought methodologically, socially, and politically. For more details, please see http://www.leedsbeckett.ac.uk/staff/dr-thomas-muskett/.

6

Understanding the Autistic Individual: A Practical Guide to Critical Discourse Analysis

Charlotte Brownlow, Lindsay O'Dell, and Tanya Machin

Learning Objectives

By the end of this chapter, you will be able to:

- Understand the key principles of critical discourse analysis.
- Understand how critical discourse analysis theorises the positioning of individuals within dominant discourses.
- Explore concepts in data such as issues of discourses, dominant repertoires, positioning, and ideological dilemmas.

C. Brownlow (✉) • T. Machin
School of Psychology and Counselling, The University of Southern Queensland, Toowoomba, QLD, Australia

L. O'Dell
Faculty of Wellbeing, Education and Language Studies at the Open University, Milton Keynes, UK

© The Author(s) 2017 **141**
M. O'Reilly et al. (eds.), *A Practical Guide to Social Interaction Research in Autism Spectrum Disorders*, The Language of Mental Health,
https://doi.org/10.1057/978-1-137-59236-1_6

- Critically consider the strengths and limitations of critical discourse analysis.

Introduction

In this chapter, we seek to explore the positioning of individuals with autism spectrum disorder (ASD) within professional discourse. We will discuss what critical discourse analysis (CDA) is and what it is not, before applying the approach to analysis to an example of data drawn from a YouTube video. In doing this, we will use the data to illustrate how the method of analysis works in practice. The chapter will also draw upon the previous work of Edley (2001) to explore issues of dominant repertoires, positioning, and ideological dilemmas operating within the therapeutic and training contexts. Finally, we will discuss the strengths and limitations of this method of data analysis, with additional implications for researchers using this approach.

In doing this, we draw on a specific understanding of ASD that is informed by critical autism studies (see Davidson & Orsini, 2013). In

---

Box 6.1 Activity 1

Activity

Before you go any further in the chapter, we invite you to reflect on the meaning of ASD and its social and medical positions in society. ASD has traditionally been thought of as a condition that is diagnosed by medical and psychological practitioners according to specific psychiatric criteria such as the DSM (*Diagnostic and Statistical Manual*). This approach to understanding autism focuses on deficit, that is, what children and adults with autism are unable to do. It compares people with ASD against 'normal' functioning. This is the dominant way in which the condition is considered in many contexts, particularly in countries such as the UK and Australia, where the authors of this chapter live and work.

In recent years, there have been critiques of this approach to understanding ASD and the development of alternative understandings, including critical approaches. People diagnosed with ASD, and other activists/advocates, have developed an alternative approach to understanding and researching this spectrum condition, which focuses not on deficit but on the skills and abilities people with ASD possess. The approach also conceptualises ASD not as a mental illness but as an identity and an alternative way of being in the world.

Box 6.1 Activity 1 (continued)

Activity

Before you continue with the chapter, take a few moments to write down what you think about this more critical perspective from your own personal position.

adopting such an approach, we argue that dominant constructions of this condition focus on medical approaches which seek to explain ASD as a deficit, whereas we argue that there is a need to focus on ASD as an identity, which is produced within certain contexts (O'Dell et al., 2016).

What Is Critical Discourse Analysis?

Critical discourse analysis (CDA) is "now part of the intellectual landscape" (Breeze, 2011, p. 493) of qualitative research. It can most usefully be thought of as a collection of approaches rather than a single 'recipe' from which to approach data analysis. CDA as a shared approached emerged in the early 1990s (Wodak & Meyer, 2015), although its epistemological roots go back much further and cross several disciplines including linguistics, sociology, philosophy and psychology. As a result, CDA is a combination of several processes, ideologies and perspectives, which while they may differ in terminology and epistemological framework, share common ground. These commonalities are typically considered to be:

- Discourse.
- Critique.
- Power.
- Ideology.
- Source: Wodak and Meyer (2015)

Important point

! Despite the use of the word 'critical' in the overall approach, this should
• not be confused with the notion that all things must be negatively evaluated when approaching research through the lens of CDA.

Wodak and Meyer (2015) point out that such an appeal to common-sense understandings of the term 'critical' are not appropriate to CDA. Rather, they argue, critique in a CDA sense concerns itself with interrogating structures of power and unmasking 'common-sense' ways of understanding issues and explore taken-for-granted assumptions and practices (Wodak & Meyer, 2015). One of the core ways that critical discourse analysts engage with issues critically is through exploring the use of understandings and which certain representations of issues become 'taken for granted' and therefore more dominant in a particular context.

One of the core principles shared by researchers drawing on a CDA approach is a focus on language, and the core role that language plays in shaping social structures and providing organised ways to view the world. A focus on language is, of course, not uncommon across qualitative approaches to research. However, one of the key elements of critical discourse analysis is that analysts approach their data from a 'macro' rather than 'micro' perspective (Parker, 2013). Rather than focusing on the individual words or phrases used by an individual as a conversation analyst might, a critical discourse analyst would be looking at the bigger picture, seeking to understand how language both constructs and is constructed by particular social contexts, subsequently positioning individuals within this. Critical discourse analysis therefore goes beyond perceiving language as just a tool for communication, instead viewing language as actively constructing what is understood (Scior, 2003).

Potter and Wetherell (1987) propose that discourse does not only reflect and express meanings, it constructs them. It is these constructions that are shared and therefore enable a shared understanding of events. Discourse is not the product of a single individual, but rather a social activity with shared understandings. This suggests that meanings, understandings and even cognition are not solely the product of an individual's thinking, but that individuals only understand the world through the discursive resources available to them in any given time and culture.

Important point

! Issues of power are central to researchers guided by critical discourse
• analytic techniques.

This is particularly evident with respect to what constructions are 'available' for speakers to use. Edley (2001) argues that there may be numerous options from which the speaker can draw upon in exchanges, but the options are not always equal in that some are more 'available' than others. Edley proposes that this is because some ways of understanding the world become culturally dominant or hegemonic (meaning that they become seen as true, or natural).

> *For example:* For many years in the UK, and other countries, heterosexuality was hegemonic; that is, it was seen as natural. In doing so, some discourses became taken for granted and were accorded factual status as a true or accurate description of events.

Edley proposes that one of the key foci of critical work is to investigate such issues of normalisation/naturalisation and to enquire whose interests are best served by the prominence of different discourses. In the work we present here, we are particularly interested in the differing levels of power between individuals who work within the ASD space, with professionals typically affording more power with respect to identification and diagnosis than either parents or individuals with the condition.

The focus of CDA on the macro level is reflected in the type of material that would comprise 'data'. Some traditions in qualitative analysis focus their attention on naturally occurring exchanges between two individuals and the structures inherent in the interchange between them (as in conversation analysis). In contrast, the material comprising data for a critical discourse analysis is much broader than that, drawing on language broadly defined as "all semiotically structured phenomena ranging from advertising images to the organisation of space" (Parker, 2013, p. 230). The focus of CDA is on the broader engagement with discourse rather than the finer grained individual expression of certain concepts.

Important point

! This has implications for how CDA conceptualises and understands individuals.

Some approaches to qualitative analysis prioritise individual perception and experience of a particular event, or the expressions used in a particular conversational exchange. However, the focus of CDA is not at the level of individual, instead focusing on the structures and institutions that function to produce certain versions of the world, and subsequently understand the role and position of the individual within this.

There are many different perspectives within CDA, which draw on different political and theoretical tools. Understandings of terms used in CDA such as *discourse* and *repertoires* can differ between individual researchers and across academic disciplines. Given the diverse range of disciplines that are drawn upon in the field of discursive psychology broadly, and CDA more specifically, analysts will carve their own analytical frameworks in approaching their work. The approach that we adopt is described next.

Our Analytical and Epistemological Framework

We have been informed by several ways of approaching CDA, including the concept of *discourses* informed by the work of Fairclough (1992), and *Interpretative Repertoires, Ideological Dilemmas* and *Subject Positions* from the work of Potter and Wetherell (1987) and Edley (2001). We define our usage of terminology in the following ways.

Discourse: Edley (2001) argues that discourses reflect a commitment to a particular ideology, and as such the term is commonly associated with approaches to analysis that are informed by a Foucauldian perspective. In our work, we share this understanding and see discourse as the overarching representation of a certain concept, something that is produced within and by particular structures of power including government, and other institutions such as medicine. For our research area of ASD, the broader discourse surrounding this condition is one that sits within (dominant) medical (re)productions of knowledges, which reflect an ideology within society. Such discourses are intertwined with embedded structures of power, which serve to marginalise and prioritise certain ways of constructing individuals, diagnostic categories and ideas about ability, disability, and impairment.

Interpretative Repertoires: Edley (2001) conceptualised interpretative repertoires as ways of talking about events or individuals, which are relatively coherent. We argue that in our own work, repertoires sit within broader discourses, not instead of them. We therefore see the possibility for several interpretative repertoires to be operating within a broader discourse. Some repertoires may draw upon the medical discourse, and may therefore be the most dominant, while others may draw upon a different understanding of ASD as a form of *differen*ce rather than as a *deficit*. Repertoires are therefore a way that individuals can both shape and be shaped by discourse, with some being more readily taken up over others, sometimes reflecting the power structures operating within the broader discursive terrain.

Box 6.2 Activity 2

Activity

Earlier in the chapter we discussed how understandings of 'discourse' can differ between researchers and disciplines. Before you have read further into the chapter, it is now a good time for you to reflect on your own understanding of critical discourse analysis by considering the following:

• How does CDA conceptualise individuals and their relation to knowledge about the world?
• How does the approach understand power?

In answering these questions, you need to think about the focus of critical discourse analysis which is on social structures and the implications of these for individuals, particularly how they are positioned, or understand themselves, in relation to dominant ideas about the world. It is not a good method of analysis if the aim of your project is to focus on individual experience. Rather, the approach focuses on broader issues, and focuses on the ways in which certain ideas about the world are seen to be normal and natural, for example, particular kinds of sexuality seen to be normal, whereas others seen as problematic or 'deviant'. Mechanisms such as diagnostic classifications, clinical discourse, and everyday language all contribute to seeing the world in this way. Furthermore, the approach is often explicitly political: "A more or less political concern with the workings of ideology and power in society; and a specific interest in the way language contributes to, perpetuates and reveals these workings. Thus the more explicit definitions all emphasise the relationship between language (text, discourse) and power (political struggle, inequality, dominance)" (Breeze, 2011, p. 495).

Ideological dilemmas: While repertoires are assumed to be relatively coherent, it is evident that people move between different repertoires, drawing on what may appear to be contrary repertoires in making their arguments. This is something that we have written about in previous work (see, e.g., Brownlow & O'Dell, 2006), where we see people who identify as being autistic drawing on two different repertoires when considering and constructing autism. One repertoire is of ASD as a distinct difference to neurologically typical (i.e., 'normal') functioning, setting up binary categories of 'autistic' and 'neurotypical' functioning. This repertoire is sometimes used within autistic identity politics to make a claim for a positive identity as an autistic person. However, the same individual may also draw on a different repertoire, one of diversity, positioning autism as just one point on a spectrum, ranging from autistic to neurotypical (NT), with everyone falling on the spectrum at some point. This second repertoire enables a framing of autism as a spectrum rather than a distinct 'condition'. Both of these repertoires position people in quite different ways. It is a good example of individuals might draw upon different repertoires at different times.

Subject positions: We can therefore see how repertoires may position individuals in certain ways, constructing particular identities. However, we would argue that individuals are both produced by and the producers of language. Individuals take up identities themselves as well as through being positioned by others, particular practices and discourses. In the example of ASD, we can see that the production of an autistic identity drawing on negative representations of 'impairment' and 'deficit', positions an individual in a particular way. However, an individual may also be able to adopt an alternative construction, which either positions them as *different* to NTs through drawing on a spectrum repertoire, or *better* than NTs through drawing on an alternative repertoire (see, e.g., Brownlow, 2010; O'Reilly, Karim, & Lester, 2016). However, such positioning, either by self or by others, operates within a broader overarching dominant discourse, which prioritises some forms of identities and marginalises others.

In sum, we would therefore argue that we both position ourselves and are positioned by others within particular interpretative repertoires. This is complex and shift within different contexts.

> *For example:* The decision to adopt a marginalised identity, such as of autism as a difference to NT functioning, as a means of empowerment may still remain marginal within the broader discourse practices because these interpretative repertoires operate within wider ideological discourses, which serve to prioritise some representations and marginalise others.

The Data

In order to demonstrate how we would approach a critical discourse analysis, we have selected a publicly available YouTube video in order for us to be able to explore how 'autism' as a diagnostic category is used within clinical consultation and training sessions. Our aim is not to examine the specifics of the individual interactions (as would happen in a more micro form of analysis) but to examine how particular discourses of ASD are taken as hegemonic within this context. We have therefore selected as an example of a YouTube video aimed at educating clinicians about developmental features of autistic traits in young children. The full video can be found here: https://www.youtube.com/watch?v=YtvP5A5OHpU.

A key concern when conducting research is one of ethics. This is a particular concern for us as critical discourse analysts because our priority is to examine/interrogate power structures and taken-for-granted assumptions about the world that position some forms of knowledge as dominant and others as marginalised. Publically available texts, such as websites, policy documents, advertisements, and so on, are often a good source of material for researchers using a critical discourse analytic approach. As critical discourse analysts, we aim to explore how repertoires, positioning, and power structures operate within everyday encounters. Even if the data you are drawing on is in the public realm, care needs to be taken in the consideration of ethical protocols and sensitive research practice. There are guidelines that can inform researchers planning research using online data (see, e.g., British Psychological Society, 2013).

The YouTube Clip

The data chosen for this chapter is a publicly available film about diagnosing ASD. It is on one hand a slightly unusual choice in that it is a type of data often used by more micro discourse or conversation analysts. However, on the other, it is consistent with a body of discourse analytic work that interrogates issues of power and classification of clinical conditions (Winter, Moncrieff, & Speed, 2015).

A YouTube clip designed to demonstrate early signs of the ASD, and produced by the Kennedy Krieger Institute was therefore selected as our analytical example for this chapter. The video showed three pairs of one-year old children, with one child in each pair identified as having ASD, and the other child who was described as not having ASD (i.e., a 'normally functioning' child). At the start of each section, a title slide that provided focal points for the viewer was displayed to guide the viewer's understanding of the material to follow. These focal points concentrated on developmental features of ASD including social opportunities through play, making social connections, and effective communication and shared enjoyment. Immediately after the focal point slide is shown, a narrator announces whether the child shows signs of ASD, as well as narrating (making sense of) the actions of the child. Intertwined with the narration are video clips from therapeutic and assessment sessions showing footage of the child and a therapist and sometimes a parent. The clip in total is 9 minutes long.

Undertaking a Critical Discourse Analysis

Our approach to analysis draws on the previous work of Edley (2001) and begins with gaining an understanding of the entire data set. While some approaches may focus on specific sub-sections of the data set, the techniques that we adopt require a full appreciation of the complete data set. By doing so, this then allows us to develop an understanding of order and flow of exchanges, as well as better interpret particular issues where understandings may require an appreciation of any power differentials that may only be evident when considering the entire exchange. It also allows for a rigorous analysis of the data (see section below in which we evaluate CDA). The data we present here is to give an illustration of how to undertake a critical discourse analysis and would not represent sufficient data for a full analysis.

Important point

! Critical discourse analysis makes visible links between theory, method,
•   and the production of knowledge.

In focusing attention on an ASD training video comprising of both narration and real-life clinical excerpts, we, as analysts, have made a choice in the material we wish to analyse. As with many other approaches to qualitative data analysis, the position of the researcher needs to be made clear. Our shared position is one of enabling marginalised voices to be represented in what are typically medically dominated arenas, and the valuing of identities of people with ASD. Therefore, our focus is one of ASD *differences* rather than ASD *deficits* and to denaturalise taken-for-granted assumptions about 'normality', in this case neurotypicality. Given our explicitly stated shared focus on *difference* rather than *deficit*, our analysis will work to highlight these repertoires in the data and seek to highlight any taken-for-granted assumptions about the children's ability. Further, we will critically interrogate and question positions of power (in this instance power to give meaning to the behaviour of children) and the interests being served by adopting certain ways of understanding and knowledge. It is with these positions that the steps of analysis to this data set are approached.

Box 6.3 Activity 3

Activity

At the beginning of this chapter, we stated our position about ASD as one of difference rather than deficit. This position informs our work and hence the analysis we offer. Before moving on to the analysis, take some time now to consider your own position on ASD, specifically:
• How does a medical discourse of ASD construct people with autism?
• What characterises alternative, critical approaches?
You could return to the activity box at the beginning of this chapter to remind yourself of the different ways in which ASD is constructed. An understanding of the different constructions of ASD is an important element of the analysis that follows.

Steps of Analysis

The approach we adopt consists of an iterative analysis, moving between the analytical themes and the data at several points in the process of analysis. The steps that we have taken in our approach to analysis are as follows:

Step 1: Listen to/watch the entire video clip. The entire video was watched several times to ensure engaged interaction and a full appreciation of the contents and order of the video material. This is an important step for you, if you choose to do a CDA project.

Step 2: Complete a verbatim transcription of the video. For our specific example here, YouTube provided a transcription. However, on closer inspection, this was not an entirely accurate record and therefore the transcription was edited for accuracy and key additions made. For this example, we also included the content of the slides used to break up the video into sections because these were considered a core part of the story being told and the representations of children within it. Because of the focus is on power and the broad, macro-level discourse, the transcript consisted of the words used in the interactions but did not include pauses, timing between words or any other notations that would be required for a more micro, fine grain analysis of conversation.

Step 3: Listen to/watch the video clip again to ensure accuracy in transcription and amend as necessary. Following the transcription, the video was watched again several times and checked for accuracy. Again, it is important that you do this in your research as it is essential to become very familiar with your data.

Step 4: Read through the transcript and highlight areas of interest. This is the point at which more applied analysis begins, although the initial engagement with the data will have already begun to sensitise us to the issues being raised in the data. It is at this stage that the analyst would highlight areas of interest within the transcript and begin an analytical interpretation of this. This is guided by Fairclough's three stages of analysis:

1. Description
2. Explanation
3. Interpretation

First, the analysis seeks to describe the main features of the text. In this instance, the film presents a series of children which the narrator describes in the following way:

```
Within each pair you will see a child with neurotypical
development followed by a child who shows early signs
of ASD.
```

In our notes, as we began the analysis we made a comment that the presentation was structured in a way to offer a clear comparison of ASD and NT assumed norms. In our description, we also noted the ways in which ASD and NT children were described, for example, in describing NT functioning behaviours were identified:

```
These include effective communication and sharing enjoyment,
making social connections and the one with which we will
begin, seeing social opportunity through play.
```

Step 5: Examine whether these areas overlap, and therefore contribute to broader discourses. Following making a commentary on the transcript, all of the individual comments were examined to consider whether there were shared aspects, and hence contributed to overarching themes within the data set. In our example, the comments made and the extracts highlighted were felt to contribute to a shared understanding of ideas that contributed to the benchmarking of norms of development.

So, we began to develop an explanation and interpretation of the data by noting that the clinician makes assumption about what is 'appropriate' social engagement. We note the taken-for-granted social norms of neurotypicality at play with a comparison (and pathologisation) of ASD behaviours. The argument therefore starts to be established that comparisons of the individual child are always made against taken-for-granted norms of development that mirror NT benchmarks. This was therefore proposed as the dominant theme within this example of data. As the data chosen for our purposes here was short, only one theme has been identified. However, we would expect in research projects that draw on multiple data sources or large data sets, several dominant themes would be identified during this stage.

Step 6: Return to the data and ensure that exemplars from the data set can evidence the themes proposed. Any themes identified must be able to be evidenced in the transcripts. It is therefore crucial that analysts return to the original, unmarked transcript to ensure that any claims made can be evidenced. This will also be an important opportunity to consider whether alternative readings of the texts are possible and whether the claims made in this particular reading can be evidenced in the data.

Step 7: Further development of the analysis—Within our identified theme of the benchmarking of norms of development, particular foci can be placed on the data that reflects core issues associated with CDA: those of power, dominant repertoires, individual subject positioning, and ideological dilemmas.

Box 6.4 Activity 4

Activity

The following excerpt is of the narrator and the participants in the film in which a 19-month-old boy plays with a toy phone. Using the information that you have been introduced to in this chapter so far, we recommend that you read the extract and sketch out how the extract provides ways in which ideas about 'normal' behaviour is assumed and used to explain the behaviour of this child:
This 19-month-old child shows signs of ASD.

Box 6.4 Activity 4 (continued)

Activity

He has an intense interest in the toy phone. He does not share his enjoyment of the phone with others. He does not look toward others and smile.

(Mom) "He really has this addiction to telephones... . It's OK if it's helping him with sounds ... There's probably like 10 telephones lying around my house. Because he walks around carrying them. Sits them down and moves on to the next one."

From the extract in the activity, we would argue that the play activities of this 19-month-old child are not framed in a positive way by the clinician/narrator. Any interest that the boy demonstrates in the toy phone is considered unusually strong and deviates from shared understandings of what such enjoyment should look like.

For example: While the boy demonstrates interest in the phone, his lack of sharing his individual interest with others contravenes common-sense shared assumptions about what enjoyment should look like; for instance, enjoyment within a shared social space with others.

This positions the boy as 'impaired' in some way because his abilities and actions are different from the dominant ways of understandings surrounding enjoyment and shared social activities. In addition, the narration of the event is provided by an individual positioned as being an expert within the field, with authority to provide commentary and to give meaning to the behaviours exhibited by the children in the film. In the extract above the child is further positioned as deficient because he is not exhibiting creativity in the expected way:

Although he puts the phone to his ear, he does not show creative play with the phone.

Step 8: Return to the data and ensure that exemplars from the data set can evidence any claims made. The analysis by this point has moved from description of the data to interpretation and analysis. However, it is crucial to maintain the iterative approach to analysis in ensuring that any claims that are being made can be evidenced in the raw data. In our example above, we can see that the claims can be evidenced in direct quotes from the transcript.

Step 9: Create a structure/flow to the analysis. In this final step, the crafting and presentation of a reading of the analysis is presented. The analysis needs to be presented as a coherent interpretation of the transcript based on the analysts' theoretical position and 'political' position in relation to understanding ASD. Our analysis of the example transcript has therefore taken the following approach.

The dominant repertoire identified in the data was 'the benchmarking of norms of development', and reflected the comparison of the behaviours of children with ASD to neurologically typical ideals. Such benchmarking clearly establishes accepted norms of development which reflect NT developmental trajectories. Transgressions from the assumed developmental pathway are observed and labelled (by the narrator and the slides) as 'atypical' or 'deficient'. Such comparisons to assumed norms are made both explicitly through the narration of the video and more implicitly within the excerpts of clinical session provided.

> *For example:* At the beginning of the video, the narrator establishes themselves as an expert within the field and establishes the focus of the videos being a comparison between children with and without ASD.

The comparisons are explicitly established through both the narrator's descriptions and the presentation of information on the slides. For example:

> You're about to watch a brief tutorial illustrating the early signs of autism spectrum disorders or ASD. You will see three pairs of videos of one-year-olds.
>
> Within each pair you offer, see a child with neurotypical development followed by a child who shows early signs of ASD.
>
> The developmental features indicative of ASD shown within these videos fall into three main categories. These include effective communication and sharing enjoyment, making social connections and the one with which we will begin, seeing social opportunity through play.

We can see from the extract above that the comparisons assume that the taken-for-granted (NT) norms of development can, and should be, considered a benchmark. The focus on appropriate social engagement explicitly links the taken-for-granted norms of NT children and enables a comparison (and pathologisation) of children with ASD.

Important point

! This positions children with ASD as 'lacking' or 'impaired'.
•

In addition to the clinical narration, the summary slides explicitly compare children with and without ASD, for example:

FOCAL POINTS: NO ASD
- Engages others in his play
- Shows meaningful, purposeful, and pretend play
- Shares enjoyment by smiling at people
- Synchronizes with others through imitation

FOCAL POINTS: ASD
- Has unusually strong interest in phone
- Does not engage with people during play
- Does not respond to name
- Enjoys tickle but does not look at mom to share enjoyment

From the aforementioned examples, we can see that the children are constructed in quite different ways based on their label. In referring to children with ASD, the slides label the group as 'ASD'. However, in contrast, those not on the spectrum are not given a label, for example, of 'NT', but rather referred to as 'No ASD'. This serves to position children on the spectrum as 'special cases' that warrant a specific label to differentiate them from the norm. The dominant group of 'No ASD' do not need a label because their behaviour is naturalised and taken for granted as appropriate and positive.

It can also be argued from the examples above that the values attached to the constructions of 'ASD' and 'No ASD' children differ. When describing NT children, positive language is drawn upon, describing a socially engaged individual, which is a valued position. In contrast, children on the spectrum are not framed in a positive way. Interests are singled out for the warranting of attention, and these are considered 'unusually strong', presumably when compared to NT norms. Further, the requirement to share enjoyment in a NT-sanctioned social manner is explicitly required, with (ASD) children not being able to enjoy tickling without it benefiting others through shared enjoyment. This positioning is further elucidated in the extracts. For example:

> This 19-month-old child does not show signs of ASD.
> He has chosen to play with the balls. He quickly integrates the lady into his play. He pretends that the balls are food and offers a bite to the lady.
> (Adult says) "Nom nom"
> [Some exchange between parent and therapist—inaudible]
> (Adult) "mmm mmm, you are making some yummy food."
> He understands that food, spoons, plates, and eating go together. As he creates a pretend play activity he remains aware of the people nearby. He enjoys incorporating social interaction into his play and offers the lady a bite.
> (Adult) "Thank you. That sure is tasty."
> He is able to pay attention to the lady, the doll, and the pretend food all at once. He shares his excitement about the toys with the lady looking at her and smiling. After the lady comments that the food is hot, he linked his play and language to her idea.

In this exchange and the accompanying narrative, we can see direct encouragement from the adult in the clinical interaction to the (NT) child, providing positive reward of the child's behaviour. The child is therefore constructed as engaging in a valued activity, which serves to position the child in a positive frame. The child has chosen the activity of interest (playing with the balls), and such focus is not positioned as problematic. The child is enjoying the activity chosen but this enjoyment for the NT child is framed positively due to the social engagement with others as part of this enjoyment.

The construction of appropriate sociality exhibited by the NT child in this example draws on an assumed 'correct' way to play, as an activity that requires the inclusion and shared enjoyment with others. No space is provided for alternative ways of playing and the interactions and narration offer no positive ways of accounting for solitary play. This prioritising of desired (NT) social ways was further discussed in the earlier stages of our analysis exemplified by the following excerpt:

> This 19-month-old child show signs of ASD.
>
> He has an intense interest in the toy phone. He does not share his enjoyment of the phone with others. He does not look toward others and smile.
>
> (Mom) "He really has this addiction to telephones... . It's OK if it's helping him with sounds ... There's probably like 10 telephones lying around my house. Because he walks around carrying them. Sits them down and moves on to the next one."
>
> Although he puts the phone to his ear, he does not show creative play with the phone.

In contrast to the interests of the NT child, this child on the spectrum does not have their interests framed in a positive way. His interest is considered unusually strong and he does not 'appropriately' enjoy his interest because he is not sharing this socially with others. Further, the label of ASD takes central importance in the presentations of understandings of the child's behaviour. The narrator comments that the boy puts the phone to his ear, an indication of engaged creative play, but this is positioned as problematic.

In addition to the requirement of the sharing of enjoyment, which has been firmly established as a benchmark for 'normal' sociality, the display of sharing also needs to conform to clear guidelines. For example, a 14-month-old boy who has been labelled as ASD demonstrates enjoyment of a social activity, but not within the prescribed ways:

> This 14-month-old shows signs of ASD.
>
> First, he flaps his hands while enjoying the bubbles. He does not share his enjoyment by looking at the man. He does not respond to his name.
>
> (Man) "Ben. Ben."
>
> Although he looks at the man's pointed finger, he does not follow the directions of the man's gesture to locate the object of the man's attention.

In this example, the child is clearly demonstrating his enjoyment of the social activity of the bubble blowing by the adult. However, this is not seen as an appropriate way of displaying happiness or engagement. The child's focused attention on the bubbles, at the expense of diverting attention towards the adult, is constructed as problematic. The child also demonstrates some skills in appropriate (NT) social ways, such as through the enjoyment of the activity and also the following of a pointed finger—both behaviours that are taken as indicative of 'normal' or non-ASD behaviour. For the narrator, this presents an ideological dilemma in that the child is labelled as ASD but appears to be demonstrating some acceptable (NT) behaviours. This dilemma is addressed through the argument that the behaviour is not 'NT enough'. So the enjoyment is not demonstrated in an NT-sanctioned manner, and the following of the finger gesture is judged qualitatively as not following the finger pointing well enough or to completion.

In this presentation of a brief analysis of the video, we argue some key points. First, the comparison of a negative construction of 'ASD' with a positive construction of 'No ASD' constructs clear benchmarks concerning norms of development, with a positive assessment of such norms clearly aligning to NT ways of being. This discourse draws heavily on 'deficit' and 'impairment' rather than 'neurodiversity' and 'difference'. We are not arguing that the children with a diagnosis of ASD in the film behave in the same way as those without a label of ASD, but we would argue that the constructions of understandings of such differences can lead to negative positioning of children (and adults) with ASD and a positive positioning of others who adhere to the taken-for-granted norms of social functioning.

Second, and linked to the previous point, the dominant discourses of ASD remain entrenched in medical model understandings, which are in contrast to discourses of neurodiversity and difference. However, more enabling discourses remain a marginalised voice within the medical profession and therefore hold less power. Within the dominant discourse there is little space for *different* behaviours, with the focus placed firmly on *deficient* and *impaired* behaviours. This precludes an 'abilities' focus on what the child *can* do, and instead focuses on what they *can't* do.

Finally, the drawing on dominant discourses further constructs *experts* within the field of knowledge about ASD. Such experts are typically considered to be professionals who hold academic knowledge rather than individuals on the spectrum who hold experiential knowledge of ASD. Such tensions therefore illuminate power differentials within the field of ASD, with a consistent prioritising of professional over experiential knowledge.

Evaluating CDA

The rich data collected from the YouTube video was analysed using techniques of critical discourse analysis drawing on the previous work of Edley (2001). Central to this approach is an examination of the implications of maintaining the dominant discourse in a particular context. Therefore, rather than describing the discourse practices occurring in the video, critical discourse analysis enables an examination of these in light of the wider social interactions and social structures.

> **Important point**
>
> ! Critical discourse analysis has enabled an examination of thinking that
> • prioritises NT traits over autistic traits, and the implications that this
> may have for an individual.

While the approach can account for the wider discourses and repertoires that serve to position individuals, it does not focus on individual's experiences and the meaning of a label for them. The analysis (and choice of data) does not provide any insight into the lives of children with autism and their families. CDA does not focus on individual agency and it is not an appropriate method of analysis for this kind of research.

There are many critiques of CDA as a method of analysis and as an orientation to research/theory. These critiques focus on theoretical issues such as the theoretical treatment of 'language' and the vast array of different epistemological and political stances within CDA research. There are also critiques of the method of analysis.

> *For example:* Breeze (2011) argues that it "can be seen as heavily conditioned by political choice, rather than scientific criteria" (p. 501) and that there is a lack of scholarly rigour and a tendency to stereotype in many research papers reporting critical discourse analytical work.

However, CDA is an approach that can provide a detailed and thorough analysis of institutional power, processes of legitimacy, and marginalisation and shifting repertoires that construct certain contexts.

Important point

! Analysts need to be rigorous and transparent about the process of
• selection of the texts to be analysed and how the analysis has been undertaken.

Summary

In conclusion, in this chapter we have discussed the key principles of critical discourse analysis and outlined the positioning of individuals within the dominant discourses and repertoires. We have also explored the key issues of power, dominant repertoires, subject position, and ideological dilemmas, as well as providing a critique of this method of analysis. Furthermore, we have practically demonstrated how to analyse a data set through the use of critical discourse analysis. We now offer a summary of the key practical messages from the chapter in Box 6.5.

Box 6.5 Summary of the practical highlights

Summary of practical highlights

1. The key understanding of CDA is that of a macro level. That is, the social structures and implications for an individual within the positioning of the dominant ideals and the identity-making opportunities that are afforded.

Summary of practical highlights

2. The steps of analysis are outlined: Listen to/watch the entire data set (e.g., video clip); complete a verbatim transcription; listen to/watch the data set again to ensure accuracy in transcription and amend as necessary; read through the transcript and highlight areas of interest; examine whether the areas overlap, and therefore contribute to broader dominant themes; return to the data and ensure that exemplars from the data set can evidence the themes proposed; examine each theme and apply the key aspects of CDA; return to the data set and ensure exemplars can evidence any claims made; create a narrative of analysis.
3. Critical discourse analysis is appropriate for a macro analysis of power structures and the workings of taken-for-granted assumptions about a particular phenomenon under study. It is not an approach that is easily used for understanding individual experience and agency.

References

Breeze, R. (2011). Critical discourse analysis and its critics. *Pragmatics, 21*(4), 493–525.

British Psychological Society. (2013). Ethics guidelines for internet-mediated research. Retrieved April 10, 2016, from: http://www.bps.org.uk/system/files/Public%20files/inf206-guidelines-for-internet-mediated-research.pdf

Brownlow, C. (2010). Presenting the self: Negotiating a label of autism. *Journal of Intellectual and Developmental Disability, 35*(1), 14–21.

Brownlow, C., & O'Dell, L. (2006). Constructing an autistic identity: AS voices online. *Mental Retardation, 44*(5), 315–321.

Davidson, J., & Orsini, M. (2013). Critical autism studies: Notes on an emerging field. In J. Davidson & M. Orsini (Eds.), *Worlds of Autism: Across the spectrum of neurological difference* (pp. 1–30). Minneapolis: University of Minnesota Press.

Edley, N. (2001). Analysing masculinity: Interpretative repertoires, ideological dilemmas and subject positioning. In M. Wetherell, S. Taylor, & S. J. Yates (Eds.), *Discourse as data: A guide for analysis* (pp. 189–228). Milton Keyes: Sage.

Fairclough, N. (1992). *Discourse and social change*. Cambridge: Polity Press.

O'Dell, L., Bertilsdotter Rosqvist, H., Ortega, F., Brownlow, C., & Orsini, M. (2016). Critical autism studies: Exploring epistemic dialogue, challenging dominant understandings of autism. *Disability & Society., 31*(2), 166–179.

O'Reilly, M., Karim, K., & Lester, J. N. (2016). Should Autism be classified as a mental illness/disability? Evidence from empirical work. In M. O'Reilly & J. N. Lester (Eds.), *The Palgrave handbook of child mental health: Discourse and conversation studies* (pp. 252–271). Hampshire: Palgrave Macmillan.

Parker, I. (2013). Discourse analysis: Dimensions of critique in Psychology. *Qualitative Research in Psychology, 10,* 223–239.

Potter, J., & Wetherell, M. (1987). *Discourse and social psychology: Beyond attitudes and behaviour.* London: Sage.

Scior, K. (2003). Using discourse analysis to study the experiences of women with learning disabilities. *Disability & Society, 18*(6), 779–795.

Winter, H., Moncrieff, J., & Speed, E. (2015). "Because you're worth it": A discourse analysis of the gendered rhetoric of the ADHD woman. *Qualitative Research in Psychology, 12*(4), 415–434.

Wodak, R., & Meyer, M. (2015). *Methods of critical discourse studies.* London: Sage.

Recommended Reading

Breeze, R. (2011). Critical discourse analysis and its critics. *Pragmatics, 21*(4), 493–525.

Davidson, J., & Orsini, M. (2013). Critical autism studies: Notes on an emerging field. In J. Davidson & M. Orsini (Eds.), *Worlds of Autism: Across the spectrum of neurological difference* (pp. 1–30). Minneapolis: University of Minnesota Press.

Wodak, R., & Meyer, M. (2015). *Methods of critical discourse studies.* London: Sage.

Charlotte Brownlow is an associate professor in the School of Psychology and Counselling at The University of Southern Queensland, Australia. Her research interests focus on understandings of diversity and difference and the impacts that constructions of these have on the crafting of individual identities, particularly for individuals identifying as being on the autism spectrum.

Lindsay O'Dell is a feminist critical developmental psychologist in the Faculty of Wellbeing, Education and Language Studies at the Open University, the UK.

Her work focuses on children, young people, and families who are in some way 'different', including autism, ADHD, young carers, and language brokers. Lindsay is an active member of the Psychology of Women Section of the British Psychological Society and co-editor of the journal *Children & Society*.

Tanya Machin is a lecturer in psychology at the University of Southern Queensland. Her research interests focus on social and developmental psychology, specifically in the context of social media and online interactions.

7

Conversation Analysis with Children with an Autism Spectrum Disorder and Limited Verbal Ability

Paul Dickerson and Ben Robins

Learning Objectives

By the end of this chapter, you will be able to:

- Identify why video data of participants with a diagnosis of an autism spectrum disorder may be useful.
- Describe the criteria for useable video data.
- Identify what will best ensure that high-quality video data is obtained.
- Understand why attention to interactional detail is important.
- Understand why attention to sequential location is important.
- Identify why data where there is little oral language is worth careful examination.

P. Dickerson (✉)
Department of Psychology, University of Roehampton, London, UK

B. Robins
School of Computer Science, University of Hertfordshire, Hatfield, UK

© The Author(s) 2017
M. O'Reilly et al. (eds.), *A Practical Guide to Social Interaction Research in Autism Spectrum Disorders*, The Language of Mental Health,
https://doi.org/10.1057/978-1-137-59236-1_7

Introduction

Chapter 5 identified some of the ways in which it is possible to use conversation analysis (CA) to examine important features of interaction involving those who have a diagnosis of an autism spectrum disorder (ASD). This chapter builds on precisely the principles outlined in Chap. 5 to consider how we might approach ASD interaction, particularly where verbal content appears sparse or impaired. However, it is possible that the very name 'conversation' analysis (CA), with its implication of a free-flowing verbal interchange, seems incongruous with those who have a diagnosis of an ASD, given that many have trouble with social interaction and communication. This chapter illustrates the way in which CA can be an invaluable tool for examining interactions where one or more of participants speak very little, as it encompasses *the whole interaction,* rather than focusing solely on talk.

One relatively early paper using CA to examine interactions in which one or more participants have a diagnosis of an ASD did not, as one might expect, involve 'high functioning' individuals, but instead focused on a child (at least as far as the data extracts were concerned) with a very restricted lexicon. Tarplee and Barrow (1999) analysed a sequence in which a child produced repetitive (or Echolalic) speech which contained an apparently restricted number of recognisable lexical items. However, despite these apparent limitations, when viewed across an extensive sequence, the child's talk could be seen as initiating a sequence of interaction in which he and his mother played out scences from a favourite book of the child's. Thus, what at first seemed to be easily dismissible as 'impaired' (Echolalic) communication was seen, on closer inspection, to be a subtle instance of interactional sensitivity. What could be seen as *merely* repetitive (or Echolalic) talk was effective in initiating a fairly extensive sequence of interaction between the child and his mother.

Important point

! Behaviour that can be seen as merely symptomatic of an ASD diagnosis
• can take on a different meaning when it is examined in terms of the sequence of interaction where it routinely occurs.

In providing a way of rethinking seemingly 'impaired' communication, CA research into ASD has echoed some of the emphasis of CA work into aphasia (Goodwin, 2003). A substantial body of CA work has thus examined some of the ways in which quite sophisticated interactional work can be accomplished in interactions where one or more participants have a communicative impairment and produce very few words.

> *For example:* Goodwin has demonstrated how gesture, prosody, and the careful placement of these in sequences of interaction can enable quite complex interactional work to be done—even when the speaker can only articulate three recognisable words—in this way features of the talk, body movement, gaze, and gesture—**and where these are situated in the interaction**—can be understood as communicative actions alongside the words themselves.

Schegloff (2003) has demonstrated that patients' interactional skill can be easily missed, demonstrating the way in which a person with aphasia fails a clinical test of pragmatic ability whilst patently demonstrating *those very same skills* during the incidental interaction around the assessment itself.

These two observations, that complex interactional work can be done—even when communication skills appear to be impaired—and that this interactional work is easily missed, identify the key argument of this chapter. This chapter seeks to illustrate that it is possible to bring a conversation analytic perspective to sequences of interaction involving a child with an ASD that could be wrongly overlooked simply because few words are uttered by the child.

The chapter begins by outlining some of the practical considerations regarding collecting data where there is relatively little verbal content and then examines some examples of data in order to illustrate ways of approaching these data analytically. Particular attention is given to the principles for good conversation analysis that can be especially fruitful for examining interactions where there is limited verbal communication.

Collecting Data

Ethical Issues

As Chap. 4 illustrates, using naturally occurring data in ASD research requires that some consideration be given to several important ethical issues. Whilst this chapter will not revisit the points raised in Chap. 4, it will outline some issues that are especially relevant when researching children with an ASD who have limited verbal ability. Gallagher, Haywood, Jones, and Milne (2010) suggest negotiating informed consent with children is in itself more complicated than is often acknowledged, this is perhaps all the truer where the research involves children with an ASD who produce relatively little in terms of verbal communication. As Arscott, Dagnan, and Kroese (1998) note, particular care must be taken in cases where participants have possible limitations in terms of their understanding of both the risks and benefits involved in participation and of their right to refuse consent or to withdraw it during the research. Even where potential participants do understand their rights, children on the autistic spectrum who speak very little may well have difficulties in expressing their desire not to participate, or, to cease participation.

By themselves these observations could lead researchers to doubt the possibility of genuinely involving children with an ASD (perhaps especially those deemed to be 'low functioning') in decisions about consent to participate in research. However, O'Reilly, Ronzoni, and Dogra (2013) provide some useful reflections on how to provide genuine opportunities for children to exercise consent that could be particularly helpful in thinking about the issue of consent amongst participants who are both children *and* on the autistic spectrum. O'Reilly et al. (2013) mention the importance of reminding participants of the fact that they have the option to withdraw and to carefully observe the behaviour of the child participants for signs of distress. One additional consideration that may be helpful for research involving children with an ASD is that the parent or caregiver's knowledge of the child can be an important source of information regarding how the child may indicate that they do not wish to commence or continue participation in the research. Ideally, the parent/caregiver themselves could be present during the data collection (regardless of whether they are participating in the research themselves). In such cases, reassuring them that the research can stop at any point should they note distress on the part of the child (or indeed themselves) provides a valuable safeguard concerning consent in cases of impaired capacity. In cases where the parent or caregiver is not present, it is worth discussing with them in some detail the scope of the research, how the child can be put at ease, and what (possibly idiosyncratic) signs of distress or discomfort should be watched for. Having introduced you to some initial key issues that are pertinent when doing research with those with ASD we would now encourage you to reflect on your learning by looking at the activity in Box 7.1.

Box 7.1 Activity on issues with video

Activity

Identifying issues with actual video recordings is an important aspect of reflexivity when doing this kind of work. We would encourage you to follow the steps below to do this:

1. Search the web for 'ASD videos' and identify about six or seven videos. It is worth locating actual videos (rather than simply imagining the issues that might come up).
2. Interrogate these recordings by investigating the following:
   • How many of the videos enable you to see the faces and actions of all who are present?
   • Who or what is unseen in the video recordings (e.g. often experimenters and other adults are not consistently visible)?
   • How many of the videos are definitely unedited and therefore have sequential integrity?
3. Now imagine that you are trying to record an interaction between an adult and a child with an ASD, both of whom are interacting with a humanoid robot, and consider the following:
   • What are the problems with not visually capturing all who are present?
   • How can this be overcome?
   • What are the problems with trying to analyse edited video recordings?

Hopefully you have managed to think about some answers to the questions we pose here. By continuing with your reading of this chapter, some of the issues you have highlighted should become clearer.

Video Recording

It may seem unnecessary to consider something as apparently straightforward and practical as video recording when thinking about collecting data of ASD interaction. The temptation is to rush straight into analysis presuming that if we know how to operate the equipment everything else will take care of itself. Things are, however, a little less straightforward than that. Issues about the placement of recording equipment can be relatively straightforward in cases where we are solely concerned with an audio record of an interaction. The two most important requirements— that are not met in most video recordings that involve children with an ASD—are:

1. that the recording captures *all participants* both audibly *and visually* and
2. that sequences of interaction are not edited down.

Most video recordings of children with ASD will capture the audio data of the child and co-present others; however, they will typically point the camera at the child and visually exclude non-ASD others from the recording except where they might briefly pass in front of the camera whilst attending to the child. This typical arrangement, of a camera pointed at the child with an ASD and not at co-present others, reflects assumptions that it is the child in isolation that is important rather than the child within an interactional environment. This arrangement at a stroke renders analysis of the interactional environment for non-vocal activity such as body movement, gaze, and gesture difficult if not impossible.

Important point

! In your research, you need to make sure that your recordings capture
• all people in the interaction, not just the child.

Those videos that do show all interactants typically fall foul of the second requirement, which can be thought of in terms of sequential integrity. If we want to examine what happens in sequences of interaction, then we need the entirety of the sequence—without this we cannot examine how one participant's behaviour is shaped by, or is shaping of, others; that is, we cannot see how participants orientate to one another, how they build action in concert. With the prevalence of measures that sample behaviour, often at fixed intervals in an interaction, it is all the more important to emphasise the importance of the integrity of the entire sequence of interaction within which any target behaviour is placed. If we do not record, or keep, the sequential context of any target behaviour, we preclude *a priori* the possibility of examining any interactional issues that the target behaviour may be orientating to.

Important point

! Video recordings often reflect certain theoretical assumptions.
• Recordings that only visually show the child with an ASD diagnosis reflect an assumption that their behaviour (e.g. 'gaze avoidance') can be understood without reference to an intricate examination of the gaze (and other) behaviour of co-present others.

In addition to these two fundamental issues, there are a number of technical considerations which can be summarised in terms of three key concerns:

- Check the equipment
- Use multiple cameras
- Test the camera positioning and view prior to recording

These technical issues can easily be dismissed as either obvious or uninteresting, yet they are very well worth addressing as it can be devastating to discover *only when it is too late* that the equipment failed to record the data. Each of these three overlapping concerns will be considered in turn.

Before even setting up the video recording equipment, there is an important consideration (which is rapidly being addressed by technological developments), namely, the definitional quality of the recording. Details such as where participants are gazing become central to this form of research and low quality definition can make judgements on this issue difficult if not impossible. Assuming that the video recorders are of sufficient quality for recording audio and visual data, it is important to check the equipment prior to recording. Though it seems patently obvious, most people who make extensive use of collecting video data will at some point have experienced issues in relation to the power (battery or mains) for the equipment and/or the memory capacity of the video recorder.

Important point

> ⚠ It is vital therefore that the equipment has an adequate power supply and that more than the minimal requirement is met in terms of memory capacity.

The second key point is to use multiple video cameras. In research that is concerned with eye gaze, body orientation, and gesture, it is frequently impossible to adequately capture all of the data using a single camera. Even when it appears that the participants are facing in the same direction, the slightest turn of a head can readily obscure potentially interesting data concerning gaze direction or facial expression. Furthermore, having at least two cameras can sometimes compensate for issues relating to positioning that are considered below—if the first camera is blocked by a participant or is sub-optimally positioned in terms of light, the second camera may provide vital useable footage.

Finally, it is important to carefully check the positioning and view of the camera. Most people who have made extensive use of video data, particularly those with an interest in all aspects of the interaction, will at some point have wished that a camera had been put in a different place. Much of this is quite straightforward, such as ensuring that the tripod is stable, that it is unlikely to be knocked over or interfered with, that it is not too much of a distraction to the participants, and that it is accessible to the researcher if necessary. Some considerations, whilst relatively apparent, do not receive as much attention as they perhaps deserve—these concern the quality and usefulness of the recorded image. The optimal camera positioning has to take into account the size and shape of the room and the sources of light within the room—without doing so, there is the risk of images being of low quality, with silhouetted figures being captured in front of a large window, or headless bodies brushing up against the cameras. These issues become more complex when we consider that our targets may move—an issue that is best pre-empted by setting up the cameras with another person playing the role of the child or children to be recorded, taking into account their height, possible head positioning, and potential movement.

In cases where participants are expected to move around rather than remain seated, extra care is needed in order to ensure that they all stay clearly within view as they move. Here it is useful to have two stationary cameras set to record a wide field of view and positioned such that between them they will best capture wherever the participants may be facing. Ideally, a third camera could be used to follow the movement by smooth panning via a tripod—though to do this well does take some practice, and doing so could have the negative consequence of drawing attention to the cameras and/or making participants feel uncomfortable about being filmed. In setting up cameras for video recording, it often pays to adopt a realistic pessimism in terms of picture quality—things may well be worse than you had hoped, so take steps in advance to address the likely problems.

Taken together, these considerations mean that it is very beneficial to set up the recording with at least one other person well in advance of the session whenever possible. There is no substitute for inspecting the equipment in advance, for using multiple cameras, and for checking the actual image in the camera monitor—allowing for the location and movement of all participants. The heart-breaking reality is that, if unchecked, it may be at the very point of data analysis that one discovers that the painstakingly collected video data may be unusable because the visual data does not clearly show the body movement, gaze, and gesture which are so vital to this form of analysis.

Analysing Data

Even when the data collected is of sufficient quality to be useful, there is a danger that really important interaction data could be overlooked simply because it does not conform to *a priori* assumptions regarding what 'interaction' or even 'useable data' should look (and sound) like. The data extracts presented below seek to demonstrate that when our concept of interaction is broad enough to include body movement, gaze, and gesture (as well as talk)—and when we look at sequences rather than isolated instances of communication—there can be real value in data, whatever its apparent limitations in terms of the amount of words or the breadth of the lexicon used. However, it is important to note that, despite the attention to visual data, the broad analytic principles outlined here still uphold CA's underpinning concerns around sequential organisation and participant orientations (see Chap. 5).

- Looking at the detail of interaction
- Looking at sequences of interaction
- Looking at data with limited talk

Looking at the Detail of Interaction

One of the key ideas within conversation analysis is that interactions can show an intricacy of organisation that can be easily missed if we do not pay careful attention to detail. The use of audio and video recording equipment and the development of a meticulous system of transcription (Jefferson, 2004) enables precisely this attention to features that we might otherwise not notice or remember. In contrast to most other systems of transcription, the conversation analytic transcription convention is highly technical and includes much detail that would be glossed over or ignored altogether. Features of how loud or quiet the talk is, the prosody shifts, and where it overlaps are all transcribed, even though, as with the extract below, they might not be referred to—the point is, as Sacks (1984) notes, we cannot know in advance what details might prove important for the interaction at hand.

In extract 1, intricate transcription of who gazed where - during a segment of interaction lasting approximately three seconds - was crucial to developing an analysis of what was being done through the shifts in gaze that are present in this interaction.

Extract 1

This extract is taken from transcripts of sessions that involved one or two children with an ASD interacting with a mobile robotic device. These two boys both have a diagnosis of an ASD, but have more verbal ability than is revealed by the participants in extracts 2, 3, and 4. In this extract, one of the two boys (Chris) has had a previous session with the robot, whilst the other (Tim) is encountering it for the first time. Tim and Chris gaze at the robot consistently until line 5.

```
01    Chris     °put [(that) on°
      Tim            [you allowed to ↑touch ↓it yeah?

                ((Tim touches the robot three times))
02              (---------1---------2---------3)

03              (------)
04    Tim       uhn?
                [((gaze at C ))   [..((moves gaze to adults))
05    Tim       [why'z ↑it   s[to[pped
                [((gaze at R))    [..((moves gaze to adults))
```

It is easy to get overwhelmed with a transcript such as that shown in extract 1—the symbols can seem unnecessarily complex and abstruse. However, as noted above, the symbols (for a brief key please see the end of this chapter) are really designed to communicate as much detail as possible about what happened in the interaction (without becoming so complex that they are no longer intelligible). This detail does not prejudge which features might prove important for understanding the interaction. Those details which do transpire to be important for a particular analysis should, as Sacks (1984) suggests, be understood as being identified through the process of analysis rather than being an *a priori* assumption or hypothesis. In this brief illustrative analysis, gaze emerged important in understanding how participants orientated to the issue of to whom a question should be addressed.

Extract 1 shows considerable detail including how the talk is delivered (for example using degree signs to indicate the quieter voice of line 1), the timing of silences (using hyphens to indicate tenths of a second and numbers to indicate seconds), and some of the non-vocal features such as body movement and gaze. These non-vocal activities are 'mapped' onto the line-numbered audio elements of the transcripts—the talk and the timed silences between spates of talk—which are shown in bold in extract 1. It should be noted that for ease of reading, in lines 1–4 the level of non-vocal detail has been simplified—with the target line (5) providing more precise detail by means of square brackets aligned with those in the transcribed talk which indicate exactly where the gaze and shift of gaze occurs. To help you contextualise this information, we provide you with some research tips in Box 7.2.

Box 7.2 Research tips

Research tips

1. Watch your data through several times to get a sense of it.
2. Transcribe the vocal components, (talk, laughter, crying, sighing, throat clearing, coughing, tutting, lip smacking, etc.) first.
3. Carefully time intervals between vocal components.
4. Try to map your visual data (e.g. body movement, gaze, and gesture) on to this vocal timeline by focusing on one element (e.g. gaze) at a time.
5. Keep checking against the recording.
6. Be easy on yourself—it really is difficult to do this accurately!

The analysis of these data (Dickerson, Rae, Stribling, Dautenhahn & Werry, 2005) centred on a very easily missed fragment in line 5. The researchers settled on this line of data as it appeared that there was something interesting going on in terms of interaction; it appeared that Tim asked a question of Chris and then both he and Chris shifted their gaze (see Fig. 7.1).

The diagrams in Fig. 7.1 show, in sequence (**a–c**), the pattern that these shifts in gaze took across the word 'stopped' in the target line (line 5), the context in which this line of transcript occurred is given in extract 1. The analysis of this data began with the identification of this easily missed detail of interaction—it was examined because it seemed to involve some potentially interesting interplay of question, followed by first gaze shift, followed by second gaze shift. In order to be as sure

(a)

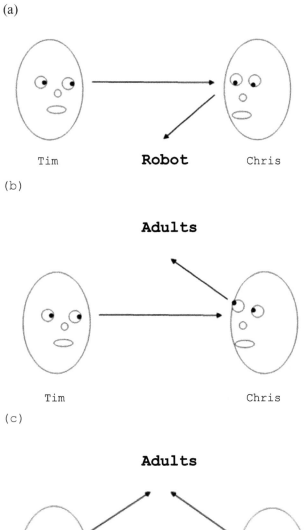

(b)

(c)

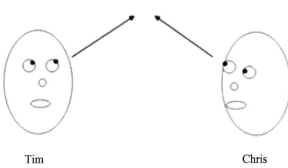

Fig. 7.1 A pictorial representation of the gaze activity of Tim and Chris. **(a)** Tim: ↑why'zit ↑sto. **(b)** Tim: <u>o</u>p. **(c)** Tim: ped

as possible regarding the precise details, the recorded sequence was played and replayed to an extent that could appear strange, if not pathological, to others not familiar with this form of analysis. Watching the target fragment perhaps one hundred times gave the researchers confidence in making the case that as Tim asked Chris why it (the robot) had stopped, Chris moved his gaze to the co-present adults in the room and that following Chris's shift in gaze to adults in the room, Tim shifted his own gaze to the adults in the room.

Important point

> ! By playing and replaying your video data many times, you will be
> • able to identify details that you would otherwise miss—yet which may hold important clues to understanding the interaction in front of you.

The analytic points that were developed from this observation were that Chris demonstrated a sophisticated way of non-verbally passing the question that Tim had asked of him to the adults in the room. That is, having been nominated as the addressee by Tim's question, Chris's gaze shift to the adults in the room nominated *them* as the appropriate addressee for Tim's question. Likewise, Tim demonstrated a sophisticated response to Chris's actions by redirecting his gaze from Chris, to the adults in the room, thereby making a response from the adults (rather than Chris) relevant. However, these observations illustrate the more general point that a fragment of data which might at first seem to offer little analytic scope can be found to be well worth analysis when careful attention is paid to detail. An important component of this attention to detail— and one that is especially relevant in data where there is limited talk—is attention not only to non-vocal features such as gaze but the precise timing of these features. It is this precision which allows an understanding of how actions (such as shift in gaze) are responsive to, or orientate to, each other, and this concern is intimately connected with looking at sequences of interaction. We suggest you now turn to the activity in Box 7.3.

Box 7.3 Transcribing

Activity

We suggest that you now try to practise transcribing.
Transcribing accurately both audio and video data is intricate work. Try and hone your skills by the following exercise:

1. Find a video on YouTube of a child or adult with ASD talking about something.
2. Try to identify a very brief segment, perhaps five seconds long, where the child or adult moves their gaze.
3. See if you can transcribe what is happening audibly, if there is vocal activity (talk, laughter, crying, coughing) use the Jefferson (2004) (or a version of it) to transcribe it; if there is no vocal activity in this segment (or part of it), transcribe this 'silence' using hyphens for each tenth of a second that elapses.
4. Try to map the gaze activity onto the timeline of the audio transcription. See how this is done in the data extracts presented in this chapter.
5. Try to identify the strengths and limitations with this video recording—what would make it better? Read the section on video recording to identify issues.

Looking at Sequences of Interaction

The emphasis that CA places on sequences of interaction stands in contrast to approaches that focus on behaviour in isolation. In the context of research involving participants with an ASD, whilst many approaches involve 'spotting' pre-specified behaviours, conversation analysis is more concerned with 'looking' at *sequences* of interaction rather than decontextualized parts (Dickerson and Robins, 2015).

The analysis of extract 1 did not adopt a decontextualized approach to understanding gaze behaviour. In contrast to some approaches, this analysis did not count separate instances of gaze, nor did it measure total gaze duration at a specific target (or targets), but instead close attention was given to the precise details of where the gaze was directed and how we might account for the shifts in gaze that were evident. This emphasis on sequence is perhaps still more apparent in extracts 2 and 3. The data presented below comes from an ESRC-funded study which examined everyday interactions at school and at home which involved one or more children who had a diagnosis of an ASD. With these data, the researchers became interested in the apparent prevalence of tapping behaviours across the pool of data that they had collected. One ready explanation for this tapping behaviour is that it could be understood in symptomatic terms—perhaps as a stereotypy—which reflects the pathology of the participants concerned. However, that would entail pushing the sequential setting to one side, dismissing it as irrelevant, without first examining whether it might shed light on what was going on with the tapping. By paying attention to where—within the sequence of interaction—the tapping occurred, the researchers started to consider what the tapping might do, or accomplish, within the interaction.

Extracts 2 and 3

Extracts 2 and 3 are taken from a single sequence of interaction between a mother (Deborah) and her son (Peter), who has been diagnosed as having an ASD. In the sequence from which these extracts are taken, Deborah has presented Peter with a flash card which has a picture on it and Peter has repeatedly tried to name the item that is depicted on the card. Two of Peter's attempts relating to the same card are shown below.

```
EXTRACT 2
                        [((Peter pushes card))
01     Peter      ↑↓o[:range
02                (------)
                         [((Peter taps card))
03     Deborah    ↑nea:r↓[ly


EXTRACT 3                    [((Peter pushes card))
01     Peter          gr↑↓[a:pes?
                                 [((Peter taps card))
02               ([---------1------ ][---2-------)
                 [((D shakes Head))]
```

One of the striking occurrences in the longer video sequence that extracts 2 and 3 were transcribed from is that Peter, the child with an ASD, intermittently taps the flash card. As mentioned previously, the

ASD diagnosis can lead to a ready explanation of these events in isolation. Knowing that Peter has a diagnosis of an ASD and that he performs occasional bouts of tapping could lead the researcher to look no further. From this perspective, it is enough to note that the tapping could be understood as a form of repetitive behaviour and that repetitive behaviour has long been associated with people who have a diagnosis of having an ASD (Kanner, 1943). However, the sequential perspective of conversation analysis provides a way of considering what sort of 'interactional action' the tapping might be accomplishing or orientating to and attention to sequence holds the key as we can ask, "why does this behaviour occur here?" (see also Chap. 5).

Important point

! When you have identified a behaviour of interest, think about it *in
• the light of the sequence in which it occurs.*

In order to address this question, the researchers carefully looked across the pool of data (involving different children and settings) to identify each instance of tapping. Careful inspection of those sequences of interaction that contained tapping behaviour enabled a consideration of whether there was something identifiable about the interactional environment in which the tapping occurred. Extracts 2 and 3 provide a representative illustration of what was found through this analytic process. In extracts 2 and 3 (and elsewhere in the data collected), tapping behaviour seemed to occur at those moments when an answer on the part of the child had been made relevant, but had not yet been given. In extract 2, the tapping occurs after a sequence which involves the child's guess (line 1), 0.6 seconds of silence (line 2) and the beginning of the word 'nearly'—it is at that point when the previous guess (orange) has been hearably declined that the child commences tapping. In extract 3, the previous guess (grapes) is followed by a shake of the head which precipitates tapping (line 2). Thus, in extracts 2 and 3 and elsewhere in our data, tapping occurred when and only when it was relevant for the child to provide an answer to a question. Furthermore, tapping ceased when the child actually provided a candidate solution to the question.

These observations, based on extracts 2 and 3 and other cases in our data, formed the basis of an argument that tapping could be understood as a means of displaying that the question is engaged with by the child *prior to a candidate answer being given.* The important point here is that, taken in isolation, it is impossible to consider any recurrent features of the interactional environment in which the tapping occurs—by examining that environment, of what people are saying and doing in interaction, we have the possibility of considering whether it is possible to characterise features of that environment. This is perhaps especially interesting and radical in cases where one or more of our participants have a diagnosis (in this case of an ASD) that might ordinarily be drawn on to explain the target behaviour. With the issue of tapping, Peter's ASD could readily explain the behaviour as a stereotypy; however, there is the danger that this ready-made explanation may foreshorten actual analysis of all of the data, treating as irrelevant precise details of where during an interaction tapping occurs. By examining the behaviour in the precise interactional location in which it takes place, we have the possibility of an analysis that does justice to any interactional dimensions that might be present - yet *unnoticed* if the focus is on the behaviour in isolation. We now offer you some further research tips in Box 7.4 to help with your learning so far.

Box 7.4 Research tips

Research tips

1. When you get an analytic 'hunch' that something interesting is going on with an action (in the case of extract 1 this was gaze movement and in extracts 2 and 3 it was tapping), try to collect together as many cases of that target behaviour from your data as you can.
2. Examine these cases and the sequential context in which they occur.
3. Develop tentative ideas about what these target behaviours might be doing in the sequential context in which they occur.
4. Revise and refine your conceptualisation of what is taking place in the light of the empirical evidence.
5. Remember that contradictory findings can assist you in developing a deeper analytic understanding.

Looking at Data with Limited Talk

The data extracts examined so far demonstrate that attention to detail and sequences reveal that more is taking place in interactional terms than might at first be apparent. However, in each of these data extracts, we find that a child with an ASD is talking—either asking a question (extract 1) or answering a question (extracts 2 and 3). This could inadvertently give the impression that although careful analysis of audio and video data can add to our analysis there is a certain minimum threshold of communicative competence that needs to be present in any specific datum that we might examine. Extract 4 presents data where this notion of a necessary minimum communicative competence is challenged.

Extract 4 (a)

```
01      Exp.      >° yes °<
02      (- - - - - - - - - 1 - - - - - -)
```

The child in this extract had quite severe communication impairment and uttered few, if any, recognisable words in the larger sequence from which this extract is taken. Furthermore, the audio transcript alone in Extract 4 (a) suggests very little in terms of possible analysis. The experimenter offers quietly spoken encouragement (yes) and this is followed by 1.6 seconds of silence. But when attention is paid to the visual data, as in Extract 4(b) it is immediately clear that much more interactional activity is taking place. For clarity, the transcript has been substantially simplified from the original (Robins, Dickerson, Stribling, & Dautenhahn, 2004) and lines have been used to link images to precisely where these captured moments occur in the transcribed sequence.

Important point
! Even 'unpromising' data can start to reveal fascinating interactional detail when we pay careful attention to every aspect of the data.

Extract 4 (b)

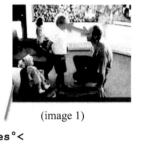

(image 1)

01   Exp.   >° yes°<

02   (- - - - - -.- - - 1 - -.- - - -)

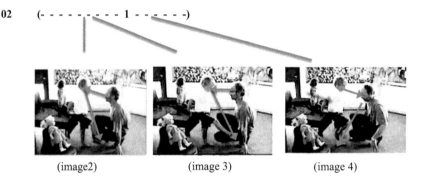

(image2)   (image 3)   (image 4)

Extract 4(b) shows, through a series of images, the movement from mutual gaze (image 1) where the experimenter and child gaze at each other, to the child lifting their foot and gazing at it (image 2), to flicking out their foot and gazing at it (image 3) to the experimenter gazing at the child's foot whilst the child gazes at the experimenter (image 4). The important point here is that the visual information contained in the four photographs adds enormously to the transcript of audio only data in Extract 4(a).

By examining what is taking place visually, we discover a somewhat intricate sequence of movements which make the data come to life with analytic possibilities. The child, who, prior to this extract, was facing away from the experimenter (at a robot whose leg had stopped moving) has turned to face the experimenter and in image 1 establishes mutual gaze with the experimenter. The child then gazes down at their foot which has been lifted off the floor (image 2). The experimenter still gazes at the child whilst the child flicks out their foot which they are gazing at (image 3). Finally, the experimenter gazes down at the child's foot as the child moves their gaze to the experimenter (image 4). What is captured here (and discussed more fully in Robins et al., 2004) is that the child has orientated to the experimenter first, by establishing mutual gaze, then by gazing down at their foot which they move, before finally monitoring the experimenter's gaze. This suggests that the child has orientated to the experimenter in a complex manner, by establishing mutual gaze and then gazing down at their own foot they make it relevant for the experimenter to also gaze at the child's foot, once the experimenter does start to move his gaze to the child's foot, the child monitors that gaze movement. In this way the child's behaviour suggests perhaps unexpected interactional sophistication on the part of the child. The child appears to demonstrate skilled orientation to where the adult is standing and where they are looking. For our current purposes, the point is that it would be easy to dismiss these data without examining them, as the child uses few, if any, lexical items, and the sequence of interaction contains only minimal talk on the part of the experimenter. By staying with these data and bringing a careful analysis to them, it is possible to discover interactional intricacies in the most unlikely of places. This very unexpectedness, finding potential interactional competencies where they were anything but anticipated, lends the analysis some import and can provide a fruitful stimulus for further investigation of data that may otherwise lie unexamined.

Summary

This chapter has suggested that we can turn to the unlikely sources, interactions where a child not only has a diagnosis of an ASD but has, or presents, limited verbal competence, and conduct a useful analysis. In order to unlock these data, it has been argued that care has to be taken both in terms of data collection and data analysis.

In terms of data collection, a certain mental shift is required which envisages all participants and all moments in the interaction as relevant (or potentially relevant). Thus, in contrast to most video recording involving a person or persons with a diagnosis of an ASD, it is necessary to record all participants (not just those with a diagnosis of an ASD) such that all of the potentially relevant audio and visual data is captured.

Similarly, in contrast to approaches that pre-specify target segments (via a checklist, clinical judgement, or timed sampling), all moments should be recorded and available for investigation such that behaviour can be examined in the sequence in which it occurs.

In terms of data analysis, this chapter has sought to illustrate how easily missed fragments that might last less than a couple of seconds can contain intricate interactional work if we take care to examine them in detail. It has attempted to illustrate that behaviour that could unthinkingly be attributed to the diagnostic label (and deemed pointless to analyse) is still worth investigating in terms of its placement within a *sequence* of interaction. Attention to the behaviour not 'in isolation' but *in sequence* can potentially reveal the relevant interactional work that it may be orientating to. Finally, the chapter has sought to underscore the point that even when we have participants who speak very little there can be extremely valuable data to be analysed by taking an analytic stance that encompasses body movement, gaze, gesture, speech delivery, and spoken words and that examines not just *what* communication occurs but also *where it occurs* within an interaction. By examining these data, we have the opportunity of both unlocking potential interactional intricacies that may have been almost completely occluded by the apparent communicative impoverishment of the participants and also of extending the boundaries of conversation analytic research itself. A summary of the research highlights from this chapter can be seen in Box 7.5.

Box 7.5 Summary of practical highlights

Summary of practical highlights

1. Taking care with video recording can ensure that we capture all of the possible data and therefore do not limit our subsequent analysis.
2. Paying attention to detail can reveal intricacies of interaction that we might otherwise easily miss.
3. Paying attention to sequences of interaction enables our analysis to become genuinely interactional and avoids simply attributing behaviour to a diagnostic label.
4. Staying with data that might seem unpromising at first can yield important analytic observations.

Transcription Conventions

The transcription conventions are a modified version of Jefferson's (2004) transcription conventions. (A full overview can be found in the introduction chapter of the volume.)

[	Left square bracket	Onset of overlap
]	Right square bracket	Termination of overlap
= =	Equals signs	Latching of talk
(1)	Numerals in parenthesis	Pause in seconds
(- - -)	Hyphens in parenthesis	One hyphen indicates 0.1 seconds
(.)	Dot in parenthesis	Untimed micro-interval
?	Question mark	Rising, or questioning, intonation
NO	Capital letters	Delivered with relative loudness
°no°	Degree signs	Enclosed talk delivered with relative quietness
↑	Upward arrow	Rising intonation
↓	Downward arrow	Falling intonation
e:::	Colon	Indicates a sound stretch
(())	Double parenthesis	The enclosed text describes actions

References

Arscott, K., Dagnan, D., & Kroese, B. S. (1998). Consent to psychological research by people with an intellectual disability. *Journal of Applied Research in Intellectual Disabilities, 11*, 77–83.

Barrow, C., & Tarplee, E. (1999). Delayed echoing as an interactional resource: A case study of a 3-year-old child on the autistic spectrum. *Clinical Linguistics & Phonetics, 13*(6), 449–482.

Dickerson, P., Rae, J., Stribling, P., Dautenhahn, K., & Werry, I. (2005). Autistic children's co-ordination of gaze and talk: Re-examining the 'asocial autist'. In K. Richards & P. Seedhouse (Eds.), *Applying conversation analysis* (pp. 19–37). Basingstoke: Palgrave Macmillan.

Dickerson, P., & Robins, B. (2015). Looking or spotting: a conversation analytic perspective on interaction between a humanoid robot, a co-present adult, and a child with an ASC. In M. O'Reilly & J. N. Lester (Eds.), *The Palgrave handbook of child mental health* (pp. 59–78). Basingstoke: Palgrave Macmillan.

Dickerson, P., Stribling, P., & Rae, J. (2007). Tapping into interaction: How children with autistic spectrum disorders design and place tapping in relation to activities in progress. *Gesture, 7*(3), 271–303.

Gallagher, M., Haywood, S. L., Jones, M. W., & Milne, S. (2010). Negotiating informed consent with children in school-based research: A critical review. *Children & Society, 24*, 471–482.

Goodwin, C. (Ed.). (2003). *Conversation and brain damage*. Oxford: Oxford University Press.

Jefferson, G. (2004). Glossary of transcript symbols with an introduction. In G. H. Lerner (Ed.), *Conversation analysis: Studies from the first generation* (pp. 13–23). Amsterdam: John Benjamins.

Kanner, L. (1943). Autistic disturbances of affective contact. *Nervous Child, 2*(3), 217–250.

O'Reilly, M., Dogra, N., & Ronzoni, P. D. (2013). *Research with children: Theory and practice*. London: Sage.

Robins, B., Dickerson, P., Stribling, S., & Dautenhahn, K. (2004). Robot-mediated joint attention in children with autism: A case study in robot-human interaction. *Interaction Studies, 5*(2), 161–198.

Sacks, H. (1984). Notes on methodology. In J. M. Atkinson & J. Heritage (Eds.), *Structures of social action: Studies in conversation analysis* (pp. 21–27). Cambridge: Cambridge University Press.

Schegloff, E. A. (2003). Conversation analysis and 'communication disorders'. In C. Goodwin (Ed.), *Conversation and brain damage* (pp. 21–55). Oxford: Oxford University Press.

Recommended Reading

Goodwin, C. (Ed.). (2003). *Conversation and brain damage*. Oxford: Oxford University Press.

O'Reilly, M., & Lester, J. N. (Eds). (2015). *The Palgrave handbook of child mental health*. Basingstoke: Palgrave Macmillan.

Richards, K., & Seedhouse, P. (Eds.). (2005). *Applying conversation analysis*. Basingstoke: Palgrave Macmillan.

Paul Dickerson is Principal Lecturer in the Department of Psychology at the University of Roehampton. He is committed to teaching, having taught undergraduates and postgraduates for 25 years and having published a pedagogically innovative textbook in the field of social psychology. Paul has undertaken a range of qualitative research, with a particular focus on conversation and discourse analysis. One particular focus of Paul's conversation analytic research has been the examination of interactions involving children with an autistic spectrum disorder.

Ben Robins is a senior research fellow in the School of Computer Science at the University of Hertfordshire. Ben's qualifications and many years of work experience lie in two disciplines: computer science and dance movement therapy. Ben completed his PhD at the University of Hertfordshire in 2005, bringing together his expertise and experience in these two disciplines. Ben's research investigates the potential use of robots as therapeutic or educational tools, encouraging basic communication and social interaction skills in children with autism.

8

Student and Supervisor Experiences of Learning and Teaching Conversation Analysis and Discursive Psychology for Autism Spectrum Disorder Focused Research: A Reflective Approach

Cordet Smart and Katie Denman

Learning Objectives

By the end of this chapter, you will be able to:

- Identify features of research supervision that are most useful to attend to when producing a discursive study of autism, including identifying possible 'threshold concepts'.
- Apply a reflective approach to research supervision for discursive psychology/conversation analysis (DP/CA) projects related to autism.

C. Smart (✉)
School of Psychology, Plymouth University, Plymouth, UK

CEDAR, Exeter University, Exeter, UK

K. Denman
Plymouth Hospitals NHS Trust, Plymouth, UK

© The Author(s) 2017
M. O'Reilly et al. (eds.), *A Practical Guide to Social Interaction Research in Autism Spectrum Disorders*, The Language of Mental Health,
https://doi.org/10.1057/978-1-137-59236-1_8

193

- Identify and consider solutions to key challenges for research supervision, including:
  - Applying a 'language-as-action' approach;
  - Reading, analysing, and writing within a 'language as action' approach; and
  - How to manage the challenges of an applied DP/CA project.

Introduction

This chapter provides a case study of a supervisory relationship to explore some of the issues of research supervision that are specifically relevant to conducting language-focused research in the field of Autism Spectrum Disorder (ASD). We focus on the specific concerns for research supervision when applying a discursive psychology/conversation analysis (DP/CA) approach to understanding ASD, offering suggestions to help students and supervisors through the process. We have used the term DP/CA to describe our approach as we used tools of conversation analysis, but took a discursive psychology informed approach. This also reflects some of the assumptions that we made that the patterns of talk in families might be related to the systemic processes of the family, and might not necessarily be solely considered as products of these conversation moments. In our experience, the challenges include:

1. the induction of the student into a new way of thinking about language, as action rather than as direct representation;
2. the implication of this for reading, writing, and analysing data; and
3. applying this approach in a way that makes practical sense to other people.

We suggest that these challenges can represent 'conceptual threshold crossings' where a postgraduate student moves from understanding a threshold concept (Meyer & Land, 2003; Neave, Collett, & Lloyd, 2017; Perkins, 2006; Wisker et al., 2010), such as that 'language is active', to deepen their knowledge, understanding, and ability to use this knowledge at postgraduate level, crossing a further level of understanding.

Facing these challenges within supervision is not always easy, as the student must negotiate difficulties with understandings (or as Perkins (2006) terms it, 'troublesome knowledge') and challenging feedback from supervisors. To try and address this, we adopted a reflective approach to research supervision. We have adapted this from Stedmon and Dallos (2009), who argued that reflection, or thinking about the supervisory relationship itself, is important for overcoming difficulties in knowledge acquisition, which can play out as frustrations in the supervision relationship and thus need to be 'contained' by the supervisor.

The importance of metacommunication in supervision is well known (Davies, 2008; Eley & Jennings, 2005; Rolls & Relf, 2006; Youselfi, Bazrafkan, & Yamani, 2015). We argue that thinking about the process is particularly important for discursive studies of ASD, where there may be several tensions to manage.

For example: Emotional investment in the concerns of people with ASD can conflict with the distanced stance required for the analysis.

Without reflecting on the interpersonal processes in supervision, there can be resistances to the use of DP/CA, or a project might be weaker as the student has not quite allowed themselves to take the risky step of trusting the method. Here we interrogate our own supervisory experiences, including the struggles that we experienced and how we overcame these. The chapter is predominantly written with students in mind, but we hope it will also be of benefit to supervisors in this area.

Background to Our Supervisory Relationship

To start then, let us introduce ourselves. We are Cordet Smart (henceforth CS), a lecturer in clinical psychology, experienced in postgraduate supervision of discursive and CA research, particularly of clinical psychology doctorates; and Katie Denman (henceforth KD), a Trainee Clinical Psychologist working with children with ASD, whose clinical doctorate focused on how families explained a child member's behaviour while the child was waiting for a diagnostic assessment. We had previously worked together in different settings where KD had been CS's research assistant. This meant that a change of dynamics needed negotiating so that KD's experience was now as a student and not as a research assistant.

Important point
❗ Reflecting on the power dynamics of the supervision relationship was crucial.

It is worth noting that a clinical doctorate works differently to other types of doctoral level study, such as a PhD. The main thesis is developed in years 2 and 3, rather than the full 3 years as in a traditional PhD. Further, thesis requirements for the final submission are substantially smaller than that of a PhD, reflecting the simultaneous clinical requirements of the doctorate. There is also a requirement for the thesis to be relevant to clinical psychology practice and theory (British Psychological Society (BPS), 2014), differing from the less applied focus of non-doctorate programmes (Quality Assurance Agency (QAA), 2011), but something we found helpful to ensure that we kept stakeholders in mind.

The course is taught in a cohort, lending greater peer supervision opportunities (McCallin & Nayer, 2012) and opportunities to develop 'academic communities of practice' (Wenger & Lave, 1991). However, one-to-one supervision is still received. On our particular doctoral programme in Plymouth, great emphasis is placed on reflective practice, which, Sedmon and Dallos (2009) argue, can improve the quality of clinical training and research through opening up different perspectives on problems. We were both engaged in this approach, with an underpinning interest in systemic perspectives on psychology, that is, how people operate in systems. Contrary to learning styles approaches where a more static relationship is envisioned between supervisor and supervisee (e.g., see Shukr, Zainab, & Rana, 2013; Honey & Mumford, 1992), we took a dynamic approach to supervision. We followed Evans and Stevenson's (2010) principles constantly reflecting on the expectations and support levels within the relationship and how these were achieved, moving the focus back and forth between the detail of the research activity and the bigger picture. Take a few moments now to work through the questions in the activity in Box 8.1 below.

Box 8.1 Activity on supervision

Activity

Spend a few moments reflecting on your own supervision environments:
- What is your relationship with your supervisor?
- Have you worked with them in the past?
- What are the advantages or disadvantages of this?
- What is the structure of your course, and what opportunities does this provide, or might it mean that you have to look for elsewhere?
- How might you make the best use of these environments to optimise your supervisory experience?

The Research Project: An Overview

We begin here by giving you some general context to the study that was undertaken by KD for her clinical doctorate. Here we provide you with just a general overview of the study and its key features to give you an overall sense of what the research was about. The title of the study and the guiding overall focus was:

> How families make sense of their child's behaviour when on an autism assessment and diagnosis waiting list.

We now offer you a short introduction to each component of the project to serve as a platform for the rest of our discussion in the chapter.

Background: KD undertook a literature review finding that families' explanations for ASD are sometimes fraught with dilemmas once a person has a diagnosis, but prior to diagnosis the literature had less to say. Based on clinical experience, she identified a need for more professional understanding of the sense making that is already going on in these families prior to receiving a diagnosis to identify how best to help and support these families.

Aim: The aim of the project was to examine how families make sense, or explain the behaviour, of a young family member who is on the waiting list for a diagnosis of ASD.

Method: KD designed a study that involved a family interview where families sat down and discussed their understandings of the child on the waiting list and the referral process. This was not by any means 'naturalistic' talk, in a 'pure' form (see Chap. 4). Nevertheless, it reflected the type of interaction that a family therapist working from a systemic lens might encounter.

Method of Analysis: The analysis drew on discursive psychology (DP) and conversation analysis (CA), and explored how the construction of meaning was constituted through family interactional patterns.

Analysis: Interruptions were a common feature of the family interactions, making it difficult for families to express how they 'made sense' of their child's behaviour, impeding the flow and development of the narratives (Hayashi, Raymond, & Sidnell, 2013). Family members worked to produce positive identities for their children and frequently acted to 'face save' or protect their young people and the family, including in accounting for interruptions. These patterns indicated that it seemed difficult for these families to produce coherent narratives about what might be going on for the focal child.

Implications: Identified patterns were used to reflect on how practitioners might interact with these families to enable or challenge sense making. Uncertainties of being on the waiting list might present as difficulties to understanding. Further, it may be harder for these families to make sense of events related to the frequent interruptions in family talk that seem to occur. At this point in the chapter we recommend you engage in the activity in Box 8.2.

The overview of our research is provided here to orientate you as a reader to our study. However, we also think that keeping the overview in mind is particularly important for applied CA studies. This is where the main focus is not the development or refinement of a 'CA' concept, such as whether a phrase is more likely to produce a response, but on the relevance to stakeholders (in this case families waiting for an assessment, clinicians or commissioners who design services). A careful balance must be struck between

---

Box 8.2 Activity on challenges

Activity

What challenges do you think might have arisen during the supervisory process of this study?

> **Box 8.3 Research tips for using DP and CA**
>
> Research tips
>
> We recommend that an important step in doing a study using CA or DP is to read three or four theses that use DP or CA. You can use these to reflect on the form your own thesis might take. Some examples are included in our recommended reading list at the end of the chapter, but there are many of these available online. You might repeat this activity during the research process, but be mindful not to become too preoccupied with the outcome before completing your own analysis.

the analytic detail and application. Further, we suggest that with DP/CA studies in particular, it can take a long time to develop the writing style required, and so gaining an overview is particularly significant. There are more research tips in Box 8.3 to help you think about your own work.

Our Research Journeys

The problem with research overviews is that they gloss over the research process itself. The work is 'cleaned up' and does not reflect the non-linear, recursive loops that were involved, or the testing points in linking concepts and exploring the data in detail. We therefore offer our own journeys through the research process as supervisee and supervisor, respectively. We present KD's voice first as the student, and encourage you to consider whether you identify with her frustrations. We then present CS's voice, which might help to understand some of the different aims that supervisors and supervisees bring to the relationship.

Our Research Journeys: The Supervisee

Developing Ideas Based on Previous Experience and Supervisor Influence

During the proposal stages of my research, I (KD) was not planning on using DP/CA. I had a broad idea that I wanted my research topic to include my interests in systemic theory, social constructionism, ASD, and labelling theory. I had previous experience of using Interpretative Phenomenological Analysis (IPA) as a research assistant and so originally intended to use this; however, these prior experiences did not prepare me fully for work at postgraduate level. I realised during a teaching session delivered by CS that shaping your research interests around a method of analysis changes the project. It appeared that if I wanted to do the project I was interested in, that was, understanding how families make sense, a language-based project such as DP/CA would fit better than an exploration of experiences.

CS's passion for the topic also influenced me. As CS had known me previously as a research assistant, she told me, 'It is now time for you to develop your own research interests'—which was in equal parts daunting and exciting. It took time to build the confidence needed to transition from being an assistant to being the 'chief investigator', trusting myself to develop a project and make the big decisions.

The way CS presented DP and CA expanded my mind to think about how qualitative analysis can be more empirical, that is, examining what is present in the data (how meanings are constructed in the here and now) rather than making interpretations based on resonating experiences as in IPA. This was appealing, knowing I would need to argue my choice of analytic approach in a viva. Additionally, it appeared to be an inclusive and validating method for families involved. I wanted to present what was 'there in the data' to make it meaningful for the families who participated, rather than what resonated with me as 'an expert'.

Completing the Project and Lessons Learnt

I chose an interview situation as a design rather than recording 'natural talk', building on previous work that CS had been involved in (Dallos & Smart, 2011; Crix, Stedmon, Smart, & Dallos, 2012; Stuart, Smart, Dallos, & Williams, 2015). I drew on Crix et al.'s (2012) method of presenting questions to the participants on a flip chart to allow the family to have as natural as possible a conversation together without me becoming part of that interaction as 'an interviewer' in the traditional sense. The DP/CA approach to analysis meant that I could include children who had communication difficulties and gave me evidence to argue that these children still add to and influence conversation (Pollock & Auburn, 2013).

My first interview lasted only 7 minutes, and the family did not include much content! This left me quite panicked. It would have been a serious concern for the IPA projects I had previously conducted. However, disaster averted—with the help of CS, I could see there was detail in that interview that would have been missed if I had chosen a different analytic method. This is when DP/CA became exciting, and I could start seeing the finite details in my data.

For example: In my data, families struggled to make sense of children's behaviours where the child in question was present.

This 'trouble' in talk often coincided with an interruption from the focal child, who had picked up on a word that was spoken and repeated that word in a different context, changing the conversation. This is illustrated in Extract 1, where Sharon is discussing the family 'understandings' and Tom, the focal child, discusses how the family should go to bed at the right time.

Extract 1: Family 1 (Sharon—grandmother; Paul—grandfather; Tom—focal child)

```
03.29
1    Sharon :   then all the fami[ly
2    Tom:                        [they all not good
3    Sharon:    all the fami[ly um some help, some understands
                don't they
4    Tom:                   [when they are um the family still
                in bed but they are these three family were all
                in bed
5    Paul:      Ok mate
6    Sharon:    ((laughs)) yeah the fami[ly um all helps and
                understands don't they
7    Tom:                               [they get up shortly
8    Paul:      yeah
03.50
```

These interruptions and the effects on conjoint sense making within the family revealed through a DP/CA analysis allowed me to consider the family processes that were affecting sense making as families spoke together. It was difficult for families to develop conjoint conversations as some family members followed different trajectories, and families accommodated this. This level of data analysis also helped me to really understand what is meant by 'language as active' and the importance of these interactional processes to enable people to display any form of understanding. Spending time analysing data was therefore central in developing a clearer understanding of the research methods and process.

Supervision Process from a Learner Perspective

Early supervisions were confusing and felt like I was 'walking in the dark'. I often came away with my head hurting, but I trusted in the method of analysis and CS. Something I found particularly helpful was CS taking my project idea and using it to explain different types of discursive methods so that I could see the differences and how each one would shape the project. This helped me choose which one fitted with my interests.

A big challenge for me was learning a new method of analysis in a very short time frame and not having the time to do all the background reading on DP/CA at this stage in the research. This meant I was learning about CA alongside doing it. I shared my concerns with CS that it felt that understanding DP/CA required its very own doctorate. It was hugely beneficial to have a supervisor who knows the method well.

Supervision was sometimes a challenge in itself, as CS would question me about my shaping project. Although this felt uncomfortable at the time, it highlighted what I didn't know and what I needed to go and find out more about. Later supervisions felt much less like I was in the dark and I started to grasp most of what was said. CS guided me in a way that felt as though my knowledge and learning of DP/CA emerged gradually and naturally for myself rather than her just telling me what to do (which I imagine is very enticing for supervisors at this stressful stage). This helped me feel like the analysis was my own and that I could talk confidently about it in my viva.

Another big challenge for me was maintaining focus on the analysis to ensure it was robust, when time pressures made me feel that I needed to get on with writing broader sections like the introduction and discussion. I also worried about the clinical relevance of conversational patterns.

Important point
> **!**
> **•** At this stage I found it helpful and reassuring to go back and read similar clinically relevant projects to see how others had completed their projects.

Additionally, CS taught me the importance of not jumping ahead too soon, to write exactly what was in the data first, and then to think more broadly. This requires trust in the supervisor and the method because, although it does come later, if you have not used DP/CA before you will not have had that experience yet. At this point in the chapter, you should be able to see what a challenging endeavour this project was and thus we provide some tips on the basis of these experiences in Box 8.4 from the student perspective.

Box 8.4 Research tips for managing a project from the student perspective

Research tips from KD

1. Think about the differences between discursive and other methods, and how each will shape your project.
2. Choose a supervisor who knows the method well.
3. Allow yourself time to work with your supervisor on background reading around CA.
4. Trust that the methodology will become clearer with time and uncomfortable experiences in supervision can lead to the strengthening of your project.
5. Keep focused on the details of the analysis and try not to impose broader understandings too soon.

Our Research Journeys: The Supervisor

A postgraduate project normally involves a supervisor as well as a student, and the supervisor goes on the journey of study with their student. This involves offering supervision, sharing ideas, sharing expertise, encouraging and motivating, and helping, amongst other things. For this study the supervisor played an important role and this is now described from the perspective of CS.

Developing Topic Ideas

During KD's supervision I (CS) held a dual role within the course, as Research Tutor for the Clinical Programme, and as KD's supervisor. For me, the supervision journey began with the initial methods teaching in the first year, where I attempted to inspire KD's cohort about the possibilities of different research approaches.

Our first supervision was in the first year. Where most students arrive at this session uncertain about their ideas and the research process, KD came with more experience and confidence around what she hoped to achieve. The first stage was to explore her ideas and interests—what did she want to say about families on the waiting list for a diagnostic assessment of autism? When students come to see me, they generally know that my interest lies in language-based approaches, but they often have not yet appreciated the nuances between different language-based methods (e.g., critical discursive psychology and conversation analysis projects)—and the implications this has on their developing project ideas.

It is for this reason that I question students about their projects—to work out their knowledge, and to think through for myself which method might be best. This process of questioning can feel uncomfortable for the supervisor as for the supervisee, especially early on, and I did not wish to knock KD's confidence. I sought to encourage her to begin to question and think at a deeper level appropriate for doctoral work. It is hard at this time to reassure students that it is acceptable not to know the answers.

Important point	
❗•︎	Perhaps this is reflective of a 'conceptual threshold crossing' where students have to develop a new level of confidence in 'not knowing' and 'how to know'.

Developing the Method and Analytic Foci

KD's initial research aim was to explore 'how families make sense of their experiences when a young person is on a waiting list for a diagnosis of autism'. Specifically, she had intended to examine discursive repertoires of perceived blame—by family member, and of any person or institution (following Wetherell, 1998). We discussed whether it would be more feasible to obtain group interview or naturalistic data. Logistics dictated that a family group discussion might be most feasible. We developed an analytic approach that would examine the discursive repertoires that family members used to make sense of the focal child's behaviours, and the associated subject positions that were created. However, research does not always go as planned.

The first interview that KD conducted was particularly short, and participants had struggled to discuss how they make sense of their child's behaviour. It was very difficult to identify any discursive repertoires. This initial pass over the data is often very anxiety provoking for students, who can feel quite overwhelmed and that there is nothing relevant in their data. To help to overcome this, I warn students in advance to expect this experience. In KD's case, she had more experience, but still it was a tricky moment. I suggest that students bring a small piece of data to me so that we can work through this together—which KD duly did.

We considered the data, but there did not seem to be very clear explanations of behaviour at all. We noticed, however, that families did start to 'make sense', but were then interrupted, drawing our attention to the details of the family interactions. We then explored whether this occurred elsewhere in the data. It did, so KD collected similar extracts which we interrogated using a DP/CA approach.

Implicit in this analytic decision was the DP/CA research dilemma: between developing a theoretically informed approach (i.e., that blaming is a central concern) and an inductive approach (using DP/CA, as interactional features seemed more relevant in the data).

> *For example:* KD's literature review revealed how parental or child blame (of all types) were significant discourses for professionals and families in understanding ASD, focusing on what the data showed allowed the revelation of new knowledge.

Certainly, what was beneficial around the inductive approach is that it challenged what both of us had expected from the data, and therefore felt more like research in the sense of discovering something new. To achieve these new understandings, however, we had to work hard in our relationship to manage the emotional anxiety around time constraints, and also to distance the beliefs about ASD developed elsewhere.

Through supervision, we recognised that expectations of parental or child blame were strong drivers for the research, but also created uncomfortable reactions for us both. This recognition, combined with the data not showing repertoires as envisaged, enabled us to put these assumptions to one side, leaving thinking space to 'reveal' new phenomena in KD's data.

Important point

!   This is an example of how supervisor and supervisee might think
 •   together about the work being undertaken.

Once the analysis was more developed, we again discussed the question of how families make sense of their experiences and how this fitted with the systemic positioning of the work. We considered the implications of applying DP/CA to non-naturalistic data and the claims that could be made from a small sample. Holding these discussions after initial patterns had been identified was another way in which it was possible to try and set aside assumptions to understand the data first. The analysis, having been completed with (relatively, at least) less distraction by theory and applied concerns, could now be treated as a finding by itself (e.g. that interruptions and face saving were key features in these family conversations) and used to produce and develop theory rather than be considered as a product of that theory.

Writing Up the Discursive Psychology/Conversation Analysis Project

During our research journey, I encouraged KD to write up short parts of her experience and progress at regular intervals, such as writing a summary after an analysis session. This task was difficult for KD, and often she reported it was time-consuming. I wanted her to develop her skills in writing up CA. However, although when in the office she engaged in active discussion of the data, when we discussed her resistance to writing she expressed that she had no clear sense of what to write and struggled with questions:

- Was the focus on the child with ASD?
- Was the focus on different CA phenomena—turn taking, pauses in talk?

What Did This Mean?

Initial writing became like longer descriptions of lots of CA features within a paragraph. However, repeated questioning about what was interesting or relevant helped KD to write in a way that described a practice in interaction—such as interruptions and parallel conversations, and then to use examples from her data to illustrate these. This journey was a reflective and practical one, and we provide some research tips from the supervisor perspective in Box 8.5.

Meta Reflections on Our Research Journeys

After writing these journeys (slightly longer ones than those included here), we engaged in discussions to identify resonances and discords. One notable difference between our journeys was our respective starting

Box 8.5 Research tips from a supervisor perspective

Research tips

1. Identify a good exemplar paper to help guide the research (e.g. Pollock & Auburn, 2013), and a good 'how to' guide, such as this book, and Potter (2012).
2. Identify a group of people who are interested in discussing qualitative data, ideally CA or DP analyses, and meet regularly and chat!
3. Reflect with your supervisor on what the work might mean and look like as a finished product.
4. Focus on a limited number of DP/CA phenomena that seem central to the focus of your analysis, especially for shorter projects, so that you can understand these in detail and don't become overwhelmed.
5. Trust your data and give the analysis time—the broader meaning will come later.
6. Start writing short sections as early as possible and let your supervisor comment on these. These pieces take less time for your supervisor to read, and help to identify writing issues and to refine the focus of the thesis.

points. KD described her initial approach as IPA, much of which CS was less aware of, as this related to thinking prior to supervision and so for CS the student's journey was considered to begin later. We suggest this difference might be difficult for students, where earlier work is not recognised, but might also reflect the different levels of expectation in terms of thinking and what can be considered to constitute doctoral level work.

Reflections on Good Supervisory Practice for Discursive Research in the Field of ASD: Tips on How to Focus Sessions

In addition to reflecting on our relationship, we identified those learning experiences that seemed most important in our journey. Some of these experiences related to 'conceptual threshold crossings' where a student changes their way of thinking about a concept (Wisker et al., 2010). We discuss three of these experiences here:

- Relational challenges in supervision
- Data analysis
- Engaging with political and clinical contexts

We relate these where appropriate to what may be 'conceptual threshold crossings' in this field.

Relational Challenges in Supervision

Wisker and Robinson (2013) suggest that a positive functional model of supervision focusing on effective communication, nurturing, and nudging through threshold concepts can overlook some of the communication challenges and breakdowns that can lead to students feeling abandoned and losing their supervisors. Although our experience was generally positive, we identified important tensions.

The first challenge for the DP/CA project on ASD is building academic confidence. This can be exacerbated where the student has previously been highly successful, and is now faced at doctoral level with an 'epistemic expansion' where everything that they thought they knew in an area is questioned as they transit through an 'ontological shift' or a shift in how to understand a topic (Wisker et al., 2010). KD reflected here on 'walking in the dark' during the early parts of supervision. We suggest that at this time, when the supervisor's and supervisee's experience can seem so different, and DP/CA quite alien, the relationship is most vulnerable. Challenges from the supervisor must be carefully done to allow development of confidence in the unknown, without the student feeling too uncomfortable to continue. We hope that recognising this tension will of itself help students to be more confident.

A second concern for supervisory processes is around belief in the feasibility of a project. The supervisor might be confident in the method and feasibility if they are experienced in DP or CA, but those with less experience might harbour concerns as the method can seem highly specialised. Thus, negotiating how the student will access support for analysis is crucial, as well as discussing how the method and findings will be interpreted for ease of access and understanding for potential participants and stakeholders to whom the research will be disseminated.

The final challenge that we see for the supervisory relationship is around the analysis, and specifically the student's anxiety, as they attempt to read and understand the expansive field of DP/CA and understand ASD as a topic. We showed here how KD's belief in DP/CA as a method improved during the analysis of her own data. As such, we advocate exposure to data analysis as early as possible, and including engagement in practice data prior to data collection. We suggest that the supervisor and student initially identify and focus on a limited number of relevant DP/CA concepts that are present in the data and relevant to the research aims and are feasible for the student to understand within the constraints of their research programme. For the clinical trainee, this might mean focusing on only one or two discursive features that are central to their research, such as in ASD research where difficulties with timings of interactions were highlighted (see Pollock & Auburn, 2013).

Viewing the Data from a DP/CA Perspective: Bracketing off Imposed Common Sense

We consider a further 'conceptual threshold crossing' to occur during the process of analysis, where students change their understanding of how language works and begin to apply in a deeper and more extended way a 'language-as-action' approach. We suggest two approaches here to help this transition.

First, we highlight the importance of 'bracketing off' (Rolls & Relf, 2006) *our own* common sense interpretations of the data so that we can reveal *participants'* common sense as displayed in the data. Parts of our respective journeys that have been 'edited out' were our own personal and professional experiences of ASD and how families cope. Rolls and Relf (2006) developed the concept of bracketing interviews, where a researcher engages in conversations about their relationship to their research at key points in the research process to help researchers deal with traumatic material. We argue that this approach is equally helpful for DP/CA research to help the researcher to become more aware of their own perspectives and to recognise these when analysing data, thereby 'freeing' the researcher to focus on conversation practices. At this point, have a look at the reflective activity in Box 8.6 to encourage you to think more about this.

Box 8.6 Reflective activity

Activity

We would encourage you to think about the importance of bracketing by answering the following two questions:

1. What are your personal and professional interests in ASD, and how might these affect your ability to identify participants' displays of understanding in talk?
2. How will you avoid evaluating the content and invoking your experience?

Second, we advocate attendance at, or the development of, data analysis groups. A data analysis group is where a group of academics and interested people come together to discuss a piece of data. The model adopted by our analysis group, CARP (Conversation Analysis Research in Plymouth) is for one member to bring a short extract of data with a sound file. The data is introduced to the group and copies of a detailed transcript are provided. Group members then listen to the audio or video recording twice, or sometimes more, firstly for transcription errors. When the group is happy with the transcript, they spend 5 minutes analysing individually. The group then discusses the transcript from the first line onwards. These groups promote development of analytic skills.

Important point

! The presence of multiple people can provide different perspectives (Elliott et al., 2013), increasing the credibility of the analysis.

Those with less expertise can contribute effectively, often observing the common-sense issues that those more focused on features of DP/CA might have overlooked. In some institutions, it is likely that such groups already exist:

For example: At Loughborough University, they run the Discourse and Rhetoric Group (DARG) for students and scholars with an interest in CA and DA.

Box 8.7 Activity on data sharing

Activity

Sharing your data in a data session with other scholars and other students is not necessarily as straightforward as it may seem, and it is important that you think about the parameters about this kind of activity, particularly in relation to ethics. Please ask yourself these questions.
• What are the ethical issues of sharing data that has not been analysed with analysis groups?
• How might you feel when your voice is part of the data being analysed in a group?

For example: At the University of Leicester and Indiana University there is an international research group, Conversation Analysis Research in Autism (CARA), which brings together scholars, students and clinical practitioners to discuss ASD research. Leading scholars at these institutions bring students together face-to-face for data sessions.

For example: As we noted Plymouth University runs a data group, Conversation Analysis Research in Plymouth (CARP) to encourage students to discuss and share data.

Of course, not all universities have these groups, and where this is not the case, we suggest that the student networks with other students and academics to organise group discussions of data themselves, which can be of mutual benefit to all attendees. Indeed, some supervisors will have two or more students using this form of analysis and may run group tutorials to encourage them to share their ideas and help each other. Turn now to the activity in Box 8.7.

Engaging with Everyday Lives, Political and Clinical Contexts

One of the most difficult issues in the management of a DP/CA based project on ASD is balancing the strict analytical procedures of DP/CA and maintaining a clinical and political awareness. Within the supervisory relationship, this can partly be addressed through regular revisiting of the topic, the research aims, the how—or the method, and most importantly, the question of what the research will produce and the 'so what?' question. A tricky issue for DP/CA is ensuring that the findings do not become an analytic exercise, but are useful to stakeholders including families and clinicians. We suggest two activities for addressing this:

- First, we think that the supervisor and supervisee should regularly discuss what will be done with the findings: the supervisor must remember to ask this question, and the student needs to be given enough space to feel able to answer such questions. These conversations might discuss current developments in DP/CA, such as Antaki's (2011) collection of applied studies, where impacts have included developing different ways of asking questions in healthcare, drawing attention to inequalities, and offering training in communications (see also Stokoe, 2014).
- Second, it can be facilitative for students (and possibly supervisors) to consult with service users and carers who have experience of ASD. This ensures that the research is relevant to service user needs. Further, it can provide external input to the supervisory relationship, challenging and revealing unacknowledged assumptions made within the supervisory relationship about ASD.

Consultation might also support the translation of technical DP/CA concepts into more accessible language, helping to break down some of the power imbalances that can be created by the highly technical language of CA in particular. Further suggestions of how to tackle the challenges of CA's language are provided by Billig (2013). Final reflections are encouraged in the activity in Box 8.8.

Box 8.8 Final reflections

Activity

We would encourage you to try to apply the lessons you have learned from this chapter to your own work and consider these questions:
- What are the realistic contributions of a DA/CA project on ASD?
- What kind of recommendations could be made from your data?

> **Box 8.9 Practical highlights**
>
> Summary of practical highlights
>
> 1. Most supervision difficulties come from poor supervision and no discussion about the supervisory process—try to reflect on this and the ways to achieve this.
> 2. Plan for the most difficult points in the research, which might be: starting the data analysis; staying with the DP/CA analysis until it is robust; and then carefully thinking about the implications and stakeholders.
> 3. Data groups are helpful to develop analytic skills and confidence and can offer additional support.
> 4. Consultation with service users and other stakeholders pre- and post-analysis can help to build understanding of the implications of your work.

Summary

This chapter has presented a case study of our experiences of research supervision as supervisee and supervisor of conducting a DP/CA study of ASD. It has taken a reflective approach and tried to consider some of the conceptual threshold crossings that students completing a DP/CA study of ASD might make. We argued that these include a deepening of understanding and application of 'language-as-action'; a transition in reading, writing, and analysing from a DP/CA approach; and ultimately a transition to apply the approach in a way that makes sense, and can be communicated, to others. We have suggested that these transitions might be facilitated by attending to both student and supervisor beliefs and confidence in the research project; analytic skills and leaving behind personal, professional, and theoretical influences; and the relevance of the research to stakeholders and clinical and political contexts. We conclude our chapter, therefore, with a summary of the practical messages you can take away from our experiences in Box 8.9.

References

Antaki, C. (Ed.). (2011). *Applied conversation analysis: Intervention and change in institutional talk*. Hampshire: Palgrave Macmillan.

Billig, M. (2013). *Learn to write badly*. Cambridge: Cambridge University Press.

BPS (British Psychological Society). (2014). *Standards for doctoral programmes in Clinical Psychology.* Leicester: BPS.

Crix, D., Stedmon, J., Smart, C., & Dallos, R. (2012). Knowing 'ME' knowing you: The discursive negotiation of contested illness within a family. *Journal of Depression and Anxiety, 1*(4), 1–8.

Dallos, R., & Smart, C. (2011). An exploration of family dynamics and attachment strategies in a family with ADHD/conduct problems. *Clinical Child Psychology and Psychiatry, 16*(4), 535–550.

Davies, C. (2008). *Reflexive Ethnography: A guide to researching selves and others.* Abingdon: Routledge.

Eley, A., & Jennings, R. (2005). *Effective postgraduate supervision: Improving the student/supervisor relationship.* New York: Open University Press.

Elliot, H., Brannen, J., Phoenix, A., Barlow, A., Morris, P., Smart, C., et al. (2013). *Analysing qualitative data in groups: Process and practice.* National Centre for Research Methods. Retrieved September 17, 2016, from http://eprints.ncrm.ac.uk/3172/1/jointanalysispaper200813.pdf

Evans, C., & Stevenson, K. (2010). The learning experiences of international doctoral students with particular reference to nursing students: A literature review. *International Journal of Nursing Studies, 47*(2), 239–250.

Hayashi, M., Raymond, G., & Sidnell, J. (2013). *Conversational repair and human understanding.* Cambridge: University Press.

Honey, A., & Mumford, P. (1992). *A manual of learning styles.* Maidenhead: Peter Honey Learning.

McCallin, A., & Nayar, S. (2012). Postgraduate research supervision: A critical review of current practice. *Teaching in Higher Education, 17*(1), 63–74.

Meyer, J., & Land, R. (2003). *Threshold concepts and troublesome knowledge (1): Linkages to ways of thinking and practising within the disciplines.* ETL Project, Occasional Report 4. http://www.etl.tla.ed.ac.uk/docs/ETLreport4.pdf

Neave, H., Collett, T., & Lloyd, H. (2017). Understanding students' experiences of professionalism learning: A 'threshold' approach. *Teaching in Higher Education, 22*(1), 92–108.

Perkins, D. (2006). *Constructivism and troublesome knowledge.* In J. H. F. Meyer & R. Land (Eds.), *Overcoming barriers to student understanding: Threshold concepts and troublesome knowledge* (pp. 33–47). Abingdon, OX: Routledge.

Pollock, C., & Auburn, T. (2013). Laughter and competence: Children with severe autism using laughter to joke and tease. In P. Glenn & E. Holt (Eds.), *Studies of laughter in interaction* (pp. 135–160). London: Bloomsbury Academic.

Potter, J. (2012). Discourse analysis and discursive psychology. In H. Cooper (Ed.), *APA handbook of research methods in psychology, Quantitative, qualitative, neuropsychological, and biological* (Vol. 2, pp. 111–130). Washington, DC: American Psychological Association Press.

QAA. (2011). *Doctoral degree characteristics*. The Quality Assurance Agency for Higher Education. Retrieved February 19, 2016, from http://www.qaa.ac.uk/en/Publications/Documents/Doctoral_Characteristics.pdf.

Rolls, L., & Relf, M. (2006). Bracketing interviews: Addressing methodological challenges in qualitative interviewing in bereavement and palliative care. *Mortality, 11*, 286–305.

Shukr, I., Zainab, R., & Rana, M. (2013). Learning styles of postgraduate and undergraduate medical students. *Journal of the College of Physicians and Surgeons Pakistan, 23*(1), 25–30.

Stedmon, J., & Dallos, R. (2009). *Reflective practice in psychotherapy and counselling*. Maidenhead: Open University Press.

Stokoe, E. (2014). The Conversation Analytic Role-play Method (CARM): A method for training communication skills as an alternative to simulated role-play. *Research on Language and Social Interaction, 47*(3), 255–265.

Stuart, K., Smart, C., Dallos, R., & Williams, F. (2015). Chronic fatigue syndrome: How families talk about psychological phenomena, a 'delicate' and 'protected' topic. *Human Systems, The Journal of Therapy, Consultation and Training, 26*(2).

Wenger, E., & Lave, J. (1991). *Situated learning: Legitimate peripheral participation (Learning in doing: social, cognitive and computational perspectives)*. Cambridge: Cambridge University Press.

Wetherell, M. (1998). Positioning and interpretative repertoires: Conversation analysis and post-structuralism in dialogue. *Discourse and Society, 9*, 431–456.

Wisker, G., Morris, C., Cheng, M., Masika, R., Warnes, M., Lilly, J., et al. (2010). *Doctoral learning journeys: Final report*. York: Higher Education Academy.

Wisker, G., & Robinson, G. (2013). Doctoral 'orphans': Nurturing and supporting the success of postgraduates who have lost their supervisors. *Higher Education Research & Development, 32*(2), 300–313.

Youselfi, A., Bazrafkan, L., & Yamani, N. (2015). A qualitative inquiry into the challenges and complexities of research supervision: Viewpoints of postgraduate students and faculty members. *Journal of Advanced Medical Education and Professionalism, 3*(3), 91–98.

Recommended Reading

Antaki, C. (Ed.). (2011). *Applied conversation analysis: Intervention and change in institutional talk*. Hampshire: Palgrave Macmillan.

Billig, M. (2013). *Learn to write badly*. Cambridge: Cambridge University Press.

Denman, K., Smart, C., Dallos, R., & Levett, P. (2016). How families understand their child's behaviour while on the waiting list for a diagnosis of autism. *Journal of Autism and Developmental Disorders.* doi:10.1007/s10803-016-2873-7

Pollock, C., & Auburn, T. (2013). Laughter and competence: Children with severe autism using laughter to joke and tease. In P. Glenn & E. Holt (Eds.), *Studies of laughter in interaction* (pp. 135–160). London: Bloomsbury Academic.

Potter, J. (2012). Discourse analysis and discursive psychology. In H. Cooper (Ed.), *APA handbook of research methods in psychology, Quantitative, qualitative, neuropsychological, and biological* (Vol. 2, pp. 111–130). Washington, DC: American Psychological Association Press.

Cordet Smart is Lecturer in Clinical Psychology at Plymouth University, and Lecturer in Clinical Research Methods at Exeter University. She completed her PhD with the Open University in social psychology, examining social influence from a discursive perspective. She has gone on to explore how discursive psychology and conversation analysis can be used in clinical psychology settings. She has a particular interest in systemic approaches to understanding how families and psychological services work as systems, and how this understanding can be developed using discursive psychology and conversation analysis to improve experiences of families and the provision of psychological services.

Katie Denman is a qualified clinical psychologist who graduated in 2015. She works for Plymouth Hospitals NHS Trust in the Child Development Centre with children and young people who have a developmental delay and their families. Katie's clinical work draws on individual techniques (CBT, behavioural, narrative) for children and young people, alongside relational (systemic and attachment) models to work with and support the whole family. Katie has a particular interest in autism, attachment, and parenting.

Part II

Examples of Empirical ASD Research

9

The Interaction Is the Work: Rehabilitating Risk in a Forensic Patient with Autism Spectrum Disorder and Learning Disability

Sushie Dobbinson

Learning Objectives

By the end of this chapter you will be able to:

- Describe why interaction is important in forensic clinical practice.
- Explain why repetition in conversation is more than meaningless parroting.
- Describe the significance of frame shifting in clinical interactions.
- Point out some of the ways in which clinicians orient to affiliation and alignment.

Introduction

Bringing about change is not a simple undertaking. One of the most frustrating things a therapist can hear, but tends to hear often nonetheless, is *'people can't really change'*. Therapists, outside of their work roles,

S. Dobbinson (✉)
Humber Mental Health NHS Foundation Trust, Hull, UK

© The Author(s) 2017
M. O'Reilly et al. (eds.), *A Practical Guide to Social Interaction Research in Autism Spectrum Disorders*, The Language of Mental Health,
https://doi.org/10.1057/978-1-137-59236-1_9

may even say it themselves, reflecting on the disappointingly predictable behaviours of friends and family as they '*revert to type*'.

For example: Drinkers 'falling off the wagon'.
For example: Relationship partners repeating earlier dysfunctional patterns.
For example: Comfort-eaters bingeing at the slightest excuse.

Indeed, there is a multiplicity of dictums on the subject, a few of which are listed below:

'You can take the man out of the small town, but you can't take the small town out of the man.'
'A leopard never changes its spots.'
'You can lead a horse to water, but you can't make it drink.'

Yet this is the task therapy sets itself: to change something personal and internal, usually both behavioural and cognitive, to the individual or, systemically, to the couple or family group (Prochaska, 1999). In this chapter, I focus on a particularly challenging therapeutic context: that of a person with autism spectrum disorder (ASD) and learning disability (LD), Malcolm (all names and identifying information in this chapter have been changed to maintain confidentiality), who has been detained to a secure psychiatric hospital under a section of the Mental Health Act (Department of Health, 2007). Extracts of interactions between Malcolm and his clinicians are analysed to demonstrate how discursive methods can contribute to rehabilitation and risk management work in the forensic setting ('forensic' here refers to the context of detention, which is required by law). Malcolm has not elected to be in hospital or made any conscious decision to engage in therapy. As well as his ASD, he also has an LD, and the family who support him are unlikely to be aware of the full extent of the offending behaviours which have led him to be in hospital. Therefore, many of the prerequisites that a therapist usually relies on before engaging in therapy are absent. Rather than enabling the patient to deal with a mutually accepted problem, the forensic SLT's focus is on working to understand what the patient understands, what and how he or she is communicating, then, armed with this information, to support them to adapt thoughts, beliefs, and behaviours so that their risks can be seen to have demonstrably reduced. As will be seen, this is quite a challenge and requires far more than the efforts of a single clinician.

What Do Forensic Wards Do?

For most SLTs, the patients they see have already been involved in some kind of decision to bring about change. Whether they have suffered an insult to previously unimpaired function, for example, a stroke or head injury, or are struggling with a developmental condition that impacts on their ability to fully access their communities, such as ASD or an LD, either they or their families have at some stage consciously responded to these conditions by purposefully seeking therapy, recognising perhaps that in order to buck the common-sense notion of *people don't ever change*, they are in need of professional intervention.

Often, there is a strong resistance to invite in a therapist, who is essentially a stranger, to play such a significant part in the arena of the personal. Support of those closest to the therapy recipient can be critical in such situations. Making behavioural changes requires a leap of faith and courage, since taking on the new inevitably involves forsaking the comfort and security of past habits. However beneficial the change is thought to be, this always has to be balanced against the threat to identity that making it will entail. There are, then, generally three components to therapy:

1. The therapy problem at hand, whether it be communication related or some other aspect of psycho-social function
2. Those who carry the main weight of the therapy problem, that is, the patient and, possibly, their supportive significant other or others
3. The therapist

Important point

! Ideally, all the people in this equation should be invested in the therapy, have some belief in its positive outcome, and should have made a conscious decision to access it. Unconditional positive regard of the therapist for the patient is essential, as is understanding, psychological acceptance, and empathy (Rogers, 2007).

Ideally, therapy recipients should be either motivated or robustly supported to make changes if the therapy is to have any chance of success. If either one of these is lacking it may be possible that an upgrading of the other can compensate, but the task is bound to become more complex and testing to the therapist. If it is hard to change behaviour and thinking when you have decided that you want to, then what hope is there when you have not (Prochaska, 1999)?

Important point
! Forensic psychiatric patients are an exception to this ideal therapeutic context due to the imposition of treatment upon them.

Forensic patients come to hospital because of the risk they pose to community and/or self. The drive to change behaviour has not arisen internally, consequent to a developing awareness of their difficulties, but has been externally and forcefully applied by legal authority. For some forensic patients (and, as the extracts illustrate, Malcolm is one of these), the idea that their behaviour should be the concern of anyone else, let alone anyone acting under the authority of the state, and made the subject of forced alteration, is a source of bewilderment and occasionally anger. Arguably, forensic patients have a greater incentive than most, since the secure hospital is the last stop. If they fail in changing themselves here and to the degree required by authority (in the UK for instance, in the imposing form of the Ministry of Justice), then there is nowhere else for them to go. Without change, they will simply remain in secure services, eventually, hopefully for their own sakes, becoming habituated to the wholesale and continuing restriction on their freedom and experience. This means several things for them as individuals:

- They will be prevented from starting new families or playing an active role in their birth families.
- They will not be able to go to work and earn money.
- They will not be able to go on holiday.
- They will not experience romance, status, or choice, other than in this restricted, unnatural environment.

For many forensic patients, the fear of this as a life outcome is enough of a motivator to access therapy. Previously incorrigible recidivists, away from the temptations that have been their undoing, can become the most radical re-inventors of themselves under such conditions.

> **Important point**
>
> ! For forensic patients with ASD and an LD, however, the
> • complexities of their profiles make risk reduction and a move
>   down the levels of security to eventual release difficult.

Many such patients have a long history of secure care, difficult family histories, and may have been victims as well as perpetrators of crime. The circumstances of their index offence (the offence which has resulted in their section) are sometimes germane to these histories.

For example: One such patient, persuaded by a relative to carry out a robbery while he waited outside, was promptly left at the scene to be arrested while the relative made his escape complete with the proceeds of the crime. Inevitably, it was the person with the LD who was convicted while the relative remained at large and free, presumably to take advantage of other vulnerable people.

What this demonstrates is that people with LDs can be vulnerable to exploitation from those closest to them, from whom, in better circumstances, they might have expected to learn more adaptive responses to the circumstances and vicissitudes of their lives. People with LDs who find themselves in criminal contexts experience particular difficulties:

- They are almost always vulnerable to exploitation.
- They cannot always judge where their actions might lead.
- Once compromised, they often lack the psychological resources to extricate themselves.

Residents on a secure LD ward may lack families who are able to offer them the kind of support that might have enabled them to escape the forensic cycle, or support them effectively once they are caught up in it. Furthermore, without having made a conscious decision to take on therapy, nevertheless, once detained under the Mental Health Act, they find themselves its recipients. Even the concept of therapy, abstract as it is, might be difficult to grasp in such a context. For some of these patients, the intention is for the clinical team to gain understanding of how best to keep them and their communities safe, rather than to make changes, that is, assessing the risks they pose so that they can be managed safely with the least possible restriction of their liberty (Department of Health, 2007). For the others, it is not clear what changes therapy will bring about until it is tried. Understanding what the patients are able to understand is then a critical aspect of the therapeutic endeavour. Nurses, assistants, psychologists, SLTs, and other therapists work together to help ensure those whose risk can be actively reduced are differentiated from those whose cannot.

As well as the personal circumstances that a forensic patient brings to the intervention table, there is also the question of the impact of an LD. Forensic LD patients are possibly the most complex in forensic psychiatry, all as unique as they are complex (Johnstone, 2005). As for most people with LDs, their LD is rarely specified, meaning that everything about the way in which each individual patient functions must be figured out. LD is simply a social label that tells us something has unfolded unexpectedly during the developmental stages. Occasionally, patients arrive with a diagnosis (e.g., foetal alcohol syndrome or ASD), which may give some clue as to what to expect, but usually the way in which a new patient functions, cognitively, emotionally, and interactionally, has to be learned by the clinical team using notes from past placements, formal assessments, and a raft of exhaustively detailed observations accumulated by a multiplicity of practitioners known as the multidisciplinary team (MDT). Most importantly, it is within the daily and therapeutic interactions that the clinical team comes to know and understand their patients, a continual, ongoing process, without which none of the formal information has any substance.

Forensic practitioners always keep in mind the risks that the patient poses, presently and in the future (Sellars, 2011). The patient's offending behaviour is exhaustively analysed and interpreted, discussed, responses unpicked, and understanding of 'what went wrong' investigated—all with the purpose of informing how this patient is to be safely managed in the future, and, according to UK law, with the least possible restriction of their liberty (Department of Health, 2007). The team aims to ameliorate the patient's own understanding of what makes them tick. If this is successful, the patient will be able to manage their own emotions and responses to such a degree that their supervision can be relaxed and they can be moved to a less secure environment. Almost entirely, this work is completed by means of interactions and is dependent on the forging of at least a few robust clinician-patient alliances.

Patient History

This section begins with an overview of Malcolm and his situation to provide context for the discussion that follows throughout the rest of the chapter. Analyses of the conversational data function as empirical exemplars to help consolidate what you have learned in part one of the book.

Malcolm arrived on the ward with no specific diagnosis, but at this initial stage, the following issues of relevance were noted:

- Malcolm's index offence was violence against a sex worker committed while under the influence of alcohol.
- Malcolm had had a previous stay on a secure forensic ward for violent offences.
- Malcolm presented as angry and lacking in a sense of responsibility towards any of the offences he had committed, expressing frequently the idea that he had been unjustly incarcerated.

Of particular note, Malcolm repeatedly told staff that he did not see why he should be punished by being locked up when other people who had committed worse offences were still at large. He seemed fearful that he would ever regain his freedom and continually asked everybody, 'Do you stay here forever?', often not waiting for an answer but recycling a theme of 'you must stay here forever because every day you wake up and it's the same'. These repetitions occurred so frequently that they became a source of great frustration for the clinical team and Malcolm's peers. Worse, from the point of view of achieving rehabilitation, Malcolm himself became more upset the more he recycled them. At times, he became extremely anxious and tearful. The team worried he was becoming hopeless—and without hope no progress would be made.

Malcolm's family were supportive of him, but unintentionally seemed to fuel his despair, by telling him (or so he told us) that he should be moving on and reinforcing the notion that people who had committed worse offences were out enjoying their lives. Malcolm repeated their words as well as similar supportive comments attributed to members of the clinical team. The MDT began to suspect that what people had said to Malcolm may not be being reported accurately. The first response was to challenge members of the team: for example, why encourage Malcolm to believe that he just needed to wait out his time on the ward rather than to work on the understanding of his offences? It gradually became apparent that phrases of encouragement underwent transformations when they entered Malcolm's understanding, into something that felt like weapons for him to combat attempts to change his ways of thinking. Long, circular arguments took place during which the ground beneath Malcolm's repetitions and recycling of the phrases of others appeared to become increasingly unstable. At the regular MDT meetings and on the ward, Malcolm's problems were discussed to try to understand where we were going wrong and what needed to be done.

Presenting the ASD Perspective

Given the nature of communication in ASD as concrete, routinized, and potentially referentially idiosyncratic, Malcolm's repetitions and his intractability suggested problems with understanding stemming from an overly rigid world view. Rather than a conscious intent to deceive or reject intervention, Malcolm's infelicitous re-castings of prior speech addressed to him were hypothesised to derive from his communicative predisposition. For example, Malcolm repeated words in the same formulaic chunks, combining them with other formulaic chunks, suggesting the words were not functioning as individually meaningful units but as referential placeholders, or a kind of shorthand to often-used concepts.

For example: '[nurse's name] says you don't stay here forever' where the nurse's name could vary and the nurse in question could not always remember saying any such thing.

Due to its continual appearance, 'Do you stay here forever' (analysed in more detail below) became a kind of catchphrase on the ward among staff and patients alike. The infelicitous re-castings caused so much confusion between staff members that some refused to interact with Malcolm when he produced them, which made him more anxious and meant that the words just burst out in his next interaction with a staff member. The clinical team decided to keep the language used with Malcolm consistent in form and take account of the context of his repetitions as much as the words, rather than viewing them as something that needed to be stamped out of his repertoire or ignored, to accept them as having a function which could be interpreted by attending to the context and paralinguistic features.

For example: when 'Do you stay here forever' was accompanied by an apparently upset Malcolm, by dealing with it as a request for reassurance and responding to it with a formula we had all agreed on, the phrase came to be understood and accepted by the clinical team as a strategy which Malcolm used to help him reduce anxiety.

To obviate Malcolm's tendency to worry out loud about who had said what and how that meant that Malcolm did not need to do any work to regain his freedom, staff set aside boundaried time periods for him to air these thoughts. In this way, Malcolm could be included in group sessions, which previously he had disrupted with his constant preoccupation on the theme of the injustice of his incarceration.

Once it became clear that these steps improved Malcolm's ability to engage with us and seemed to help boundary his anxiety, the MDT made the decision to formally assess Malcolm for ASD. Once obtained, the diagnosis made it possible for those who did not know him to understand a little more how he functioned. The reasons an ASD diagnosis is often missed in forensic settings are outlined elsewhere (Dobbinson, 2016). It is not always helpful to diagnose an adult with ASD, particularly when they seem to be functioning more or less adaptively in everyday life.

However, Malcolm's recidivism, rigidity of understanding, and difficulty engaging with the clinical team, let alone internalising strategies to reduce his risk, made diagnosis a potentially important element of our patient management, not least to alert future placements about the best way to manage him.

Taking into account the above, the decision was made to work with Malcolm using visual comic strips (Gray, 1994). I met with him every week and drew out the planned steps of his care to help him understand what was going to happen next.

Important point

! An important component of these visuals was Malcolm's eventual return to the community as this gave him hope and helped orientate him to our mutual goal.

Malcolm sometimes carried his visuals with him on the ward, as he did with his favourite DVDs or pictures of his favourite soap stars. The visuals thus became incorporated into Malcolm's anxiety-reducing behaviours. By anchoring us all to something concrete beyond Malcolm's confused verbal re-castings of past conversations, the visuals also helped frame future discussions with Malcolm as well as summing up earlier ones.

Talk with Malcolm

The extracts below were taken from programmed sessions with Malcolm between March and November 2015 as Malcolm was preparing to undertake an external assessment that it was hoped would lead to his move-on. Within the context of the book, the data analyses serve empirically as examples to demonstrate ways to deal with this kind of interaction in practice. The clinical practitioners included:

- two LD-trained forensic nurses, Cat and Kevin, and a nursing assistant, Seth, who all worked closely with Malcolm, and
- an occupational therapist, Alan, who saw Malcolm regularly, but far less than the nurses.

In CA terms, the overarching frame of risk reduction work is the same for all of the extracts, although each of the clinicians aligns to it differently.

Seth and Kevin: Alignment, Affiliation, and Moving on

The first extract is taken from the opening of a session between Malcolm and Seth, the nursing assistant. Seth starts the session with an open question in a conversational register, allowing Malcolm to set the agenda. This type of opening is a topic initial elicitor and, as can be seen in the other extracts here, is a regular way for staff to begin programmed sessions with Malcolm (Button & Casey, 1984).

Malcolm responds with a variant of one of his most commonly used formulas, '*[name] says you don't stay here forever but every day you wake up in ere.*' Malcolm produces it here with the hopeless element, *every day you wake up in ere*, first, immediately followed by its complementary hopeful adjunct, '*it's not forever*', the latter reported as the words of Malcolm's favourite member of staff, Paul Logan, who spends a great deal of time patiently listening and talking with Malcolm. Seth's repetition at line 4 accords with the clinical team's agreed response to neither shut down formulaic phrases, nor unpick whether or not [name] did in fact say what Malcolm reports them to have done, but instead to respond to what seems to be the socio-emotional function of the words in the present context.

Extract 1

```
S    what's on yer mind
M    (2.0)((sniff)) (5.0) bout (1.0) in here every day you wake
     up in ere (.) then Paul Logan says it's not forever
S    that's right it's not forever
M    hmm?
S    it's not forever. you only need to be here while there's
     work we can do with you obviously finish doing that work
     won't need to be   here anymore (1.0) you can move on
     and we can look after somebody else that needs our help
```

Malcolm's opening tells of his hopelessness, but then immediately supplies the hopeful response, putting the latter into the mouth of Paul Logan, as if Paul were present supporting Malcolm in that framing.

Seth's immediate repetition of the formula '*it's not forever*' in line 4 both affiliates and aligns with Malcolm (and, indirectly, with Paul Logan). At line 6, Seth follows Malcolm's minimal response with a second repetition (more alignment and affiliation), to which he adds context, '*you only need to be here while there's work we can do with you*', a kind of mitigated directive, implying that while Malcolm will not stay here forever, he still needs to do the work required by the ward team. The next turn construction unit (TCU), '*obviously finish that work won't need to be here anymore*' increases the directive force.

Important point

!
• Remember that a Turn Construction Unit (TCU) (as introduced by Sacks, Schegloff, & Jefferson, 1974) refers to a unit of a conversation which is complete in its own right.

So, if you look closely at the extract, the phrase '*finish that work*' is the only component of Seth's turn with directive syntax, albeit softened by being tied both in contour and structure to another mitigating element of hope, '*you won't need to be here anymore*'. This restates the hoped for result of the work. Seth completes his turn with a recast of the hope message, '*you can move on and we can look after somebody else that needs our help*'.

Thus, initially, Seth supports Malcolm emotionally and interactively by affiliation and alignment, then contextualises, by reminding Malcolm of the condition to move on: that he needs to keep working. Thus Malcolm's immediate orientation to Seth's repetition of his words at line 4, as well as Seth's second repetition (line 6) at the start of Seth's most rehabilitation-focused turn, demonstrate how use of Malcolm's words forms the foundation by which progress of therapy along the lines of the institutional requirements is achieved by the two interlocutors.

Lastly, in his turn final TCU, '*and we can look after somebody else that needs our help*', Seth orients to his responsibility as a clinical practitioner to prepare Malcolm for the clinical team's eventual detachment from him. Conditionality is embedded in the clinical relationship at many levels.

Important point

! While Malcolm and his peers are almost entirely dependent on
• clinical practitioners for support and guidance as they navigate
    forensic services, the relationship is bound to be temporary.

Move-on is inevitable, thus practitioners need to maintain clinical distance from their patients. Caring for patients without them becoming too dependent on individual staff members can be a tricky element of the professional relationship to manage, particularly with patients such as Malcolm who have social deficits. Seth's turn final TCU indicates that Seth is working to manage this even while he deals with Malcolm's immediate concerns.

I have undertaken quite a lot of analysis here and unpacked much of what has been said by those in the interaction, so I would encourage you to pause and reflect at this point and try the activity in Box 9.1.

Seth maintains the frame of risk reduction work while adopting an informal register. His use of Malcolm's words, by virtue of repetition aligning and affiliating, at the same time keeps the tone of the interaction conversational. This does not always happen, however. In Extract 1a, Malcolm has just mentioned '*responsibility*' in conversation with the nurse, Kevin, which Kevin then picks up.

Box 9.1 Reflecting on the analysis

Activity

The analysis presented is quite dense and it is quite easy to skim over the points made. At this point, I would encourage you to make a list of the key things you have learned from the analysis of Extract 1 so far.

Extract 1a

```
K    (3.0) ↑yeah well once they you're responsible for what you
     do aren't yer (.) the choices that you make (.) you're
     responsible for being here now n you'll be responsible
     for getting yourself moved on (2.0) so if you come back
     you've- it will be your responsibility
     n'av anyone to blame but yourself (3.0) famous saying
M    (2.0) yeah but I thought you said (2.0) when people go you
     don't wanna see people again
K    (1.0) well no we don't wanna see em come back we wanna see
     em go out n do well in life n use their skills that we
     try n give them (4.0)
```

Despite Malcolm making first mention of '*responsibility*', and regardless of Kevin's repetition of it, Malcolm does not take it up as a topic, and instead orients to '*if you come back*'. '*Responsibility*' is a term associated with the more formal register of forensic therapeutic work. Its sophisticated meaning relies on understanding moral obligations of self in relation to others and environment, hence it is an important concept within the institutional discourse frame of the psychiatric hospital. Institutionally important terms, however, often seem far less salient to patients. Forensic LD patients rarely have complete understanding of emotions and, despite them sometimes using it, the language of self-control used to guide their responses to situations is not always completely accessible to them. Kevin's repetitive TCUs at lines 1–6 can be understood as, at least in part, an attempt to align Malcolm's talk with the formal register of forensic work.

Malcolm's '*yeah, but I thought you said…*' in adjusts the footing from a discussion about abstract to concrete matters with personal relevance for Malcolm. Kevin responds somewhat adaptively, by giving a less formal account of his expectations for Malcolm, focusing on actions rather than concepts: to him '*doing well*' by applying the skills he has learned, rather than '*being responsible*'. Kevin's line 1 self-repair from '*they*' to '*you*' also brings talk into the frame of Malcolm's personal experience. Kevin's final turn not only adapts to the simpler conceptual basis of Malcolm's turn but also repeats Malcolm's lexis and structures, '*We don't wanna see 'em come back, we wanna see 'em go out 'n' do well…*', aligning and affiliating with Malcolm, just as Seth has done earlier.

Box 9.2 Kevin's reflections on talk with Malcolm

Kevin's reflections

If you repeat things enough, expose someone to it, eventually you hope it will sink in. In our conversations it was always emphasising the same key things, the same key points bringing it back, his offending, to rights and responsibilities cos they're what he needed to demonstrate in his behaviour and conversations to show minimisation of risk. He was never going to get the future he wanted for himself if he did not take on board some of the things we were giving him, but he rarely demonstrated much evidence of learning, as he was just too fixated on wanting to get out.

Thus, Kevin pushes Malcolm conceptually where he can thereby open up the possibility of entering the formal register of forensic risk reduction, but retreats to the less formal, more concrete, and personally relevant when Malcolm offers nothing that suggests he is taking up a concept.

Your reflections from earlier should have helped you to see how a conversation analysis is done in this context. It is useful to continue this reflection, and therefore, it would be helpful to examine the reflections on Kevin in Box 9.2.

Cat: Matching Frames and Empathy

The start of Malcolm's session with Cat is similar to Seth's. Cat starts with a topic eliciting open question which, in the second TCU, targets more specifically the activity of airing Malcolm's worries, giving him explicit permission to vent his concerns. Cat leaves lots of space for Malcolm to formulate his response.

Extract 2

```
C   right (1.0) what d' you want to (1.0) discuss (.)
      what's been worrying yer today (7.0)
M   what when I was upset earlier
C   yeah
M   (2.5) bout being in ere
```

```
C    m ok
M    (2.0) nnd er Paul Logan was saying (1.0) th there is a
     light (.) under the tunnel tht (0.5) it's not gonna be
     forever
C    nyeah (.) what does he mean by er (1.0) a light under the
     tunnel
```

The interaction in lines 1–6 becomes a negotiation about what is to be discussed, during which both participants orient to any specific cause of Malcolm's upset as not being a matter for discussion at this point. Despite line 2 *'today'* and line 3 *'earlier'*, Malcolm's *'bout being in ere'* does not include any mention of recent events on the ward that may have precipitated him being upset, an issue which, in the interests of getting patients to acknowledge and take ownership of their actions and emotions, Cat may have, but chooses not to prioritise as a topic for talk here. Cat's minimal response, *'m ok'*, to Malcolm's rather generalised construction of being upset as a result of *'being in ere'* indicates that she is leaving the task of identifying any more specific cause up to Malcolm. At the same time, *'m ok'* suggests Cat may have another interpretation of Malcolm's being upset earlier, which she elects not to open up here. Malcolm's use of first pair parts, *'what when I was upset earlier'* and *'about being in ere'* effectively enables him to get Cat's permission for determining choice of topic.

Malcolm's next TCU, as with Seth's extract, is a complement to the expression of hopelessness, a message of hope once again attributed to favourite staff member Paul Logan. This time Malcolm presents a new idea, *'there's a light under the tunnel'*. Instead of repairing the misrendering (by replacing *under* with *at the end of*), Cat orients to the aphorism by probing Malcolm's understanding of it. Thus, in this early stage of the session Cat chooses to focus neither on disputing reasons for Malcolm getting upset earlier nor on who said what nor on the correct use of the aphorism, but instead on what Malcolm understands: *'what does he mean by light under the tunnel'*. Indeed, in repeating Malcolm's words exactly, Cat chooses repetitive affiliation with Malcolm over repair.

Extract 2a shows Cat dealing with Malcolm's understanding of psychiatric concepts differently to Kevin's attempts to relate them to the frame of institutional forensic discourse. Instead, she is minutely focused on

Malcolm and his actions. At line 8, her affiliating repetition of Malcolm's *'a situation like that again'* contextualises her question. When Malcolm hesitates to supply a response, she directs him to concrete events rather than abstract concepts, leading Malcolm to make the connections himself. In this way, Malcolm recovers from memory the forensically important concept of empathy in his last turn. Cat manages to do this without shifting frames from personal to institutional, or registers from informal to formal.

Extract 2a

```
M    (2.0) I then I then (1.0) I then e-e n e was saying a-
     (1.0) a then er:: a then Seth s'used a say to me (.) if
     I get into a situation like that again what got me in
     ere (.) I'- say you be able to errr- (2.0) ss n stop n
     er think (.) that (1.0)hh wa-w-w- what was it like when
     I was in ere (.) n I didn't like being in ere
C    (2.0) are there other reasons why you'd ss-(.) act
     differently (.) if you got yerself into a situation like
     that again
M    (6.0) er:: (4.0)
C    think about the stuff you've been doing (.) in yer
     sessions=
M                                        =nyea::h
C    wha-(.) what else migh- (.) might stop yer
M    (1.0) ooh bout Jules (1.0) the art therapy e was talking
     to me about (.) what I was telling Shauna today the
     psychologist
C    yeah
M    empathy about (.) about (.) about I wunt like people to
     hurt me for what I did an an an n-an then Kevin start
     telling me about (.) my aunty down south (0.5) she
     didn't bring you up to be like that=
C    = mm
```

In Extract 2a, Malcolm begins to give an account of his understanding of *empathy*, nested on a bed of prior mentions of earlier conversations with Jules the art therapist, Shauna the psychologist, and Kevin. Malcolm substitutes the leap of imagination that empathy requires, from '*what I'm feeling might be similar to what others might be feeling*', to '*my behaviour might cause a reaction in other people that might make me feel bad*'. Malcolm misses out the role of the other's feelings in his causal chain.

We see here that Malcolm is only able to handle topics around feelings and abstract forensic concepts by collocating them with people (e.g., in Extracts 1 and 2 Paul Logan is mentioned in the context of hopefulness). In Extract 1a, Malcolm diverts talk about *responsibility* by citing Kevin's own words on the topic of move-on. In 2a, mention of *empathy* collocates with mention of the people who Malcolm recalls talking to him about it.

Important point

> **!** Importantly, while Malcolm adopts these key items of institutional vocabulary, and in so doing makes a partial shift towards the forensic register, this feature of always collocating these sophisticated concepts with mentions of people reminds us that Malcolm has not moved from the frame of his own personal experience.

Cat's closing of the topic is shown in Extract 2b.

Extract 2b

```
C    so you shouldn't do those things to other people(.) nyeah
     (.) nyeah (.) n'also think about yer aunty n you
     wouldn't want people  you care about to think bad of yer
M    (1.5) no::: (.) yea::h
C    so that's the reasons:: the reasons not to offend again
     (1.0) ↑good (1.0) so (2.0) reasons not to offend
M    ((clears throat)) (7.0)
```

As she moves into closing, Cat's line 2 mention of '*yer aunty*' shifts to the frame of Malcolm's personal experience. Malcolm's response at line 4 orientates to both components of this turn. Cat's final turn however, uttered almost as an aside, sees her frame-shifting back to forensic lexis. The final TCU, '*reasons not to offend*', suggests a heading such as would precede a list. Notably, Malcolm's final turn gives no indication that he orients at all to this as being relevant to him.

Box 9.3 Cat reflecting on talk with Malcolm

Cat's reflections

I really thought that bit with the art therapist was a step forward for him because it was the first time he really started thinking about how other people felt and his aunty seemed to be key. He started saying things like *'If I did something like that it'd upset my aunty, she wouldn't be proud of me'*. I'd never really heard him talk like that before we started exploring empathy. He'd come back from sessions to start with saying, *'Oh, I've been doing about empathy'*, but couldn't actually say what, and then one day he just said, *'Well, I wouldn't like it if someone treated my aunty like that'* and *'My aunty wouldn't be proud of me'*, and was thinking about other people's perception or feelings, and I thought, *'Actually, yeah, he has got that bit'*. To start with, it was all to do with how it affected him and the consequences for himself, very rigid and focused on himself, so I just thought that was a real step forward.

It is useful at this point to continue your reflection on the analysis presented and therefore it would be helpful to examine the reflections of Cat in Box 9.3 below.

Alan: Disaffiliation as a Therapeutic Choice

Practitioners do not always choose to affiliate with Malcolm. As for Extracts 1 and 2, Extract 3 is taken from the start of a session. Alan sees Malcolm only occasionally 1:1, so the two are less familiar interlocutors. Malcolm is clearly angry when he arrives, red faced and speaking rapidly with forceful intonation. As with Extracts 1 and 2, Malcolm begins with formulaic reference to his present situation (in bold). Unlike Extracts 1 and 2, Malcolm does not wait for an initial topic elicitor before speaking. Despite some initial affiliation by repeating '*happy*' and '*on Friday*', unlike Cat and Seth, Alan attends to the verifiable items in Malcolm's turn at line 1 rather than providing a second pair part with a countering message of hope to Malcolm's first parts of hopelessness. In line 3, Malcolm sidesteps the specific response requested by Alan at line 2, just as he does with Cat in Extract 2, using two of his formulas '*being in ere*', and '*my aunty said ....*' Alan's second attempt at contextualising Friday, by taking up mention of '*aunty*', critically takes the talk within the frame of Malcolm's personal experience. This time Malcolm does orient specifically to Alan's question, albeit formulaically, and in fact, despite long, unfilled silences, goes on to provide relevant second parts to Alan's subsequent questions.

Other than in his initial turn, Alan shows this preference for disregarding affiliation and alignment at the same time as maintaining the frame of Malcolm's personal experience throughout the conversation. Alan is the only clinician who chooses not to repeat the second pair parts of Malcolm's formulas, asking direct questions instead of providing hopeful second parts to first parts of hopelessness (e.g., *'what are we working towards Malcolm'*).

A few lines after this extract, Alan directs Malcolm to fetch the visual produced by Malcolm and I in our last session, which they then go through together. This provides a focus for talk away from whatever has caused Malcolm to feel angry, by providing a topic of personal relevance represented visually, that is, concretely.

Extract 3

```
M    (4.0) not very happy. (0.3) on Friday they got no right to
     keep me in ere (1.5)
A    why weren't you happy on Friday?
M    (5.0) it's being in this place (1.5) ( ) my aunty said
     I've a right to be out I've been in ere long enough
A    (2.0) were you talking to your aunty on Friday.
M    (5.0) no I weren't talking to my ↑aunty ( ) (.) I was
     talking to (1.5) I was talking to the staff (0.5) n then
     nthen Paul Logan said   they can't keep me locked up
     (1.0) n Paul Logan said no they can't keep you locked up
     (1.0)
A    hmhh (4.0)
M    nh you don't stay here forever n every day you come back
     in ere (2.0)
A    what are we working towards Malcolm
     (5.0)
     what's the next step
     (13.0)
M    low secure (1.0)
A    low secure (2.0) so what we waiting for for low secure
     (16.0)
M    referral (2.0)
```

Of all the clinicians' talk, Alan's is the least reliant on immediate repetition (although Alan still makes use of formulas familiar to Malcolm, as can be seen by the way in which Malcolm is able to provide the second to Alan's first pair parts). Alan's turns at lines 12 and 15 are the only instances of clinician disalignment in the extracts.

Important point

! • Disalignment can be used to challenge without recourse to direct confrontation, such as to assert disaffiliation to racist dialogue (Pagliai, 2012).

Alan's disaligning choices in Extract 3 occur in the context of Malcolm's presentation of anger at the time of the interaction, and include the use of closed questions which directively project Malcolm's next turns towards the institutional frame by constraining him to use forensic lexis: *low secure* and *referral*. Alan's first pair parts project Malcolm into the future, focusing him on the pathway out of his current position, and indirectly away from further expressions of hopelessness, frustration, and anger. Thus, even while disaligning and disaffiliating, Alan still orients to familiar formulas. Alan's moves can then be understood as attempts via the therapeutic interaction to organise Malcolm's own internal responses to his feelings of anger and frustration, co-opting his formulaicity to move him towards a more hopeful perspective.

Summary

In attempting to rehabilitate Malcolm, clinicians are presented with a challenging task: to overcome a cognitive predisposition with sufficient effect to impact on future choices and actions. The disjunction between Malcolm and the clinicians emerges interactively as a mismatch of frames (Goffman, 1974); despite his occasional use of forensic psychiatry lexis, Malcolm remains firmly embedded in the frame of his own personal experience. As we see when Kevin tries unsuccessfully to take up the *responsibility* topic, Malcolm's occasional mention of forensic vocabulary does not denote a shift in frame for him. In Malcolm's talk, concepts such as *responsibility* and *empathy* collocate with people-mentions, suggesting these words remain tied to the events in which they were produced. The clinicians, on the other hand, by definition on their interactive and informational home ground, adjust dextrously between frames (Goffman, 1974), moving between institutional and personal, formal and informal.

Tannen and Wallet noted that a clinician shifting frame to accommodate a patient can be triggered by a mismatch between knowledge schemas (1987); that is, the expectations which interactants bring to contexts of how an interaction is likely to unfold. Since construction of new knowledge schemas depends on interactants having the cognitive flexibility to sift and select information, Malcolm's inability to shift frame is likely to have arisen as a consequence of the ASD difficulty in using information to achieve central coherence (Frith, 1989; Vanegas & Davidson, 2015). Despite this, the turns following Malcolm's in which he uses forensic lexis suggest the clinicians interpret it as indicating that meaningful talk on forensically important topics is both viable and relevant. Thus, adaptively pushing forward constitutes at least some of the therapeutic work, for example, by making the relations between the frames explicit for Malcolm. We see this perhaps most clearly in Kevin's self-repair at line 1 from *they* → *you*, which can be read as an attempt to incorporate the forensic concept of *responsibility* into Malcolm's personal experience frame. Cat's *reasons not to offend* turn also designates the foregoing talk as relatable to the forensic frame, while Alan uses first pair parts to direct Malcolm to provide the forensic terms himself.

The extracts show how frame shifts progress risk reduction work, by accommodating to Malcolm in three critical ways:

1. Focusing on the concrete (i.e. actions, events, people) rather than the conceptual
2. Using Malcolm's words (repetition)
3. Using informal rather than institutional register

Focusing on the concrete enables Malcolm to engage with institutional concepts. For example, in Extract 3, Alan defuses Malcolm's anger by projecting his mention of events. As another example, in Extract 2a, Cat's mention of events projects Malcolm's mention of *empathy*. Conversely, when conceptual rather than concrete language is used, any such progress stalls. For example, in receipt of Kevin's *responsibility* turn (Extract 1a), Malcolm attempts to organise the therapeutic discourse to more specifically accommodate his interactional needs by topic-shifting away from conceptual to events-based matters.

Far from being empty parroting of prior talk, repetition can serve many interactional functions, including rendering a discourse coherent (Norrick, 1987). As such, it is an important interactional resource for people with ASD (Bottema-Beutel, Louick, & White, 2015). Cognitively speaking, the cycling of known information in new contexts both allows for and attempts to co-opt the weakly coherent nature that is often associated with ASD, guiding Malcolm about where to incorporate new information and modelling how to accomplish its integration into his own thoughts and ideas. The clinical practitioners' use of words which Malcolm recognises, through the use of both repetition and informal register, lets him know his interactants are cognizant of his world and aware of his emotional stance. In taking Malcolm forward, they imply that they do not intend to leave him behind. The clinicians' choices can be seen, then, as attempts to help Malcolm achieve, if not central, then a less weakly functioning coherence. Most importantly the extracts show how, far from residing solely within the domain of the more interactively competent clinician, successful therapeutic interaction emerges as a negotiated product of both the clinician and patient.

I suggest you now try answering the question in the activity in Box 9.4 as a way of consolidating what you have learned in this chapter.

Box 9.4 Activity to consolidate your learning

Activity

From reading through the analysis presented in this chapter you should be able to see that Kevin and Cat expressed very different ideas about their work with Malcolm.

- How far do you think this is reflected in the extracts of their interactions with him?

> **Box 9.5 Summary of practical highlights**
>
> Summary of practical highlights
>
> 1. While clinicians shift frame adaptively, Malcolm struggles to move from his personal experience frame.
> 2. The clinicians' frame shifts enable progress in the work of risk reduction by incorporating three key elements: focus on the concrete (events, actions, people) rather than the conceptual, use of Malcolm's words (repetition), and informal register.
> 3. Affiliation and alignment are used to maintain therapeutic alliance.
> 4. Disalignment and disaffiliation also have a therapeutic use.
> 5. At times, repetition may be an important interactional resource in conversations that include people with ASD.

This empirical chapter has been designed to show you a working example of how CA is done in practice. It has taken you through the steps of analysis using a step-by-step process of a real example of naturally occurring data in a forensic ward with one patient. There are therefore a number of practical messages from the chapter, and these are summarised in Box 9.5.

References

Bottema-Beutel, K., Louick, R., & White, R. (2015). Repetition, response mobilization, and face: Analysis of interactions with a 19-year-old with Asperger syndrome. *Journal of Communication Disorders, 58*, 179–193.

Button, G., & Casey, N. (1984). Generating topic: The use of topic initial elicitors. In J. M. Atkinson & J. Heritage (Eds.), *Structures of social action: Studies in conversation analysis* (pp. 167–190). Cambridge: Cambridge University Press.

Department of Health. (2007). *Mental Health Act.* London: HMSO.

Dobbinson, S. (2016). Conversations with adults with features of autism spectrum disorders in secure forensic care. In M. O'Reilly & J. Lester (Eds.), *The Palgrave handbook of adult mental health.* Basingstoke: Palgrave Macmillan.

Frith, U. (1989). *Autism: Explaining the enigma.* Cambridge: Blackwell.

Goffman, E. (1974). *Frame analysis.* New York: Harper & Row.

Gray, C. (1994). *Comic strip conversations: Illustrated interactions that teach conversation skills to students with autism and related disorders.* Arlington, TX: Future Horizons.

Johnstone, S. (2005). Epidemiology of offending in learning disability. In T. Riding & C. Swann (Eds.), *The handbook of forensic learning disabilities* (pp. 15–30). Oxford: Radcliffe Publishing.

Norrick, N. R. (1987). Functions of repetition in conversation. *Text and Talk, 7*(3), 245–264.

Pagliai, V. (2012). Non-alignment in footing, intentionality and dissent in talk about immigrants in Italy. *Language and Communication, 32*, 277–292.

Prochaska, J. O. (1999). How do people change, and how can we change many more people? In M. A. Hubble, B. L. Duncan, & S. D. Miller (Eds.), *The heart and soul of change: What works in therapy* (pp. 227–255). Washington, DC: APA.

Rogers, C. A. (2007). The necessary and sufficient conditions of personality change. *Psychotherapy: Theory, Research, Practice, Training, 44*(3), 240–248.

Sacks, H., Schegloff, E., & Jefferson, G. (1974). A simplest systematics for the organization of turn-taking in conversation. *Language, 50, 696–735.*

Sellars, C. (2011). *Risk assessment in people with learning disabilities* (2nd ed.). Oxford: BPS Blackwell.

Tannen, D., & Wallat, C. (1987). Interactive frames and knowledge schemas in interaction: Examples from a medical examination/interview. *Social Psychological Quarterly, 50*(2), 205–216.

Vanegas, S. B., & Davidson, D. (2015). Investigating distinct and related contributions of central coherence, executive dysfunction and systematizing theories to the cognitive profiles of children with Autism Spectrum Disorders and typically developing children. *Research in Autism Spectrum Disorders, 11*, 77–92.

Recommended Reading

Muskett, T., Perkins, M., Clegg, J., & Body, R. (2010). Inflexibility as an interactional phenomenon: Using conversation analysis to re-examine a symptom of autism. *Clinical Linguistics and Phonetics, 24*(1), 1–16.

Robinson, J. D., & Heritage, J. (2014). Intervening with conversation analysis: The case of medicine. *Research on Language and Social Interaction, 47*(3), 201–218.

Sterponi, L., de Kirby, K., & Shankey, J. (2014). Rethinking language in autism. *Autism.* doi:10.1177/1362361314537125

Sushie Dobbinson works for Humber Mental Health NHS Foundation Trust, where she is the lead speech and language therapist (SLT) at the Humber Centre for Forensic Psychiatry as well as a diagnosing clinician for the Humber Adult Autism Diagnosis Service. She has a particular interest in conversation analysis (CA) in autism spectrum disorder (ASD) and uses this and other discursive techniques in her work with forensic patients. Prior to SLT training, Sushie taught linguistics at York St John University. Linguistics continues to inform her analytical methods.

10

Children's Use of "I Don't Know" During Clinical Evaluations for Autism Spectrum Disorder: Responses to Emotion Questions

Trini Stickle, Waverly Duck, and Douglas W. Maynard

Learning Objectives

By the end of this chapter, you will be able to:

- Recognize how, even when answering test questions insufficiently according to ADOS evaluation guidelines, children with autism deploy what we call *concrete competence*. That is, these children are able to produce practices of talk and embodied behaviours which contribute to the achievement of orderly engagement with another participant.

T. Stickle (✉)
Western Kentucky University, Bowling Green, KY, USA

W. Duck
University of Pittsburgh, Pittsburgh, PA, USA

D.W. Maynard
Department of Sociology, University of Wisconsin-Madison,
Madison, WI, USA

© The Author(s) 2017
M. O'Reilly et al. (eds.), *A Practical Guide to Social Interaction Research in Autism Spectrum Disorders*, The Language of Mental Health,
https://doi.org/10.1057/978-1-137-59236-1_10

- Identify displays of concrete competence as a type of *ability* and, in particular, the selective and skilful deployment of phrases such as *I don't know.*
- Offer insights to caregivers and practitioners on some of the challenging questions about experiences and expressions of emotions for persons with autism.

Introduction

In this chapter, we present our observations on children's responses to evaluation prompts about their experiences with emotions and their perceptions of others' emotional experiences. In doing so, these observations speak to the social-communication *abilities* of children on the autism spectrum. Our focus on *I don't know* responses by children during their evaluations provides insights into the perplexing questions on the experience and expression of emotions for children on the autism spectrum as well as with their interactions with others such as the testing experience affords.

Our Participants and Methods of Discovery

Our data come from children engaged in answering evaluation questions for autism spectrum disorder (ASD) at a clinic for developmental disabilities. Five clinicians participated by asking these questions as part of the evaluation for ASD using the Autism Diagnostic Observation Schedule (ADOS-II) Modules 3 or 4 (as specified for different ages and verbal abilities) (Lord, Rutter, DiLavonre, Pickles & Rutter, 2012). Specifically, we examined the use of *I don't know* (IDK) utterances in seven high-functioning, verbally fluent children (aged 6–17) who subsequently received an ASD diagnosis. Questions about emotional experiences on the ADOS are designed to provide insight into how children who might have ASD express both their own emotional experiences and how they may perceive others' emotional experiences (Lord et al., 2000).

Using conversation analytic methods (Schegloff, 2007; Sidnell, 2010), while also drawing upon interactional linguistics (Couper-Kuhlen & Selting, 2001), we investigate how IDK utterances work within the evaluation context. We examine children's IDK utterances in two ways:

- Turn composition—the effects of the exact wording chosen by all participants
- The sequential placement—where in the back and forth of turns utterances occur

We also look closely at each clinician's orientation to those utterances and we pay close attention to participants' eye gaze, other bodily behaviour, and prosody. We would encourage you to think about the relevance of this for your own analysis.

Important point

! Multimodal aspects of interaction both contribute to and help
reveal how the participants make sense of their interactions.

Empirically, we consider what contributes to the children's use of the IDK construction by examining the following key questions:

1. Are there types of information requested that lead to the use of IDK utterances?
2. Do clinicians' grammatical formulations and specific word choices of the ADOS questions contribute to the children's use of IDK utterances?
3. How does turn design affect children's responses to emotion questions?

A Brief Summary of Observations

Children's responses to examination questions in one-on-one encounters, particularly the use of IDK utterances, are orderly rather than haphazard. As such, the children contribute to the "interactional substrate" (Maynard & Marlaire, 1992) of standardized psychological testing: they, like the clinicians, are displaying skills which contribute to a valid testing experience. These interactional skills represent what Maynard and Turowetz (2017) call "first order", concrete competence. Concrete competence is situated in lived experience, and includes the basic capacity (among others) for orienting to question-answer sequences regardless of whether the content of an answer is correct.

However, using concrete competence does provide for the display of correct, abstract, or what Donaldson (1978) calls "disembedded" knowledge, an ability that has consistently, since Kanner (1943), been described as absent or poorly developed in children on the autism spectrum. While the capacity to use concrete competence is not itself being tested, as part of the interactional substrate, such competence may be taken for granted and, as such, is somewhat invisible. Our observations help make these *abilities* visible, and, for our readers (e.g., parents, caregivers, practitioners) more recognizable in other interactional contexts.

In this chapter, we report on four patterns in children's use of the IDK utterances as they undergo evaluation for ASD. These utterances demonstrate competencies and interactional skills that we believe are ordinarily obscured and, thus, invisible:

- First, children, like others, do use IDK utterances to display epistemic stance, or an uncertainty or a lack of knowledge regarding the information requested by the evaluation question. Consequentially, clinicians display their orientations to the utterances as such.
- Second, in many cases, the IDK utterances resist fulfilling the action of the question: children produce IDK utterances in place of providing the information requested by the evaluation question. Often the children provide information (previous to or post the IDK) that suggest both access and the ability to convey knowledge of emotions that would sufficiently answer the question at hand.

- Third, we examine how clinicians' syntactic (grammatical) variations of each question contribute to valid and non-valid responses (e.g., IDK utterances, "no", lateral headshake, and silence). Our report suggests that children with ASD may have difficulty responding to questions formulated with vague "what about" or "how about" phrases. Yet, when either phrase is coupled with a more concrete reference forms, children with ASD are able to answer validly.
- Fourth, we consider the clinicians' practice of formulating a question using the inclusive *we* that works to encourage the production of valid responses from the children.

Overall, we show how the children's displays of concrete competence during the administration of the ADOS exam broaden our understanding of their abilities to participate in the testing process and, we believe, other participatory activities like testing. Moreover, we suggest that while such abilities often lie outside what is officially being tested, these abilities, when noticed, provide evidence of the children's social and communicative strengths.

I Don't Know as Responses to ADOS Questions About Emotions

The children frequently used epistemic clauses while being tested. These clauses consist of a first person pronoun plus a verb that expresses a mental state, both with and without negation (e.g., *I think, I don't think, I guess, I know, I don't know*). The children's level of commitment to or uncertainty about their ability to acknowledge and describe their emotional experiences generally falls along a cline of increasing doubt (for a general description of knowledge claims in interaction, see Heritage, 2012); see Fig. 10.1.

However, of the epistemic clauses used by the children, *I don't know* occurs nearly twice as often as the next most frequent epistemic clause,

I know > I guess > I think > I don't know

+ knowledge_____−knowledge

Fig. 10.1 Epistemic level

Table 10.1 Epistemic clauses

1. Epistemic clauses selected by children with ASD in ADOS-II, Module 3	
I don't know	84
I think	43
I guess	19
I know	8
I don't think	7
I remember	1
Total	162

I think. In other words, children with ASD use typical epistemic expressions indicating their difficulty in expressing or recollecting their emotional experiences. In doing so, they overwhelmingly opt for negative epistemic expressions as shown in Table 10.1.

Our findings, shown in Table 10.1, led us to question the relationship between the interactional function of such clauses—epistemic and otherwise. As shown in our analysis below, an understanding of the various functions of IDK may allow for better communication with persons—children and adults—diagnosed with ASD.

Displaying Knowledge

While the children frequently use IDK utterances to express their epistemic stance in response to the emotion questions, these utterances are also frequently accompanied by corresponding verbal and/or embodied behaviours. Clinicians tended to accept and, in some cases, show agreement with a child's knowledge claim.

> **Important point**
>
> ! These observations are consonant with what has been noted in
> • conversations of non-impaired persons (Pomerantz, 1984).

In extract (1), the child's IDK utterance plus the added clause, or complement, identifies his difficulty with describing his emotions.

Extract (1) Case 46, Gordon, age 11;2 (Happy II, p. 12, original lines 566–574)

```
PY:  And, uhm ah so can you describe how you feel when you're happy.
CH:  Like (.) some (.) like (.) well I don't really know how to
     describe when like I'm happy, like ((diverts gaze upward toward
     ceiling)) it's like, ah feeling- ((takes right hand with index
     finger pointed toward abdomen and makes circular motion))
     you can't describe- like jealousy, you can't describe that
     feeling.
PY:  M'huh. m'huh. m'huh, yeah. it's hard to describe that,
     really hard. okay and, uhm what things are you afraid of?
```

In line 2, Gordon begins his turn with features that exhibit some difficulty with his formulation of the answer to the evaluation question. He restarts his turn three times, with each restart separated by a pause, that is, represented by a (.) in the transcript. Additionally, Gordon begins his turn with *well*, which is often an indicator that the subsequent response is not going to be straightforward (Schegloff & Lerner, 2009). The IDK utterance contains the adverb *really*, which emphasizes the negative verb *don't really know*. The child completes his claim of insufficient knowledge by identifying his difficulty: "*how to describe when like I'm happy*" (line 3). Simultaneously, Gordon uses his body to possibly show additional signs of difficulty. He looks toward the ceiling, which could serve as a display to his recipient that he is searching for an answer (Rossano, 2013; Wilkinson, 2007). He next begins another unit of talk only to cut it off: "*it's like, ah feeling-*" (line 4). This utterance is soon followed by a second gesture (lines 4–5) that suggests an attempt to provide an embodied version of an answer that he has not been able to verbalize: he makes a circular motion with his index finger pointed toward his abdomen as if his stomach were churning. Gordon ends his turn with a tacit claim that potentially anyone would have difficulty: "*you can't describe- like jealousy, you can't describe that feeling*" (lines 6–7), particularly if "you" is heard as a general reference.

The clinician produces a response that shows an acceptance of the child's characterization of the task and agreement with his characterization that it is difficult to express what happiness feels like. She produces a series of three minimal tokens and then an agreement token, followed by her shared assessment that describing happiness is *"really hard"* (lines 8–9). She then moves to the next emotion question (end of line 9), which displays to the child that his attempt to answer the question is sufficient.

Careful attention to the child's IDK utterance along with co-occurring verbal and nonverbal behaviours—perturbations, halts in his turn, shift in gaze, the use of gestures, and the syntactic composition of his turn—may help clinicians and caregivers identify the difficulty children with ASD have providing a description of their emotions from other uses of IDK, as will be discussed further. Here, Gordon's gestures evidence that, while he cannot describe at the moment how it feels to be happy, he is engaged in a search for the information to the question being asked and that he does have in his memory experiences of happiness. This is a form of concrete competence that the test itself does not measure, but that may be informative about the range of skills children on the spectrum have even if they are unable to provide the abstractly correct answer.

In extract (2), Justin produces a valid response (lines 4–5) to the question of what kinds of things make him sad (lines 1–3). Notice that the clinician's question has a turn-final "or", which device interlocutors may use when working out a stance of uncertainty regarding a proposition in a speaker's utterance (Drake, 2015). Yet when asked what it feels like when he is sad (lines 6–8), he mobilizes, as part of his answer, an IDK utterance (line 10).

Extract (2) Case 44, Justin, age 10;0 (Sadness II, pp. 11–12; original lines 529–540)

```
PY:   We all have times when we feel sad what kinds of things make
      you ((looks at CH)) feel sad. ((looks down at booklet))
      (0.4)
CH:   Like when my little brother breaks something that
      belongs to me.
PY:   Oh, my. Yeah that's kinda sad. So when you feel sad, what's
      that like=can you describe what that's like
      when your brother breaks somethin' or-
CH:                                   [((gazes up toward
      ceiling)) It's like you're mad and sad, I dunno.
PY:   M'huh, m'huh. (.) .tsk okay what bout feeling relaxed ((directs
      gaze at CH)) what kinds of things make you feel relaxed.
```

Justin formulates his response by drawing upon the syntax of the clinician's question ("...*what that's like*", line 7): "*it's like you're mad and sad, I dunno*". The turn-final or tag-positioned IDK utterance works as an epistemic downgrade (Heritage, 2012; Raymond & Heritage, 2006) that attenuates the certainty of his characterization, but it is clearly responsive to the suggested stance initiated by the clinician within her question. Again, we can see that even though the answer is not valid in terms of the task to "describe" what it is like when he feels sad, there is concrete, interactional competence exhibited in the very form or practices by which he assembles his answer.

An interesting feature about our next example is that it includes a question for which a valid answer requires what is called "theory of mind" (Baron-Cohen, 2001). In other words, the question requires that the child infer mental states or perspectives of others. Previously in the interview, Gordon, who receives an ASD diagnosis, has stated in response to a series of questions that he "*sometimes*" feels lonely, that he does many things to help himself feel better when he is lonely, and that he believes other children his age also feel lonely.

Extract (3) Case 46, Gordon, age 11;2 (Loneliness II, p. 24, original lines 1203–1211)

```
PY:   M'hm. M'hm. okay, and what and what about other things that
      people do to help themselves feel better when they're lonely.
      (0.3)
CH:   I donno 'cuz they never tell me.
PY:   M'huh. [okay.
CH:          [or show me.
PY:   Uh'huh, okay. yeah, but, hopefully they have something that helps
      them feel a little bit better. ((turns to cabinet)) Okay, very
      good, we've got one more thing to do, this is real simple.
```

After a brief pause, however, the child is clear that he makes no claim of knowing of how others manage their loneliness. Instead, through his turn composition, the child makes an epistemic claim, "*I donno*," and then includes the reason he lacks this knowledge: "*cuz they never tell me*" (line 4). As the clinician produces two minimal tokens (line 5) that display receipt of the child's claim of insufficient knowledge, the child continues in overlap with an additional reason for his lack of knowledge regarding what others do when they are lonely: "*or show me*" (line 6). By constructing his turn in this way, the child displays that any claim to knowledge of what others do, for him, would require explicit information—seeing or hearing—what others do.

Attention to the child's exact response provides evidence for the child's need to have concrete, and not inferential or abstract, knowledge of others emotional states. The child's response does meet the goal of the ADOS evaluation questions on emotions: the degree to which the subject can display verbal fluency for engaging emotional experiences of others in an abstract, disembedded way. However, we emphasize that Gordon's literalistic answering, although departing from what would be a neurotypical answer and can be described as an absence of abstract thinking, does demonstrate, once again, a form of concrete competence. He is participating in the testing parameters and he is providing interactional support for the answer he is issuing.

The examples we have presented so far show how children use IDK utterances to make claims of their lack of knowledge or about uncertainty regarding the topics at hand. These topics are about what may make themselves or others feel a particular emotion and how to describe a particular emotion. When children struggle, and then fail to answer the questions by formulating valid responses, their use of "*I don't know*" shows various kinds of skilful deployment that is intelligible in various concrete ways. Clinicians acknowledge the children's IDK utterances as displaying lack of knowledge.

Resisting the Question

As neurotypical children use standalone IDK utterances as a strategy of resistance to avoid responding to questions (Hutchby, 2002, 2005), children being tested for ASD also use IDK utterances to resist providing a valid response to evaluation questions. Moreover, these standalone IDK utterances are not accompanied by verbal or nonverbal behaviours that suggest them to be knowledge claims or by cues that additional talk is forthcoming. Any accompanying physical responses seem to suggest the IDK utterance works to end the topic at hand.

As a point of clarification, by resistance, we mean that a child fills the answer slot in a questioning sequence with an IDK utterance with no accompanying talk or effort at explication. This practice, we see, is a form of competence, insofar as the use of IDK attends to the task—the question—that is, the practice does "answering". Thus, rather than an absent response, which could suggest that the child is inattentively "away" in a Goffmanian (1963, pp. 69–70) sense, the child is co-participating.

In extract (4), the child uses an IDK utterance to resist a single evaluation question. Before the extract begins, Malcolm has provided examples and descriptions of his emotional experiences.

> *For example:* Video games make him happy; being afraid makes his body stand still; people saying stupid things makes him mad.

The clinician then poses a follow-up question about his experiences of anger.

Extract (4) Case 28, Malcolm, age 13;1 (Angry II, p. 15, original lines 1933–1941)

```
PY:   And ((gestures with hand toward self)) how do you feel inside
      when you're real angry.
      (0.2)
CH:   I dunno. ((directs gaze to left)) ((CH rubs cheek with right
      hand))
      [            (0.4)                    ]
PY:   [((observes CH; writes in booklet))]
PY:   That's okay. (.) And, most people have times when they feel
      sa:d, what kinds of things make you feel that way.
```

After a slight pause (two-tenths of a second), Malcolm responds with the standalone IDK utterance "*I dunno*" (line 4). As he does so, he directs his gaze away from the clinician and begins rubbing his cheek. The clinician takes 0.4 seconds (lines 6–7) to observe the child's behaviour, while she adds notes to the evaluation form. Then she responds with the palliative

"*That's okay*" (line 8), which works to accept his standalone IDK utterance. In this way, Malcolm's IDK resists providing a valid response to this question and serves in the closing of this sequence, which is completed by the clinician's move to the next question-answer sequence on sadness.

In the next example (5), we can see how a child may use resistive IDKs in an iterative fashion. That is, after successive questions regarding "*feeling mad or angry*" (lines 1–2; 5), Dan answers either with an IDK produced with hesitation (line 3) or in standalone fashion (6). At line 7, the clinician reformulates the child's response as "not sure", and suggests that feeling "*mad*" is a "*sometimes*" feeling for "*most people*".

Extract (5) Case 24, Dan, age 9;3 (Anger I & II and Sadness I & II, p. 17, original lines 785–807)

```
PY:   What about feeling mad or angry? ((CH looks down)) What kinds
      of things make you feel that way.
CH:   Ah:: I dunno.
      ((CH looks over at MO))
PY:   How does your body feel when you're mad or angry.
CH:   >I dunno<.=
PY:   =not sure. Most people feel mad sometimes.
CH:   I'm making this go backwards ((talking about the fire truck))
      [on two wheels.    ]
PY:   [It's going backwards?]
      ((CH sideways glance at PY))
PY:   And Dan, most people have times when they feel sad, what kinds
      of things make you feel sad.
      ((CH playing with truck))
CH:   Uh:m, (.) ((turns truck in a circle)) ah: I dunno.
PY:   Not sure?
      (0.3)
PY:   How do you feel when you're sad. (.) Can you describe it. How
      does your body feel.
CH:   Ah:: (.) uh I don=know.
PY:   That's okay. you're doing a great job answering all my
      questions. We're gonna switch to something a little bit
      different.
```

After a brief exchange regarding the toy fire truck on the table (lines 8–10), the clinician, addressing Dan, also invokes "*sad*" as something "*most people ... feel*" (lines 12–13). Dan continues to play with the fire truck before responding with yet another IDK utterance, this time prefaced by two perturbations. Those perturbations, the micropause, and the child's continual engagement with the toy work with the standalone IDK utterance to again resist providing the information requested by an evaluation question.

The clinician now produces a clarification question that again formulates Dan's resistance as a kind of uncertainty (line 16). This utterance, with its rising intonation, renews the relevance for a valid response. When no response is forthcoming, the clinician issues a multiunit turn of three questions, "*How do you feel when you're sad? (.) Can you describe it? How does your body feel?*" The child responds with another IDK utterance (line 20). Here again perturbations and a micropause, which may be dealing with the series of questions Dan has been asked, precede the IDK utterance. Given the persistence with which the clinician pursues questions about "*mad*" and "*sad*", Dan's iterative resistance could be said to show some kind of equal persistence. Dan's answer does not display either his understanding of emotions or the ability to describe them. Consequently, with regard to the testing protocol, he would not receive "credit" for an abstract display of emotions. Yet, his responses do display a competence that concretely and uncomplainably shows him to be co-oriented to the testing environment and its interactional substrate.

These examples show how children undergoing testing for and who ultimately receive an ASD diagnosis respond to the emotion questions in competent interactional ways, although the substance of their answers may be invalid in an abstract sense. The children do so using IDK utterances that may be accompanied with additional information, verbal and nonverbal responses, that work to convey their difficulties in particular ways. The next section of the chapter illustrates this point.

Formulating the Question

We now take a closer look at the evaluation question preceding the IDK utterance to see whether something in the syntax of the questions could account for the frequent use of IDK utterances used to resist them. We examine the syntactic variations of each of the clinician's questions in relation to valid and non-valid responses.

> *For example:* We explore IDK utterances, 'no', or other negative responses such as 'm'hm', lateral headshakes, and silence.

In particular, we examine how the children's responses may, indeed, display an interactional competence to the structural ambiguity inherent to the "*what about/how about*" questions.

"What/How About" Question Formulation

The question construction linked to non-valid responses is the "what/how about" formulation. In the ADOS manual these constructions form the first part of the two-part question series that are used across three emotions: fear, anger, and relaxation. The model questions are as follows:

a. What about things that you're afraid of? What makes you feel frightened or anxious?
b. What about feeling angry? What kinds of things make you feel that way?
c. How about feeling relaxed or content? What kinds of things make you feel that way?

The clinicians generally present both questions of the series within a single turn. When they do so, the questions do not pose much difficulty to the children and 80% of the two-part questions are responded to with a valid answer (see Appendix). In extract (6) we illustrate this phenomenon with the question series on fear.

Extract (6) Case 24, Dan, age 9;3 (Fear I, p. 16, original lines 763–765)

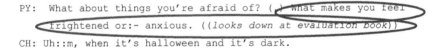

```
PY:  What about things you're afraid of? (  ) what makes you feel
     frightened or:- anxious. ((looks down at evaluation book))
CH:  Uh::m, when it's halloween and it's dark.
```

The clinician issues the two-part question series (lines 1–2), and the child produces a valid response (line 3). Dan begins his turn with the perturbation "*Uh::m*" that is produced with a sound stretch and continuing intonation projecting more talk. He then produces the information requested by the second part of the question, naming "*what*" makes him frightened or anxious.

It turns out that the two-part question series that begins with either a *What about* or a *How about* construction rarely poses problems for the children. There are, however, four instances within the data that the clinicians only present the first part of the series, the "what/how about" question, and not the second part. In all of the instances in our data set, a non-valid response results: an IDK, silence, or an inapposite answer:

For example: A lateral head shake, a verbalized "no".

Extract (7) begins with the child describing how it is he knows when he is happy, followed by the clinician's acceptance of this response and her move to a question on the child's experiences with fear. She issues only the first part of the two-part question series.

Extract (7) Case 44, Justin, age 10;3 (Fear I, p. 11, original lines 497–502)

```
CH:   'Cuz when I unlock something I start to laugh.
PY:   M'huh ((vertical head nod)) m'huh, okay.
      And what about things you're afraid of.
CH:   I don't know.
PY:   M'huh. okay. tsk. When you feel frightened and you're anxious
      how does it feel.
```

In response to the single question that employs the "*what about*" formulation, Justin produces a standalone IDK utterance (line 4). The "*what about*" question in extract (7), as compared with the one in extract (6), is vague. Whereas in (6), there is an accompanying "*What makes you feel frightened or anxious*" that then further defines the "*what*" to be things or experiences related to fright and anxiety—in (7), the "*what about*" phrase stands on its own and has no exemplars to delimit or clarify the phrase. The clinician immediately moves to another question about fear in which the structure of the question assumes the child's experience with fear and being anxious, and the level of specificity of the question is clear: "*how does it feel*" (line 6).

In extract (8), the clinician provides a transition from the previous question-answer sequence on happiness, which the child has answered at length. She asks the child the single "*what about*" question on fear.

Extract (8) Case 28, Wade, age 13;7 (Fear I, p. 13, original lines 592–601)

```
PY:   Okay let's try a different one.
CH:   ((yawns))
PY:   What about things you're afraid of?
      [                    (12.7)                        ]
CH:   [((makes faces in one-way mirror across from him))]
CH:   I dunno.
      [                    (7.9)                         ]
      [((PY writes in booklet; child makes faces in mirror))]
PY:   ↑Anyth↑ing? (0.3) you can think of? (.) n↑o. (.) n'kay.
      (0.4)
```

Although Wade did engage at length with the earlier questions on the emotion "*happy*", he provides no initial verbal response to this new question, but instead stares ahead and begins making faces into the one-way mirror immediately in front of him. After nearly 13 seconds of silence during which the clinician observes his actions, he produces a standalone IDK utterance: "*I dunno*" (line 6). The vagueness of the question is palpable, and Wade's response may be indicative of literally not knowing what question he is to respond to:

- Is it the question, does he experience fear? Or
- Is he to provide examples of what makes him afraid?

In other words, with "*I dunno*", Wade may be responding competently to the ambiguity of the single "*what about*" question.

For nearly eight seconds (lines 7–8), the clinician continues to take notes, and Wade continues to make faces in the mirror. The clinician then presses the child, initiating a multiunit turn in which she produces the utterance, "↑*Anyth*↑*ing?*" with questioning intonation that renews the relevancy of a next response from the child. After a 0.3 second pause in which he provides no response, she adds the increment: "*you can think of?*" The clinician does not wait long for a response; the notation here indicates a micropause—that less than two-tenths of a second passes before she continues her turn with a candidate understanding "*(.) n*↑*o*" (line 9). After another micropause (.), the clinician closes this question-answer sequence regarding "*things you're afraid of*". She never issues the second part of the model question, instead moving to the next emotion.

Further evidence for the difficulty created when the "*what/how about*" question is posed alone is shown in a subsequent non-valid response from Wade.

Extract (9) Case 40, Wade, age 13;7 (Emotions III, p. 12, original lines 602–605)

```
PY   What about feeling angry?
CH:  ((vertical head shake))  Yeah.

     [              (4.6)              ]
CH:  [((stares into mirror/making faces with hands))]
```

Wade responds with a vertical head shake and a quietly produced "*Yeah*". His nonverbal and verbal responses are fitted to a yes/no question; they serve to affirm that he recognizes the vocabulary of "*feeling angry*" and may serve as a kind of "*go-ahead*" for a fuller question. Through the child's response we can see where the trouble originates. When the "*what/how about*" question is produced alone—that is, there is no follow-on question referring to "*what things*"—there is a lingering vagueness that a child may handle by way of an IDK answer or by way of treating the question as a yes-no interrogative.

In extract (10), a third example of a "*what/how about*" question formulation, the child produces no response. When the second question in the series is issued by the clinician in her next turn, however, the child issues a valid response.

Extract (10) Case 40, Wade, age 13;7 (Relaxed, p. 13, original lines 622–626)

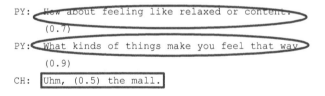

```
PY:  How about feeling like relaxed or content.
     (0.7)
PY:  What kinds of things make you feel that way
     (0.9)
CH:  Uhm, (0.5) the mall.
```

Wade's answering is helped by the second part of the question series. Like the children who produce valid responses when issued both questions in the series within the clinician's single turn, he has more information as to what specifically is being requested, and he, too, provides a valid response.

The possible link demonstrated here between "*what/how about*" question constructions and the emergence of non-valid responses warrants further investigation. Several lines of evidence here suggest that these question formulations are problematic:

- First, in each of the four cases in which a *what about* or *how about* construction is presented alone, the child produces a non-valid response.
- In contrast, in eight of the ten instances in which the "*what/how about*" question is joined to a second question that more clearly specifies the information sought, the response from the child is valid.
- Finally, in those cases in which the child was presented only with the "*what/how about*" construct and produced a non-valid response, subsequent presses by the clinician with what should have been the second part of the series produces a valid response two of the three times such a press is used.

More important to our focus in this chapter, this evidence suggests that the children are providing competent, although not necessarily correct, responses to the subtle nuances of the test questions.

Inclusive *We*

The ADOS-II manual provides a prefatory statement to the first emotion question on sadness: "*Most people* have times when *they* are sad. What kinds of things make you feel that way?" (emphasis added). The formulation of this question, which is sometimes used for other emotion questions, presents the experience of sadness as an abstract, possibly "other-experience" that does not, necessarily, include the child. These two factors—abstract and other-experienced—may predispose children with ASD to hear and subsequently respond to this question as something particularly challenging.

In our data, this "*most people*" construction is employed in four of the six evaluations. Three of the four questions are responded to with an IDK utterance. There are two evaluations, however, in which the clinician substitutes "*we all*" for "*most people*" and "*we*" for "*they*"; both receive a valid response. The contrast provides evidence that the children are assembling their responses through careful attention to the design of the questions posed to them. To explore this contrast, we first present the effectiveness of inclusive *we* in extracts (11) and (12). In extract (11), the clinician uses the "*we all*" and "*we*" construction.

Extract (11) Case 44, Justin, age 10;0 (Sadness I, p. 11, original lines 529–531)

```
PY:   We all have times when we feel sad what kinds of things make
      you ((looks at CH)) feel sad.
CH:   Like when my little brother breaks something that belongs to
      me.
```

Justin's response is immediate and valid; additionally, his response is a personal account of sadness (lines 3–4). In the next extract (12), a different child responds to a nearly identical "we" formulation and assembles his response to include himself as well as others.

Extract (12) Case 46, Gordon, age 11;2 (Sadness I, p. 14, original lines 602–605)

```
PY:  Okay, well, we all have times when we feel sad. What kinds of
     things make you feel sad.
CH:  Maybe it's sad when you listen uh music.
PY:  M'huh.
```

Gordon responds by providing an activity that could invoke sadness. He hedges his response with the adverb "*maybe*" and then formulates the experience using the generic "*you*" (line 4). His usage suggests that Gordon is carefully focused on the collective aspect of the question as it is posed to him. Like "*we*", "*you*" opens up the experience as one that is available to the clinician, others, and himself.

In extract (13), the clinician uses the "*most people*" form within the prefatory statement and/or question (lines 1–2). While the child produces an IDK utterance in response (line 3), his answer demonstrates that he was attentive both to the prefatory statement and the question.

Extract (13) Case 28, Malcolm, age 13;1 (Sadness I & II, p. 16, original lines 736–743)

```
PY:  And, most people have times when they feel sa:d, what
     kinds of  things make you feel that way.
CH:  I dunno.
     (.)
CH:  I just feel sad.
     (.)
CH:  I usually just feel sad at night.
PY:  Okay.
```

While his line 3 utterance is formulated with finality (a downward pitch in the prosody), after a micropause (line 4), Malcolm expands his answer by continuing his turn with two utterances (lines 5, 7). His "*I just feel sad*" is a claim that he, like "*most people*", experiences sadness. His next unit of talk provides a temporalizing of when he feels sad: "*I usually just feel sad at night*" (line 7), which ties back to "*times*" of feeling sad in the question. This careful assembly of his response suggests Malcolm's attention to the concrete details of the question put before him.

While the *we* construction (e.g., "*We all* have times when *we* feel x") is similar to the preface provided by the ADOS-II manual for the emotion sadness ("*Most people* have times when *they* feel sad"), the first person plural form provides concrete personalization in its inclusion of both the child and the clinician (and everyone, by extension) as having experienced the emotion in question.

Important point

!•   In this way, the *we* construction is a way the clinician, and by extension others, may build into the turn formulation an expectation that the child does have the requisite knowledge to answer the question (Pomerantz, 1988).

With limited observations, we speculate that the *most people* construction presents the emotional experience as one that only a subset of people experience, something "*they*" feel, which could allow the child to identify as someone who is not a part of "*most people*" or "*they*". Moreover, the inclusive *we* may be one way to build social solidarity between the child and clinician, fostering a rapport within which the child is better able to see him/herself a part and, thus, share his or her emotional experiences. The combination of increased expectation for an answer, the inclusiveness of the statement, and the potential for social solidarity may all work to elicit a valid response more effectively than the alternative construct presented in the ADOS manual.

Summary

We present these observations on the children's responses to evaluation questions and the use of *I don't know* utterances in order that their interactional competencies—concrete, syntactic, and social—are made visible and, thus, more easily recognizable. We report that these children use *I don't know* utterances to display epistemic stance and resist providing the requested information of evaluation questions. We also show that syntactic variation in the clinicians' formulations of the ADOS-II evaluation questions contribute very little to the frequency of *I don't know* utterances, with the exception of the "what/how about" construction. We tentatively note that the use of inclusive *we* in the formulation of questions may achieve valid responses. The IDK utterances paired with accompanying verbal and nonverbal displays show that children with ASD are co-oriented and contributing to an interactional substrate that makes testing possible. Their consistent use of IDK, as well as other responses showing that they pay careful attention to question design, illustrates a form autistic intelligence. That is, these children deploy practices exhibiting concrete competence independently of what is required in terms of the disembedded or abstract analysis as required for correct answering.

Our findings begin to answer the call put forth in earlier accounts (Grandin, 1995) and observations (Losh & Capps, 2006) for better understanding of the difficulties persons with autism encounter in the social milieu. We contend that examining emotion talk in the testing frame (as well as within social interactions) broadens our understanding of concrete competence, a part of autistic intelligence, which is overlooked when emphasis is placed on whether or not a child answers correctly and validly. When a child cannot recall or respond, this can index problematic syntax or types or knowledge that children with ASD find particularly challenging; yet, the child often uses mundane expressions such as IDK in interactionally competent ways. As seen in our data, both non-valid and valid responses require skilful participation in the interactional substrate of testing and concrete interactional competence.

In this chapter, we have demonstrated a conversation analysis and given you empirical examples of the analytic claims we have made. These were grounded in the data and you can see how they have been made on that basis. From this, you should be able to translate those key messages for your own work and we summarise the practical messages you can take away from the chapter in Box 10.1.

Box 10.1 Practical summary

Summary of practical highlights

1. Children with ASD use IDK utterances to display epistemic stance.
2. Children with ASD use IDK to resist fulfilling the action of the question.
3. Children with ASD may have difficulty responding to questions formulated with a vague "what about" or "how about" construct.
4. When formulating a question for a child with ASD, using the inclusive *we* may encourage the production of valid responses from children with ASD.
5. Children with ASD respond to test questions in ways that display a reliance on first-order, "concrete" competence, whether or not they obtain correct, second-order, "abstractly" competent answers.
6. Children with ASD do exhibit a joint participatory stance—that is, skilled participation in the interactional substrate of testing—and do so through ordinary linguistic and interactional practices.

Appendix: "What About/How About" Question Formulation and Responses

When a two-part question is administered ($n = 10$), 8 responses are valid (80%).

When a one-part "What about/How about" question ($n = 4$) is administered, all 4 responses are non-valid.

Fear

```
ADOS (2-part question): What about things that you're   afraid
of? What makes you feel frightened or anxious?        RESPONSE
1)  What about things you're afraid of? What makes you feel
    frightened or anxious?                              (valid)
2)  What about things you're afraid of?                  (IDK)
3)  And what about things you're afraid of?              (IDK)
4)  And what about things that you're afraid of? Kinds of
    things that make you feel afraid.                    valid)
5)  How about things that you're afraid of? Is there anything
    that you're afraid of?                              (valid)
6)  What things are you afraid of?                      (valid)
```

Anger

```
ADOS (2-part question): What about feeling angry? What kinds
of things make you feel that way?                    RESPONSE
```
7) What about feeling mad or angry? What kinds of things make
    you feel that way?   (IDK)
8) What about feeling angry? What kinds of things make you
    angry?   (valid)
9) Now, what about feeling angry? What kind of things make
    you angry?   (valid)
10) **What about feeling angry?**   **(No Response)**
11) What about angry? Do you know what things make you
    angry?   (valid)
12) We all get angry from time to time. What kinds of things
    make you angry?   (valid)

Relaxed

```
ADOS (2-part question) How about feeling relaxed or content?
What kinds of things make you feel that way?         RESPONSE
```
13) **How about feeling like relaxed or content?   (No Response)**
14) What about feeling relaxed or content? What kinds of things
    make you feel that way?   (valid)
15) What about feeling relaxed or content? What kinds of
    things make you feel that way?   (valid)
16) What 'bout feeling relaxed? What kinds of things make you
    feel relaxed?   (IDK)

References

Baron-Cohen, S. (2001). Theory of mind and autism: A review. *International Review of Research in Mental Retardation, 23*, 169–184.

Couper-Kuhlen, E., & Selting, M. (2001). Introducing interactional linguistics. In M. Selting & E. Couper-Kuhlen (Eds.), *Studies in interactional linguistics* (pp. 1–22). Amsterdam; Philadelphia: John Benjamins.

Donaldson, M. (1978). *Children's minds*. New York: W.W. Norton.

Drake, V. (2015). Indexing uncertainty: The case of turn-final or. *Research on Language and Social Interaction, 48*(3), 301–318.

Goffman, E. (1963). *Behavior in public places: Notes on the social organization of gatherings*. New York: Free Press.

Grandin, T. (1995). How people with autism think. In E. Schopler & G. B. Mesibov (Eds.), *Learning and cognition in autism* (pp. 137–156). New York: Springer US.

Heritage, J. (2012). The epistemic engine: Sequence organization and territories of knowledge. *Research on Language and Social Interaction, 45*(1), 30–52.

Hutchby, I. (2002). Resisting the incitement to talk in child counselling: Aspects of the utterance "I don't know". *Discourse Studies, 4*(2), 147–168.

Hutchby, I. (2005). "Active listening": Formulations and the elicitation of feelings-talk in child counselling. *Research on Language and Social Interaction, 38*(3), 303–329.

Kanner, L. (1943). Autistic disturbances of affective contact. *Nervous Child, 2*, 217–250.

Lord, C., Rutter, M., DiLavore P. C., Pickles, A., & Rutter, M. (2012). *Autism diagnostic observation schedule* (2nd ed.) (ADOS-2 Manual (Part I): Modules 1–4), Torrance, CA: Western Psychological Services.

Lord, C., Risi, S., Lambrecht, L., Cook, E. H., Jr., Leventhal, B. L., DiLavore, P. C., et al. (2000). The Autism Diagnostic Observation Schedule-Generic: A standard measure of social and communication deficits associated with the spectrum of autism. *Journal of Autism and Developmental Disorders, 30*, 205–223.

Losh, M., & Capps, L. (2006). Understanding of emotional experience in autism: Insights from the personal accounts of high-functioning children with autism. *Developmental Psychology, 42*(5), 809–818.

Maynard, D. W., & Marlaire, C. L. (1992). Good reasons for bad testing performance: The interactional substrate of educational exams. *Qualitative Sociology, 15*, 177–202.

Maynard, D. W., & Turowetz, J. J. (2017). Doing Testing: How concrete competence can facilitate or inhibit performances of children with Autism Spectrum Disorder. *Qualitative Sociology, 40*(4). Advance online publication. https://doi.org/10.1007/s11133-017-9368-5

Pomerantz, A. M. (1984). Agreeing and disagreeing with assessments: Some features of preferred/dispreferred turn shapes. In J. M. Atkinson & J. Heritage (Eds.), *Structures of social action: Studies in conversation analysis* (pp. 57–101). Cambridge: Cambridge University Press.

Pomerantz, A. (1988). Offering a candidate answer: An information seeking strategy. *Communications Monographs, 55*(4), 360–373.

Raymond, G., & Heritage, J. (2006). The epistemics of social relationships: Owning grandchildren. *Language in Society, 35*(5), 677–705.

Rossano, F. (2013). Gaze in conversation. In J. Sidnell & T. Stivers (Eds.), *The handbook of conversation analysis* (pp. 308–329). Malden, MA: Blackwell-Wiley.

Schegloff, E. A. (2007). *Sequence organization in interaction. A primer in conversation analysis* (Vol. 1). Cambridge: Cambridge University Press.

Schegloff, E. A., & Lerner, G. H. (2009). Beginning to respond: Well-prefaced responses to wh-questions. *Research on Language and Social Interaction, 42*(2), 91–115.

Sidnell, J. (2010). *Conversation analysis: An introduction.* Chichester; Malden: Wiley-Blackwell.

Wilkinson, R. (2007). Managing linguistic incompetence as a delicate issue in aphasic talk-in-interaction: On the use of laughter in prolonged repair sequences. *Journal of Pragmatics, 39*(3), 542–569.

Recommended Reading

Maynard, D. W., & Marlaire, C. L. (1992). Good reasons for bad testing performance: The interactional substrate of educational exams. *Qualitative Sociology, 15*, 177–202.

Ochs, E., & Solomon, O. (2004). Practical logic and autism. In C. Casey & R. B. Edgerton (Eds.), *A companion to psychological anthropology* (pp. 140–167). Oxford: Blackwell.

Solomon, O. (2015). "But- he'll fall!": Children with autism, interspecies intersubjectivity, and the problem of 'being social'. *Culture, Medicine, and Psychiatry, 39*, 323–344.

Turowetz, J. (2015). The interactional production of a clinical fact in a case of autism. *Qualitative Sociology, 38*, 58–78.

Trini Stickle is Assistant Professor of English at Western Kentucky University, Bowling Green and Glasgow. Her main research interest is the linguistic and interactional competency of persons of special populations, in particular, children diagnosed with autism and older persons diagnosed with dementia. She has also published on the communication strategies of persons in meeting settings, as well as the age demographics of regional American dialects.

Waverly Duck is Associate Professor of Sociology at the University of Pittsburgh. Waverly has done research on orderly properties of communication in settings troubled by autism, poverty, welfare reform, and gender. His approach is ethnographic and ethnomethodological—analysing the social detail through which social orders of inequality are produced and maintained. He is also the author of the book *No Way Out* (2015; finalist for the 2016 C. Wright Mills Book Award).

Douglas W. Maynard is the Conway-Bascom Professor, and Harold & Arlene Garfinkel Faculty Fellow, in the Department of Sociology at the University of Wisconsin – Madison. His research on the testing and diagnosis of ASD is supported by a grant from the National Science Foundation. In collaboration with a palliative care physician at UW Health, he is conducting research concerned with quality-of-life conversations in oncology care.

11

Discursive Methods and the Cross-linguistic Study of ASD: A Conversation Analysis Case Study of Repetitive Language in a Malay-Speaking Child

Nor Azrita Mohamed Zain, Tom Muskett,
and Hilary Gardner

Learning Objectives

By the end of this chapter, you will be able to:

- Discuss the value of applied conversation analysis (CA) in cross-cultural research.
- Interpret analyses of interactions involving a Malay-speaking child with a diagnosis of autism spectrum disorder (ASD).
- Discuss findings in relation to existing, primarily English-language CA work on ASD.

N.A. Mohamed Zain (✉)
International Islamic University Malaysia (Kuantan Campus), Kuala Lumpur, Malaysia

T. Muskett
Leeds Beckett University, Leeds, UK

H. Gardner
University of Sheffield, Sheffield, UK

© The Author(s) 2017
M. O'Reilly et al. (eds.), *A Practical Guide to Social Interaction Research in Autism Spectrum Disorders*, The Language of Mental Health,
https://doi.org/10.1057/978-1-137-59236-1_11

275

Introduction

The diagnostic category of autism spectrum disorder (ASD) emerged from the practices of Western European and North American psychiatry. As has been discussed across social and critical psychiatry, the under-standings of human behaviour and subjectivity that underpin these prac-tices are culturally specific. Unsurprisingly therefore, there is variation across historical, cultural, and geo-political contexts in the description of children who would, in the contemporary West, fit the diagnosis. For instance, Ellenberger (1968) noted that children termed *Nitkubon* ("mar-vellous children") in Senegal demonstrated many features that may have led them to be diagnosed with ASD elsewhere in the world, whilst Westermeyer (1979) reported that the comparable category of *Samqng Uan* is used in rural Laos to describe children with social difficulties and a lack of adaptability.

In recent decades, Western practices of psychiatry have spread perva-sively across much of East Asia and into urban areas of West Asia, as is reflected by the translation of the *Diagnostic and Statistical Manual for Mental Disorders* (DSM) into 20 languages (Kawa & Giordano, 2012). This expansion has prompted attempts to undertake international and/or transcultural research into ASD. However, it has been argued that such research, when undertaken within positivist traditions, may implicitly adopt an ethnocentric perspective which assumes the universality of the DSM and the practices through which it is applied (see Bhugra & Bhui, 2001). The international adoption of diagnostic terms such as ASD (Cohen & Volkmar, 1997) may obfuscate significant cross-cultural varia-tions in the individual and social meanings associated with these diagno-ses. This includes accepted lay understandings of causation of the condition. Consider the contemporary Western neurological and bio-logical discourses of ASD against, for instance, an account grounded in reincarnation proffered by a Sri Lankan family (Leonard, 1985) or meta-physical explanations within the Jewish Ultra-Orthodox community (Bilu & Goodman, 1997).

Such variations result in the likelihood of the diagnosis being used with considerable variability across the world, even by clinicians working within Western models of psychiatry. Diverse interpretations of specific diagnostic criteria (such as what constitutes a "delay", "social play," or "inappropriate interaction") across cultural contexts are almost inevitable (Daley, 2002). We argue therefore that conversation analysis (CA) is a useful way of examining this area, as the focus on social interaction and the close attention to language enable an interrogation of the communication between those with ASD and others.

Important point

! • Conversation analysis offers a potentially valuable contribution to transcultural research on ASD. This is because the methodology enables a novel solution to issues of cross-cultural validity.

First, CA's findings are grounded in features of interactions that are demonstrated to be important or relevant by the participants themselves. Hence, into the methodology are built safeguards against researchers imposing their own culturally specific understandings onto data (an *emic* research approach; cf. Harris, 1976). This feature of CA's architecture has resulted in cross-cultural applications of the approach within ethnography and anthropology (e.g. Ochs, 1982), and to language systems other than English (e.g. Tanaka, 1999). In the context of ASD, CA enables emic identification and/or examination of apparent language and interaction difficulties across different language systems, empirically grounded in the responses of speakers in the interaction.

Second, CA offers a novel perspective through which to explore lay cultural understandings of conditions such as ASD. This position builds on the ethnomethodological precept that participants' real-time responses in interactions involving individuals diagnosed with ASD demonstrate practical forms of everyday social and/or cultural knowledge of the category. Hence, participant lay understanding of ASD is recast as an accomplished set of shared cultural practices rather than representing solely individually held beliefs and attitudes.

Before you go any further with the chapter you might find it useful to pause and reflect on the issue of culture and ASD as we have introduced so far. We suggest you try the activity in Box 11.1.

In this chapter, we aim to illustrate the opportunities for transcultural ASD research offered by CA. To do so, we present a single case study of a six-year-old Malay-speaking child with a diagnosis of ASD. During initial stages of analysis of data involving this child, initially generated as part of a large CA research project, a specific phenomenon was identified—that being the child's ostensibly repetitive and unusual use of a particular turn form (*apa tu*—"*what is that*"). *Apa tu* contains the pre-interrogative word *apa* ("*what*") (cf., Steensig & Drew, 2008), and therefore in typical use in Malay could be predicted to be received by a listener as a question, particularly when uttered with a rising pitch (Karim, Onn, Musa, & Hamid, 2000).

However, an initial scoping of the frequent instances of *apa tu* in these data indicated that such turns were often deployed in unconventional manners and, crucially, were not always treated as questions by the co-speaker. Along these lines, this case study examines the different manifestations of *apa tu*, demonstrating that the emic approach offered by CA enables empirically grounded interpretation of behavioural features associated with ASD across linguistic contexts, in a manner that is accessible to readers without specific understanding of Malay culture.

Box 11.1 Activity on culture and ASD

Activity

Try to make a list of at least ten diagnostic features of language, communication, and social interaction associated with ASD that you might predict to vary cross-culturally.
• What aspects of this activity feel difficult?
• What was it that made this feel difficult?

Method

Context of Data

The analysed data were collected within a multi-participant project examining gaze, reference, and joint engagement in parent-child interaction involving Malay-speaking children with and without diagnoses of ASD. Participants were children aged 3 years to 6 years 11 months and their mothers. Participants with ASD were recruited from *Autisme Malaysia* society and had all been diagnosed by multi-disciplinary teams of Malaysian healthcare professionals. The project had received full ethical review and clearance from the host university prior to recruitment. Names used in this chapter are pseudonyms.

Case Study: Participants and Data

This case study's data consists of two 30-minute undirected recordings involving Irfan (I), a six-year-old boy with a diagnosis of ASD, and his mother. "I" was diagnosed with mild ASD when he was four years old. When recordings were made, "I" was observed to speak in short utterances, typically of four to five words in length. Recordings were made two days apart at the participants' home. During the first recording, a set of investigator-selected toys were used, whereas in the second, some of "I's" were included. Participants also made use of a set of flash cards depicting illustrations of objects and simple situations.

As noted above, analysis of "I's" talk was inspired by the frequency of the *apa tu* ("*what is that*") phrase in the recordings. There were 32 complete instances of *apa tu* across the 60-minute data set, with 14 in session one and 18 in session two. All instances of *apa tu* were transcribed for comparative analysis using CA.

Transcription

The transcriptions presented below use an adapted version of the Jefferson format. Relevant non-verbal features of the interaction have been included. All talk is presented in its original form, which was primarily in Malay with some English code-switching. Beneath each turn of talk is up to two levels of translation provided to facilitate understanding of the extracts for non-Malay-speaking readers: a literal word-for-word English translation, and where necessary an edited natural English interpretation.

Analytic Findings and Discussion

As described above, this case study focuses on sequences containing *apa tu* ("*what is that?*") turns. Close scrutiny of these using CA demonstrated that there were distinct types of such sequence, differing both in relation to the placement of *apa tu* and its sequential implicature. In the following analysis, we will focus on three of these sequence types with the aim of illustrating the diverse functions performed by "I's" *apa tu* turns. These are:

- *apa tu* as a question form
- *apa tu* as a mechanism through which "I" influenced the present focus of the interaction
- *apa tu* as apparently self-directed talk by "I".

As will be demonstrated, a key theme across these distinct types of sequence was that the different actions apparently realised by the frequent *apa tu* turns did not necessarily correspond to the literal meaning of this utterance ("*what's that?*"). As a cross-cultural research team, use of CA enabled us to adopt an emic perspective to understand these variations within their micro-social context. It also enabled consideration of cross-cultural similarities with and variations against previous interactional research on ASD, which has historically typically only involved English-speaking children.

Sequence Type 1: *Apa tu* as a Question Form

In its literal translation, *apa tu* is a specific question form ("*what's that*"). Consistent with questions across other languages (Steensig & Drew, 2008), Malay speakers then modify this basic function by appending additional constructions. There were several instances in the recordings where "I's" mother (M) responded to such *apa tu* turns as if questions. However, *apa tu* was sometimes used in a sequentially unconventional way during such sequences. To illustrate these variations of *apa tu*, we now present analysis of example extracts in which one or both participants orient to such turns as questions.

Extract 1 below demonstrates a typical and fitted use of an *apa tu* question by "I". The participants have been engaging in a spontaneous picture naming activity, where M shows flash cards to "I" and asks questions about them. In this case, the flash card depicts a boy who has fallen down the stairs. M has just been asking "I" about the picture, describing aspects of it herself before producing an evaluation (see line 1). "I" then produces an *apa tu* turn, literally translating to "*because what's that?*". This form in Malay is conventionally used by speakers to mean "*why?*".

Extract 1 [Because he ran]

```
1     M:     kesian di↓a: jatuh ↑kan
             poor hi↓m: fall ↑right
2    →I:     sebab apa tu
             Because what's that?
3    (0.6)   ((M looks at the picture card))
4     M:     sebab dia lari:
             Because he runs
5     I:     t[engok- (.)[tengok dia la     ]ri.
             Look-        look he runs
```

In line 4, M clearly demonstrates understanding of "I's" question as if projecting the conventional meaning of "*why did he fall?*". There is a brief pause before M's answer, which may reflect that she has already talked extensively about reasons for the child falling prior to the extract. "I's" subsequent response in line 5, which enthusiastically picks up the idea of the boy running, indicates that M's interpretation and therefore answer of his question was acceptable and appropriate.

A similar function of *sebab apa tu* can be seen in extract 2. During the same spontaneous picture naming activity, M is showing "I" a picture of a man lying under a car in a garage. As in extract 1, "I" uses *sebab apa tu* ("*because what is that?*") in line 8, which again is responded to as if a conventional 'why?' question. However, the prior sequence differs in this extract, as this *sebab apa tu* follows an earlier conventional *why* question, formulated without *apa tu*, in line 4:

Extract 2 [Mechanic]

```
1     M:     i↑ni
             this
2     I:     LA:
             La:
3     M:     kenapa?
             Why
4     I:     dia >kenapa< dia kena langgar?=
             He >why< he got ran down?
5     M:     hehhhheh
6     I:     kere↑ta
             car
7     M:     bukan langgar: dia mekanik dia baiki kereta kereta
             rosak: ((M points to the picture as Irfan looks on))
             Not ran down: he is a mechanic he repairs car car
             has broken down
8   →I:      sebab apa ↓tu ((still gazing at the picture))
             Because what (is) ↓that
9     M:     sebab kereta rosak >ni nam<pak kereta rosak ((M
             points at the picture))
             Because the car has broken down>this se<e car has
             broken down
10    I:     cam↑ni ((points to the picture))
             Like ↑this
11    M:     hm:
```

In the above extract, it is evident that "I" uses *two* appropriate yet differing forms of "*why?*" (lines 4 and 8), one of which contains an *apa tu*. There are potential sequential reasons for use of these different turn forms. First, "I's" "*kenapa*" turn in line 4 follows a use of *kenapa* by M, and therefore this construction may serve to tie the answer to her prior question. Second, "I's" question in line 4 indicates a perception of the picture as showing a person who has been hit by a car. However, the picture is actually intended to be of a mechanic, and "I"'s misperception is demonstrated through M's laughter (line 5) and clarification attempt (line 7). It is here that "I" produces *sebab apa tu*, which is received as a more general query of "why is the mechanic repairing the car?". M treats this second question as fitting within the existing topic of talk (and, in fact, as a request for clarification).

In both extracts 1 and 2, *sebab apa tu* is treated conventionally as a 'why' question based upon a topic established in the previous turn. However, elsewhere in the data, such questions were less well fitted to the prior talk, and accordingly were not necessarily treated as conventional "why" questions by M. Extract 3 illustrates such an instance. At this point in the recording, the participants were playing with a set of kitchen toys. M then looks for a plastic knife:

Extract 3 [No knife]

```
8     M:     la: mana pisau? Takde p[un pisau ((takes toys out
             from the kitchen set bag, "I" looks on))
             la: where is knife? There is no knife
9    →I:                        [sebab apa tu?
                                Because what is that?
10    M:     sebab apa pisau takde:?
             Because what there is no knife:?
11    I:     sebab >dia kena< apa tu.
             Because >it is being< what that
12    M:     ↑mana: takde pisau pun (1.2) Cari. Cari.
             Where: there is no knife pun (1.2) search. Search.
```

"I's" first question in line 9 is of the form discussed in extracts 1 and 2. Where this differs from the *sebab apa tu* turns in those extracts is that it does not clearly relate to the prior turn, which appears to be a question form produced by M. Its lack of fittedness is demonstrated by M, who reformulates "I's" line 9 into the contextually relevant *sebab apa pisau takde* ("*because what there is no knife?*"), in doing so seeking to establish the meaning of *tu* ("*that*") (cf. Chouinard & Clark, 2003). Rather than confirming or rejecting this reformulation, however, "I" revises into the grammatically unusual second question *sebab dia kena apa tu* ("*because it is being what that?*"). M appears not to treat this as a question as she provides no answer, and instead returns to searching for the knife. Here then, there are two unusual forms of *apa tu* turn:

- The first is apparently ill-fitted to its sequential context and therefore, whilst treated as a question, is not interpreted as reflecting a conventional meaning (of "why").
- The second is apparently not treated as a question, as it receives no answer at all (Stivers & Rossano, 2010).

There were numerous other instances where *apa tu* was treated as a question of sorts, but not with a conventional 'why?' meaning. Consider extract 4 below, in which the participants are playing cooking with a toy stove. In line 1, "I" pretends to turn on the stove, which is narrated by M subsequently. "I" then asks an *apa tu* question in line 3 which, in this context, appears to be unconventionally interpreted by M as meaning 'what happens next?' (see her response in line 4). Tentatively, "I's" use of *tiba tiba* ("*suddenly*") at the start of his turn may contribute to this hearing of his question:

Extract 4 [Big fire]

```
1   I:    (('turns the gas on' as M looks on))
2   M:    ha: Irfan buka api
            ha: Irfan turns on the fire        ⌐
3   I:→   (tiba tiba: (.) (tri) apa tu      │  ((Irfan looks at M))
            (suddenly) (tri) what is that?    ├
4   M:    jadi api besar:                   │
            Becomes big fire                  ⌐
            (0.58)
5   M:    terbakar
            Burning
```

Important point

> ! When examining interactions across cultures, it can be easy to assume
> • or amplify the extent of potential differences. What you should be
>   able to see, however, from extract 4 is that there is a strong
>   tendency of speakers to interpret utterances dynamically and
>   according to the immediate context of the prior turn(s). Therefore,
>   this feature of human interaction appears to be universal.

Sequence Type 2: *Apa tu* Initiates or Develops a Shared Focus

Extracts 1–4 suggest that, at points in these data, *apa tu* was both designed and interpreted as a question form. There was, however, variation in "I's" design of question turns featuring *apa tu* and M's responses to these. The analyses above demonstrated that even comparatively designed *apa tu* turns did different work in different contexts, illustrating the contextually specific and dynamic nature of *apa tu* as a question form. Crucial factors in M's responses to "I's" questions appeared to be:

- the extent to which these could be contextualised against prior turns and
- their fittedness to the present activity that the participants were undertaking.

Indeed, as demonstrated above, M would repair or even overlook the question in instances where *apa tu* was particularly ambiguous or ill-fitted.

Analysis also demonstrated that there were other manifestations of *apa tu* which were consistently *not* explicitly treated as if questions. In this subsection, we will discuss *apa tu* turns that functioned to initiate a new topic or develop an existing one. This represents a very different function of *apa tu* than that described above, and not one in line with the turn's conventional social usage in Malay. However, as can be seen from the extracts, both "I" and M treated *apa tu* as serving such a function in certain interactional contexts.

Extract 5 provides an example of this phenomenon. Here, the participants are in free play. M is removing toys from a bag, before prompting "I" to name them:

Extract 5 [Mama open]

```
1    M:     ni (.) Duck: la:
            This? Duck: la
2    I:     duck
3    M:     duck:. Su↑sun (1.6) Ada bera↑pa. ki↑ra.
            Duck:. Arrange (1.6) Have how many? Count.
4           (("I" turns to the bag))
5    M:     Ada berapa
            Have how many?
6   →I:     (("I" gazes at toy bag, and removes smaller bag of
            cars)) apa ↑tu ma↓ma
            What is that mama
7    M:     mm:: ni ada apa lagi: ((M reaches out to touch bag
            of cars))
            oo this has what else:
8    I:     mama buka↑kan
            Mama open
9    M:     ((M takes bag of cars from "I")) bu↓ka↑kan:
                                           open:
```

At the start of the extract, M unsuccessfully attempts to initiate an object-counting activity on two occasions (lines 3 and 5). "I" then produces an *apa tu* turn. This turn's literal, conventional meaning ("*what is that?*") fits "I's" current activity, as he is removing a bag of cars from the main toy bag, and moreover is appended with the response mobilising nominal form *mama* (see Stivers & Rossano, 2010). Hence, through design and placement, this turn strongly projects for M to produce an answer. Unlike in the extracts above however, M does not answer the question but instead shifts her focus to the vehicle bag, moving the live joint topic of talk away from the proposed counting activity that she had been pursuing previously (see lines 7 onwards). It appears therefore that *apa tu* here functioned as a mechanism through which a subsequent joint focus is established—a means by which "I" could start a new joint project at a point in the interaction where M was pursuing her own agenda.

Important point

! Note that "I" does not repeat *apa tu* following M's lack of explicit
• answer, unlike in earlier extracts. This, from a CA perspective, suggests that "I's" turn was designed to shift M's current focus rather than generate an answer.

Similar turns—in which *apa tu* was not received as a question, but instead served to modify the joint focus of the current talk—were evident throughout the data, although operated in a variety of ways. Consider extract 6, in which participants are playing with plastic food. Here, *apa tu* is again not responded to as if a question, but rather than initiating a new topic as in extract 5 appears to serve to further develop an *existing* joint focus.

Extract 6 [Chilli]

```
1    I:     mama nak (.) cili: ((holds the chilli out to M))
            Mama want chili
2    M:     ss:: cili pe↑das
            Ss: spicy chilli
3   →I:     cili pun kena apa tu?
            Chili also being what's that?
4    M:     ha?
5    I:     kena zombie
            being zombie
6    M:     haah
7    I:     (makes a shooting-like sound))
8    M:     meletup::   ((M looks to the toys on her right))
            Exploding
```

In line 1, "I" offers M a toy chilli as part of their play. However, her subsequent talk about the chilli in line 2 merely expands "I's" prior utterance without driving forward the play episode. Notably, "I's" subsequent *apa tu* turn ties specifically to "chilli", to which M provides a minimal response projecting for further talk from "I". "I's" next turn in line 5 takes the form of an (ultimately accepted) suggestion to pretend that the chilli is a zombie. Hence, *apa tu* in line 3 does not appear to function as a question, particularly because "I" *himself* ultimately "answers" his own turn in line 5. Instead, "I's" turn results in the topicalisation of a (pretend) attribute of the chilli, whilst simultaneously opening an interactional position for he himself to develop the topic further in subsequent turns. In this way, the turn has some similarities to the "*do you know what?*" floor-gaining questions that are typically used by children in interaction with adults when bringing up a new topic or digressing from an adult-led interactional episode (Sacks, 1972; in relation to ASD, see Muskett, Perkins, Clegg, & Body, 2010).

Important point

⚠   In English adult-child dyads, "do you know what?" questions
•   have been argued to reflect issues of social and interactional
     rights.

In other words, by using these children demonstrate an appreciation that they are not positioned to simply start a new topic without somehow announcing it first. In the above (atypical) Malay adult-child dyad, a comparable phenomenon appears to occur where "I" produces an unconventional turn, which opens a space for him to introduce subsequently a new aspect of an imaginative play scenario. This suggests there may be key social similarities in the positioning of adults and children between Malay and English-speaking dyads.

Sequence Type 3: *Apa tu* Treated as Self-talk

The sections above illustrate instances in which socio-interactional actions are clearly performed by "I's" repetitive *apa tu* turns, whether acting as questions (see section "Introduction") or alternatively influencing the joint focus pursued by participants (see section "Method"). In both cases, M was responsive to the *apa tu* turn. However, there was another variety of such turns which was characterised by M's *irresponsiveness* towards "I's" prior talk. As will be demonstrated, in these instances M appeared to receive *apa tu* turns as non-communicative and/or representing self-directed talk on the part of "I". Notably, this variability seemingly is an artefact of features of the design of these kinds of turns.

In extract 7, the participants are playing with toy animals. M begins by initiating a toy naming activity similar to that seen in some of the above extracts, before beginning to look for a mouse in line 3. This topic is discussed until line 6, when Irfan produces a *sebab apa tu* ("why?") question. Unlike in earlier extracts, M provides no receipt for this and instead recommences her toy naming activity:

Extract 7 [No mouse]

```
1    M:    Ha Irfan:: apa ni
           Ha Irfan:: what's this?
2    I:    Lion
3    M:    ha lion (1.7) lion and the mouse. Mouse ada takde.
           Mouse takde: ::
           Ha lion (1.7) lion and the mouse. Mouse present
           absent. Mouse absent::
           Ha lion (1.7) lion and the mouse. Is there a mouse
    (or) not. no mouse::
4    I:    sebab dah hilang
           Because has disappeared
5    M:    mm↑m[m:↓
6    I:→        [(("I" looks forwards and downwards)) sebab
                apa tu
                 Because what is that?
7    ((M picks up chicken))
8    M:    ↑ni: (("I" looks towards chicken in M's hand; M
    looks up at Irfan))
           ↑This:
```

```
9     I:     °chicken°
10    M:     chicken. Dekat Ayamas.
             Chicken. At Ayamas.
```

Given that neither participant attempts to recover the apparently unanswered line 6, it is reasonable to suggest that this *sebab apa tu* must be somehow different than that in previous extracts. Utterances being treated as meaningful in one context and disregarded in another has been discussed previously in relation to ASD by Wootton (1999). In a discussion of an English-speaking child's demonstration of delayed echoing, Wootton described a range of sequential, prosodic, and embodied features of delivery that occasioned either a co-speaker response to apparently echoed turns, or alternatively a glossing over as if self-directed talk. Whilst "I" has significantly more linguistic resources than the child discussed by Wootton, we suggest that participants orient to the *apa tu* turn in extract 7 as if self-directed talk in a comparable way, given that neither participant attempted to repair the sequence around line 6. Crucially, the specific discrepancy in "I's" delivery of *apa tu* appears to lie in his gaze pattern, because unlike in previous examples, he is looking down and away from M (and not towards M or the shared referent) as he produces this turn.

Extract 8 provides another example of this phenomenon. Here, the participants are playing imaginatively with a doll and play food. In line 1, M is "voicing" the doll as asking for corn. "I" offers the doll a pear, a proposition which M (appropriately) disattends in order to look for the corn. M's absent response is received playfully by "I" (line 4). However, "I" then produces an apparently ill-fitted *sebab apa tu* in line 6. Unlike in the examples discussed in sections "Introduction" and "Method", M does not attempt to contextualise this turn as either acting as a question or occasioning a shift in joint focus, and instead continues searching for the corn without response (line 7). Hence, she appears to receive "I's" turn in line 6 as if self-directed and without interactional consequence. Crucially, as in extract 7, "I" is gazing down at the point of question delivery (between lines 4–8). Moreover, following the glossing over of his turn by M, "I" then continues to participate in the feeding play without problematising the absence of M's response (line 8). This further reinforces the suggestion that line 6 was self-, rather than socially, oriented talk.

Extract 8 [Corn]

```
1    M:     makan car<u>rot</u> (.) saya nak:: ja<u>gung</u>: ((shakes doll
            in front of Irfan's face))
            Eat car<u>rot</u> (.)          i want::       <u>corn</u>
2           (("I" picks pear up and puts near to doll's face,
            eyes looking up at M))
3    M:     ((shakes doll) ja:gung
                           corn
4    I:     (("I" looks up, smiling)) no (("I" gazes down))
            no
5    M:     nak jagung (.) <u>mana</u> jagung,?
            Want corn.     Where corn
6    I:  →  sebab: ↑apa ↑tu
            Because what is that
7    M:     saya nak makan ja<u>gung</u>: mana jagung?
            I want to eat corn: where corn
8    I:     ((picks up an orange and puts it near doll's face))
```

We have presented an in depth analysis through the chapter and illustrated our claims through the data. As we pull this chapter to a close, we recommend you reflect on what you have learned and try the activity in Box 11.2.

Box 11.2 Activity on ASD

Activity

During your own project on ASD we recommend that you keep a diary of your interactions with children diagnosed with ASD. In this diary, focus on observing and recording which behaviours you might instinctively associate with a child speaking in a self-directed manner. As you do so, ask yourself this question:

• Do you note that eye gaze or any other physical action is a recurring factor in your experiences of these behaviours?

Summary

This chapter aimed to illustrate the value of CA in cross-cultural research on ASD by presenting a case study of a Malay-speaking child. In this study, we investigated the variation in design and use of a repetitive turn element, *apa tu*, which frequently occurred in this child's talk. Use of CA enabled us to ground analysis of the functions of this feature of the child's communication in the real-time responses of his co-participant. Findings demonstrated that whilst *apa tu* was often used unconventionally by the child, it was not necessarily treated as problematic by his co-speaker, and indeed served a range of interactional functions including direct questioning, establishment of joint engagement between the participants, or as a tool to extend or maintain a current topic. On other occasions, both speakers apparently treated it as if self-directed.

Through analysis, it was demonstrated that several sequential features of the above functions are directly comparable to those found in English-speaking dyads, with both typically- and atypically developing children. As noted above, it is only too easy to amplify possible cross-cultural differences in relation to ASD. Whilst we do not deny that interactional differences are likely to exist between any cultural groups, the case study reported above has demonstrated that, at least in relation to the turn element examined, there are broad interactional consistencies in how adult-child dyads organise between speaking and linguistic contexts. Two particular themes are worthy of further consideration. First, in interactions involving European speakers with communication difficulties, it has previously been observed that repair does not occur as frequently as might be anticipated given the level of interactional problems that might potentially emerge (e.g. Body & Parker, 2005; Paoletti, 1998; Muskett, Chap. 5, this volume). This phenomenon was arguably evident in the data presented above: M rarely initiated repair and would often work to receive impressionistically unconventional turns by "I" as fitted and meaningful. The consistent manifestation of this phenomenon in both European and Malay dyads could be argued to reveal that certain practical understandings about the competency of people with communication difficulties (including children with ASD) cross-cultural barriers. Second, it is strikingly difficult to identify consistently what categorically constitutes an "interactional difficulty" in the above data, given that similar behaviours or turns are responded to differently in different contexts. Again, this variability within interactions involving people with ASD has been similarly noted in English data (e.g. Stribling, Rae, & Dickerson, 2007; Muskett et al., 2010), and hence is likely to reflect universal issues associated with psychiatric diagnoses.

To conclude, we wish to highlight an important practice implication of the above findings. In the modern globalised world, practitioners are likely to work with families and children from diverse cultural and linguistic heritages. It is well acknowledged that available assessment materials and tools, particularly in relation to language, are both ethno- and lingua-centric, which presents a significant challenge for modern services and their users. Whilst readers who are not from a Malay-speaking background will have likely used the English translations extensively during their reading of the extracts in this chapter, they may have noticed that use of the CA approach enables them to *understand* this communication *in context* and, therefore, follow data-informed hypotheses about the social function of the verbal behaviours demonstrated by the child in the case study. Along these lines, CA may be a useful tool to use in cross-cultural professional practice, given that it provides an emic means by which to interpret behaviours and their social meanings—thereby avoiding imposition of assumptions or personal values onto such interpretation.

We have presented an empirical analysis of Malay-speaking interlocutors and have guided you through CA. We have demonstrated how to do this practically and summarise these in Box 11.3.

Box 11.3 Summary of practical highlights

Summary of practical highlights

1. Regardless of language or cultural context, ostensibly atypical behaviour by children with ASD inevitably has interactional consequences and is treated as relevant by co-speakers.
2. As an artefact of its methodology, conversation analysis (CA) has significant potential application as both a research and practical tool in cross-cultural working. This is because it partly mitigates the necessity to make personal judgements about the meaning of social behaviours in different linguistic and/or cultural contexts.
3. Cross-cultural linguistic differences may obfuscate similarities in how people from different heritages respond interactionally to children who demonstrate behaviours consistent with an ASD diagnosis.
4. The moment-by-moment, unconscious interactional behaviours demonstrated by people around an individual with ASD can be interpreted as an indication of their practical understanding of ASD. This means that CA can be used to complement work with families or professionals, including in transcultural contexts.

References

Bhugra, D., & Bhui, K. (2001). African–Caribbeans and schizophrenia: contributing factors. *Advances in Psychiatric Treatment, 7*(4), 283–291.

Bilu, Y., & Goodman, Y. C. (1997). What does the soul say? Metaphysical uses of facilitated communication in the Jewish ultraorthodox community. *Ethos, 25*, 375–407.

Body, R., & Parker, M. (2005). Topic repetitiveness after traumatic brain injury: An emergent, jointly managed behaviour. *Clinical Linguistics and Phonetics, 19*, 379–392.

Chouinard, M. M., & Clark, E. V. (2003). Adult reformulations of child errors as negative evidence. *Journal of Child Language, 30*(3), 637–669.

Cohen, D. J., & Volkmar, F. (1997). Conceptualizations of autism and intervention practices: International perspectives. In D. J. Cohen & F. R. Volkmar (Eds.), *Handbook of Autism and pervasive developmental disorders* (pp. 947–950). New York: Wiley.

Daley, T. C. (2002). The need for cross-cultural research on the pervasive developmental disorders. *Transcultural Psychiatry, 39*, 531–550.

Ellenberger, H. F. (1968). Psychiatric impressions from a trip to Dakar. *Canadian Psychiatric Association Journal, 13*, 539–545.

Harris, M. (1976). History and significance of the emic/etic distinction. *Annual review of anthropology, 5*, 329–350.

Karim, N. S., Onn, F. M., Musa, H. H., & Mahmood, A. H. (2000). *Tatabahasa Dewan (Edisi Ketiga)* (3rd ed.). Kuala Lumpur: Kementerian Pelajaran.

Kawa, S., & Giordano, J. (2012). A brief historicity of the diagnostic and statistical manual of mental disorders: Issues and implications for the future of psychiatric canon and practice. *Philosophy, Ethics, and Humanities in Medicine, 7*, 2.

Leonard, C. J. (1985). Brief outlines of the parent/family reaction to childhood disability in families from 3 ethnic minority groups. *International Journal for the Advancement of Counselling, 8*, 197–205.

Muskett, T., Perkins, M., Clegg, J., & Body, R. (2010). Inflexibility as an interactional phenomenon: Using conversation analysis to re-examine a symptom of autism. *Clinical Linguistics & Phonetics, 24*(1), 1–16.

Ochs, E. (1982). Talking to children in Western Samoa. *Language in Society, 11*, 77–104.

Paoletti, I. (1998). Handing 'incoherence' according to the speaker's on-sight categorization. In C. Antaki & S. Widdicombe (Eds.), *Identities in talk* (pp. 171–190). London: Sage.

Sacks, H. (1972). On the analyzability of stories by children. In J. J. Gumperz & D. Hymes (Eds.), *Directions in sociolinguistics: The ethnography of communication* (pp. 325–345). Oxford: Blackwell.

Steensig, J., & Drew, P. (2008). Introduction: Questioning and affiliation/disaffiliation in interaction. *Discourse Studies, 10*(1), 5–15.

Stivers, T., & Rossano, F. (2010). Mobilizing response. *Research on Language and Social Interaction, 43*(1), 3–31.

Stribling, P., Rae, J., & Dickerson, P. (2007). Two forms of spoken repetition in a girl with autism. *International Journal of Language & Communication Disorders, 42*(4), 427–444.

Tanaka, H. (*1999*). *Turn-taking in Japanese conversation: A study in grammar and interaction*. Amsterdam: John Benjamins.

Westermeyer, J. (1979). Folk concepts of mental disorder among the Lao: continuities with similar concepts in other cultures and in psychiatry. *Culture, Medicine and Psychiatry, 3*, 301–317.

Wootton, A. J. (1999). An investigation of delayed echoing in a child with autism. *First Language, 19*, 359–381.

Recommended reading

Daley, T. C. (2002). The need for cross-cultural research on the pervasive developmental disorders. *Transcultural Psychiatry, 39*, 531–550.

Ochs, E. (1982). Talking to children in Western Samoa. *Language in Society, 11*, 77–104.

Nor Azrita Mohamed Zain is Lecturer in Speech-Language Pathology at the International Islamic University, Malaysia. She has obtained her PhD in human communication science from the University of Sheffield, the UK. Azrita's research interests include typical and atypical speech, language, and communication development in children, interactional (in)competencies in individuals with autism, and conversation analysis.

Tom Muskett is Senior Lecturer in Psychology at Leeds Beckett University, the UK. Tom's professional background is in speech and language therapy. He has worked in clinical and educational roles with children with diagnoses of autism and their families, and previously led a clinical training programme at the University of Sheffield, the UK. Informed by his experiences in these roles, Tom's teaching and research aims to explore how children's "development" and "disorder" can be rethought methodologically, socially, and politically. For more details, please see http://www.leedsbeckett.ac.uk/staff/dr-tom-muskett/.

Hilary Gardner has been a speech and language therapist for several decades and is Senior Lecturer in Human Communication Sciences at the University of Sheffield. Her passion for conversation analysis and interest in therapeutic interactions of all kinds, particularly adult-child dyads, have spanned as many years as her professional practice.

12

Conversation Analysis: A Tool for Analysing Interactional Difficulties Faced by Children with Asperger's Syndrome

Johanna Rendle-Short

Learning Objectives

By the end of this chapter, you will be able to:

- Describe some of the interactional difficulties faced by children with Asperger's syndrome.
- Understand what social interaction difficulties might mean in practice as you interact with a child with Asperger's syndrome.
- Describe four key terms within conversation analysis, namely, turn-taking, adjacency pairs, first pair parts, second pair parts
- Describe the difference between intra-turn pauses and inter-turn pauses or gaps
- Understand how pauses or silences can interrupt the progressivity of talk
- Describe how conversation analysis can be used as a pedagogic tool for parents, teachers, and children diagnosed with Asperger's syndrome.

J. Rendle-Short (✉)
The Australian National University, School of Literature, Languages and Linguistics, Canberra, ACT, Australia

© The Author(s) 2017
M. O'Reilly et al. (eds.), *A Practical Guide to Social Interaction Research in Autism Spectrum Disorders*, The Language of Mental Health,
https://doi.org/10.1057/978-1-137-59236-1_12

• Understand the importance of empowering children to become their own mini-analysts so that they can understand how interaction works and how to improve their interactional skills.

Introduction

Children who have been diagnosed with Asperger's syndrome find social interaction difficult (e.g., Attwood, 2000; Fine, Bartolucci, Szatmari, & Ginsberg, 1994; Gillberg & Gillberg, 1989; Minshew, Goldstein, & Siegel, 1995; Rendle-Short, 2003, 2014; Rendle-Short, Cobb-Moore, & Danby, 2014; Tager-Flusberg & Anderson, 1991; Wing, 1981; Wootton, 2003). These individuals might find it difficult in several areas:

• They might find it hard to know what to say at the right time.
• They may not look at the other person when they are talking to them.
• They may not be able to successfully initiate a conversation or to keep it going.

As a result, children with Asperger's syndrome may find themselves socially isolated at school, especially given the importance of social inter-action in developing peer relationships and in forming friendships (e.g., Erwin, 1993; Margalit, 1994).

Even within the family, siblings and parents of a child with Asperger's syndrome may experience periods of interactional difficulty when trying to include the child into everyday family conversations. Not being able to express themselves easily to others may result in low self-esteem, loneli-ness, anxiety, and depression (e.g., Diehl, Lemerise, Caverly, Ramsay, & Roberts, 1998; Dunn, 2004; Erwin, 1993; Margalit, 1994).

In this chapter, the focus is on individuals with Asperger's syndrome. The chapter provides descriptive detail of the condition to provide con-text for the empirical analysis that follows. The main focus of the chap-ter is to demonstrate how conversation analysis (CA) may serve as a useful pedagogical tool for practitioners to better understand the condition.

What Is Asperger's Syndrome?

Although the label of Asperger's syndrome was officially defined in the *Diagnostic and Statistical Manual of Mental Disorders IV* (DSM-IV),[1] the label has now been removed from the latest edition (DSM-5). Children who were previously diagnosed with Asperger's syndrome are now diagnosed with autism spectrum disorder (ASD). Conversely, in the 4th edition 'autism' was defined in relation to a triad of impairments, namely:

- Problems in development of social skills
- Communication impairment
- A lack of flexible thinking

> **Important point**
>
> ! Under the more recent description, social and communication
> • dimensions are classified together. The diagnosis, and its definition, however, has been controversial. It has resulted in diverse and at times contested responses, with some positioning the diagnosis as a 'core identity' and others questioning its very existence.

The data that will be presented in this chapter was recorded between 1996 and 2008, before the more recent DSM-5. As a result, the children in this data set were diagnosed with Asperger's syndrome (DSM-IV), and the label of Asperger's syndrome will be used throughout this chapter.

Conversation Analysis as a Tool for Understanding Interaction

Conversation analysis is a talk-in-interaction methodology that permits detailed analyses of the 'technology' of interaction (Sacks, 1984, p. 413). It analyses how participants in naturally occurring conversation mutually orient to, and collaborate with, other interactional participants to achieve orderly and meaningful communication (Goodwin & Heritage, 1990).

If 'problems' within the interaction arise, such 'problems' are predominantly dealt with by participants as they emerge. Problems that might arise in everyday conversations include problems of turn-taking, topic initiation, or problems in understanding the content of the previous talk.

Important point

> ! Participants display their understanding of the prior turn through the
> • production of a sequentially relevant next turn (Heritage, 2009).

One important feature of CA is the turn-taking system.[2] It ensures that speakers will design their turn to build on the context of the prior turn-at-talk, and that hearers will attempt to understand a turn with reference to the sequential context provided by the prior turn (Heritage, 1984). Turns-at-talk are thus both 'context-shaped', in that a turn exists within the context of a prior turn, and 'context-renewing', in that any turn becomes the context for the turn which follows (Heritage, 1989, p. 21). The hearer interprets the meaning of an utterance in the light of previous utterances, as exemplified by the analytic question, 'why that now?' (Schegloff, 2007).

Turns build on the concept of adjacency pairs (Schegloff & Sacks, 1973) with the first pair part (FPP) making the next action, the second pair part (SPP), relevant. There are constraints on the timing and the form of the SPP action. In terms of timing, if an SPP is not forthcoming, it is heard as being in some way missing or 'absent', with absences seen as being accountable (Schegloff & Sacks, 1973). The absent SPP, as well as the accompanying silence, 'belong' to the participant who should have produced relevant talk at this point in time. Silences of more than the 'standard maximum' of silence of about 1.0 second (Jefferson, 1989) tend to be 'noticed' and interactionally responded to.

Absences of talk can be evidence of a problem of achieving intersubjectivity or a state of mutual understanding in conversation. Generally speaking, the achievement and management of intersubjectivity or mutual understanding is rarely made explicit in that intersubjectivity is most commonly constructed, demonstrated, and maintained by means of implicit procedures, woven into the procedural infrastructure of interaction (Heritage, 2007; Schegloff, 1992). Problems of intersubjectivity tend to disrupt the progressivity of talk as any lack of understanding must be resolved before the talk can move forward. For this reason, pauses or silences within talk that jeopardise progressivity are treated as evidence that intersubjectivity or mutual understanding has also been jeopardised.

Important point

! As will be shown in the data below, long silences in a conversation
• are problematic and a potential indicator that mutual
understanding has not been achieved.

There are several benefits to using a conversation analysis methodology for exploring interactions with individuals with Asperger's syndrome:

• CA allows you to examine social interaction in detail.

The methodology provides a powerful lens for examining social interactivity through its rigorous and finely tuned analysis of ordinary conversations in naturally occurring settings. Such fine-grained analysis is important given the subtle social and pragmatic difficulties experienced by children who have been diagnosed with Asperger's syndrome.

• CA is grounded in naturally occurring data.

The second advantage relates to the fact that conversation analysis works from the premise that any claims made *about* the data must be demonstrable *in* the data. Instead of drawing on abstract theories or predetermined analytical constructs, conversation analysts treat the data as the participants' phenomena, providing evidence as to how the participants themselves understand and act upon each other's contributions.

• CA treats a typical interaction positively by focusing the analysts' attention on interactional competencies rather than deficiencies.

The third advantage arises from the way in which the methodology of conversation analysis encourages analysts to apply a competence model with emphasis placed on what it is that the children *can do* rather than adopting a deficit model that emphasises poor social interaction skills.

Naturally Occurring Interaction: A Rich Source of Evidence for Investigating Communication Difficulties

Children are competent manipulators of verbal and interactional resources (e.g., Bruner, 1983; Cromdal, 2009; Forrester, 2008; Garvey, 1984; McTear, 1985; Schieffelin, 1990; Sidnell, 2010b; Wells, 1981; Wootton, 1994, 2006, 2007). They are able to share concerns, interests, and other activities with each other as well as voluntarily show mutual respect (Margalit, 1994). For children who have been diagnosed with Asperger's syndrome, however, social interaction is not so straightforward (e.g., Attwood, 2000; Bauminger & Kasari, 2000; Knott, Dunlop, & Mackay, 2006). They may find it difficult to be a 'good listener', to initiate a conversation, or to respond in a timely and appropriate manner.

Important point

! Children who have been diagnosed with Asperger's syndrome may
• not always have the interactional control required for successful social interaction.

This is not to say that children diagnosed with Asperger's syndrome are not competent interactionists. It is the very fact that they are *so good* at interacting that can create difficulties. Because children diagnosed with Asperger's syndrome are often able to 'pass', their conversational partners may not know how much 'work' is going on underneath as the children try to keep up with the conversation and try to ensure that there is no threat to the progressivity of the talk. It is for this reason that we need a more nuanced understanding of how children with Asperger's syndrome communicate and participate in everyday interaction within naturalistic settings (see also Macintosh & Dissanayake, 2006). Naturally occurring interaction can be a rich site for evidence of collaboration, careful monitoring, and demonstration of the way in which affected children pay attention to the emerging talk (see, e.g., Geils & Knoetze, 2008; Stribling, Rae, & Dickerson, 2009; Muskett, Perkins, Clegg, & Body, 2010).

The rest of this chapter will focus on two types of pauses within interaction to show you how CA can be used as an analytic tool in contexts where one or more of the interlocutors have communication difficulties. The focus of analysis is on how pauses or silence can interrupt the progressivity of talk. This chapter therefore has several sections:

- The first section presents extracts from two children who have been diagnosed with Asperger's syndrome showing how they pause within a turn (intra-turn) as they are initiating a new topic. In both cases, topic initiation is delayed.
- The second section shows how an interlocutor responds to an inter-turn pause or gap following an FPP. The example shows how a person (an adult) waits for 4 seconds before checking whether the child diagnosed with Asperger's syndrome is still on the phone.
- The third section builds on the previous two sections by analysing a small video interaction of two children engaged in a spontaneous activity. In this instance, the pause occurs after the friend of a child diagnosed with Asperger's syndrome falls down because she has hurt herself. This third section explores how the principles of CA can be used as a pedagogic tool for teachers, parents, and children.

All extracts were transcribed according to Jefferson's transcription conventions (see Appendix) to include pauses, overlap, latched talk, as well as prosodic variation in talk. When transcribing pauses, intra-turn pauses are generally shown as 'belonging' to the speaker who is currently talking; inter-turn pauses or gaps are generally shown on a separate line as they 'belong' to the next speaker.

Now that the context has been set for the chapter, it is worth taking some time to reflect on the issues that I have begun to raise. Take a look at the activity in Box 12.1 before you go any further with the empirical analysis example that is presented.

Box 12.1 Activity in understanding CA

Activity

Think about how participants might display their understanding of the prior turn through the production of a sequentially relevant next turn (Heritage, 2009). For example: One way that participants display their understanding of the previous turn is at the beginning of a conversation. When the first person says 'Hello', the second person (the recipient) says 'Hello' in response.
• Can you think of another example?

Delayed Progressivity: Intra-turn Pause During Topic Initiation

---

Important point
! Having a conversation with a child with Asperger's syndrome can be
• variable.

Sometimes the conversation with a child with Asperger's syndrome runs quite smoothly with minimal delays, minimal repetition of ideas, and with coherent topic development; sometimes the conversation feels more awkward with a lot of repetition, with confusion as to what exactly was intended, or with a lack of topic coherence. Because interaction evolves moment by moment, conversational participants have to constantly monitor what was said and how it was said in order to know what to say next. In other words, talk is highly contextualised and locally managed (Sacks, Schegloff, & Jefferson, 1974) such that there are no context-free norms of interaction against which one can identify the *right way* or the *wrong way* to talk.

One potential difficulty occurs when a child diagnosed with Asperger's syndrome tries to initiate a new topic of talk. *Initiating* a topic can be more difficult than *responding* to someone else's topic of talk, a comment or question. When responding, there is an inbuilt predictability because it is clear what type of response is required and that the response should be forthcoming with minimal gap and minimal overlap (see Jefferson

(1989) for the maximum expected silence between turns). On the whole, participants know what to do or how to respond. However, when the child with Asperger's syndrome has to initiate an action by him or herself, it is not so predictable as they have to appropriately position the question, the comment, or the new topic within the interaction as a whole (Rendle-Short, 2014). The following two extracts, taken from Rendle-Short (2014), exemplify the interactional difficulty of trying to get a new topic of conversation into the talk.[3]

Extract 1 was recorded while Jancis[4] (an 8-year-old child who had been diagnosed with Asperger's syndrome) was talking to her friend Tiffany (also 8 years old) on the telephone. Jancis had rung up her friend after school one day because she (Jancis) had been ill and unable to pick up the boiled egg that the children had been painting for Easter: (See Appendix for transcription conventions.)

Extract 1 [Jancis and friend] (Rendle-Short, 2014)

```
1.    T:    are you still there?
2.    J:    yes.
3.    T:    good.
4.          (1.2)
5.    J:  → I wanted t'a::sk, hh (1.2)
6.    T:    Jancis guess what you missed.
7.    J:    wha'
8.    T:    a big easter egg 'cos
9.          you brought all your homework in.
10.         an' a li'le one too.
11.         (1.0)
12.   T:    but [never mind.] you'll get i- them=
13.   J:        [(          )]
14.   T:    = on the first day back.
15.         (0.8)
16.   T:    heh heh
17.   J:    hh .hh ((sniffing))
18.   T:    yeah.=what did you want me [to a::?-what] do=
19.   J:                               [uhm      hh ]
20.   T:    =you want t' ask?
21.   J:    did you bring back my boiled e:gg?
```

Jancis initiates her new topic in line 5, '*I wanted t' a::sk*', after a short checking sequence confirming that her friend, Tiffany, is still on the phone and is still listening (lines 1–3). Although Jancis' turn beginning indicates that a question is going to follow, there is a vulnerability of execution highlighted by the slow delivery and long intra-turn pause of 1.2 seconds. The vulnerability becomes a reality when Tiffany highjacks the turn by asking her own question in line 6. Tiffany orients to her question being 'out of place' in two ways:

- First, she uses an address term at the beginning of her interrogative turn (line 6) to both create social closeness and to emphasise the sequence initiating nature of the turn (see Rendle-Short, 2007).
- Second, Tiffany indicates in lines 18 and 20 that Jancis' yet unasked question is still relevant '*what did you want me to a::?- what do you want t' ask?*'

So although Jancis does eventually get an opportunity to ask her question (line 21), this example highlights how progressivity of talk can be delayed due to the hesitant way in which Jancis introduced the new topic into the conversation in line 5. Jancis' opportunity to actually ask her question only comes after Tiffany has told her own story about the Easter egg (lines 6–17). Being able to finally ask her question relied on her conversational partner remembering that Jancis' question was still outstanding. So although Jancis successfully chose a sequentially appropriate position to launch her reason for call, delayed execution meant that the talk did not progress as anticipated and eventually it relied on her conversational partner to reintroduce the new topic.

The second extract shows a different way of introducing or initiating a new topic. Extract 2 was recorded while Will (an 8-year-old boy with Asperger's syndrome) was talking to his older brother (a 10-year-old boy) on the couch in their home.[5] The Mother (M) was also present and listening to the conversation.

Extract 2 [Will and brother] (Rendle-Short, 2014)

```
1.    W:    there's one last thing I need to talk about.
2.    Br:   okay?
```

```
3.     W:   <o::h I don't have to start,>
4.          (1.5)
5.          a::nd, (2.0)
6.          the first of all the people you need
7.          to know about Asperger's Syndrome,
8.          that we enjoy TALKING ABOUT,
9.          is that (1.5) even if it's a disability
10.         and you don't have any strong (or        ),
11.         it's just (1.0) you don't have to go
12.         around the world complaining about it,
13.    Br:  yes. they are very special.
14.     W:  [AND]
15.    Br:  [so ]
16.      →  (2.0)
17.    Br:  I think I might go and watch:
18.         some TV so [I'll
19.     W:             [but there's one more thing
20.         I meant to say.
21.    Br:  okay.
22.     M:  you can go now
23.    Br:  no. you can s[ay.   [me
24.     W:               [I::   [I:::
25.    Br:  talk to me.=
26.     W:  =me and many other people in the world
27.         about 300 or something (2.0)
28.         have ASPERGER'S SYNDROME.
29.         see ya.
```

In Extract 1, Jancis initiated a new topic with '*I wanted to ask*'. By contrast, in Extract 2, Will introduces his new topic with '*there's one last thing I need to talk about*' (line 1). However, during the setting up of the new topic, he also hesitates and delays the topic initiation. Following elongated pauses (lines 4 and 5), he explains what it is like to have Asperger's syndrome, although his extended turn has intra-turn pauses (lines 9 and 11) and unclear grammar (lines 6–12). His comment is responded to with an agreement and an assessment: '*Yes, they are very special*' (line 13).

However, in spite of having said '*first of all*' to show that there will be at least two parts to his turn at talk (line 6), the second part isn't so easily forthcoming. Will says a louder '*AND*' to foreshadow the second part, but as with Jancis in Extract 1, the intra-turn pause of 2 seconds (line 16) creates a continuity vulnerability and his brother says he might go and watch TV. As Will is about to lose his audience, he overtly indicates there is '*one more thing*' he wants to say (lines 19 and 20). At this point, the child's mother intervenes. The brother decides to stay and listen, thus providing the necessary scaffolding so that Will can complete the second part of this idea (lines 26–29).

The analysis highlights similarities between Jancis and Will, even though they were initiating their topics in different ways. It enables us to see the two children as competent interlocutors even though their topic initiation may not have been executed as smoothly as it could have been. They both still got their topic out in the open and could say what it was that they wanted to say.

However, the two extracts have not been presented to demonstrate that all children diagnosed with Asperger's syndrome *will have difficulty* initiating a topic or that the interactional partner will *always* have to take responsibility for ensuring that a topic is eventually produced. The extracts do not even tell us that Jancis and Will's conversations will be replete with intra-turn pauses—there are many instances where Jancis and Will produce well-connected, well-timed talk and where they produce unrecorded, unnoticed, and unanalysed instances of successful topic initiations.

Important point

! What the extracts allow us to 'see' or investigate is what *can happen*
• when hesitancies, pauses, or difficulties arise during a conversation.

So, you can see that these extracts of data

- allow us to go into depth within a single instance of topic initiation and to understand what it might mean for the certain interactional participants;
- allow us to see how much 'work' or scaffolding the conversational partner is doing to enable the conversation to continue and not to stall;

Box 12.2 Activity to reflect

Activity

People engage in interaction all the time and most of this is taken for granted. I would encourage you to be more reflective about your own talk and interaction in order to help you think about your own analysis. Next time when you are talking to someone, listen to how they talk and what happens when they pause in the middle of a turn and ask yourself these questions:

- Do they repair their own talk or does the next speaker say something?
- How long does the pause tend to last before the speaker 'sorts out the problem'?

- put the spotlight on the way in which pauses create interactional vulnerabilities, thus delaying the progressivity of talk.

The analysis adds to previous studies showing how children diagnosed with Asperger's syndrome tend to be less skilled at initiating topics (e.g., Jones & Scwartz, 2009) and that they tend to sit back and allow their conversational partner to take the lead. Wootton (2003), in a broader discussion of the 'pragmatically unusual', similarly showed that young children with autism, Asperger's syndrome, and pragmatic impairment can find it difficult to initiate interaction, as did Hale and Tager-Flusberg (2005), who showed that such children tend not to take the listener's perspective into account, thus affecting their ability to engage in conversations in a sustained or meaningful way.

This is a good point in the chapter to stop and reflect. I would encourage you to think about what you have learned so far by reading the chapter. Try the activity in Box 12.2.

Delayed Progressivity: Inter-turn Pause or Gap Following FPP

Schegloff (1968) demonstrates that one of the defining characteristics of an adjacency pair is the property of conditional relevance: a first action creates a slot or space for an appropriate next action such that even in the absence of that next action, the first action (usually a first turn, FPP) can be perceived as a relevant and noticeable event (Duranti & Goodwin, 1992). The following extract provides an example of how an FPP (first action) makes the SPP (second action) the next relevant action.

Just prior to the beginning of Extract 3, Jancis had rung her friend's (Tiffany) number. However, she had hung up the phone just as her friend's mother (M) was about to answer it. So Extract 3 begins with M answering the phone for the second time.

Extract 3 [Jancis and friend's Mother] (Rendle-Short, 2014)

```
1.  M:  hell:o::.
2.  J:  hello. (.) it's Jancis.
3.  M:  hello Jancis,=did you just call a minute
4.      ago an' then hang up?
5.      (1.6)
6.  J:  y:es:, hh
7.  M:  wh:y did you do that.
8.  →  (4.0)
9.  M:  ↑yoo hoo::,↓
10. J:  he he .hh
11. M:  are ya there?
12. J:  ye::s, hhh
```

As soon as M responds to the greeting and identification sequences in the opening, she asks Jancis if she had rung a few minutes ago (lines 3–4). Jancis pauses 1.6 seconds before replying with a minimal '*y:es:*' (line 6). However, in response to why she did that, Jancis pauses for 4 seconds (line 8).

As with the intra-turn pauses in Extracts 1 and 2, the inter-turn pause or gap also interrupts the progressivity of talk. The difficulty this time is that intersubjectivity has also been compromised. Due to Jancis' non-response to M's '*wh:y did you do that?*', M is not sure what has happened. M treats the delay as a problem of hearing, as demonstrated by her next talk '*yoo hoo*' (line 9), which also functions to check if

Jancis is still on the phone. As it turns out, Jancis' non-response was due to a problem of not knowing what to say—as shown in Extract 4—when she explains to another person how M wanted to know why Jancis had hung up the phone the first time. Jancis says, '*n I couldn't explain it prop'ly.* (line 41).'

Extract 4 [Jancis and other adult]

```
38.        (1.6)
39. J:   uhm she asked .hh why hh .hh hh I-I rang up
40.        and then put the phone do::wn¿ heh heh ugh,
41.        'n I couldn't explain it prop'ly. hh .hh
42.        (5.4)
```

Extracts 3 and 4 demonstrate Jancis' awareness that a response to a question is the next relevant action, with a clear understanding of the rules of turn-taking. However, in this instance, she is unable to provide the required response. As a result, the progressivity of talk is compromised and the mother has to rectify things. So although the conversation continues, there is a vulnerability at that point and Jancis is put in the position of not quite knowing how to proceed.

As before, I would encourage you to reflect at this point and again think about your own conversations. Try the questions in Box 12.3 to help promote reflective thinking about the issues being raised in the analysis so far.

Box 12.3 Reflective activity

Activity

Like before, think about interactions you have had with your own peers. Next time you are talking to someone, focus on what happens if there is a pause after a question (FPP). Ask yourself this important question:
- How long does the pause last before the person who asked the question says something to sort the 'problem' out?

Using CA as a Pedagogic Tool for Analysing Delayed Progressivity

CA can be used as a pedagogic tool for teachers, parents, and children. Children, in particular, are receptive to being taught the principles of interactional sequence organization, including adjacency pairs, FPPs and SPPs, how to open a conversation, and what it means to continue a conversation. They enjoy becoming their own mini-analysts, empowering them to better understand interactional contributions and how such contributions might be responded to. This is particularly important for girls who have been diagnosed with Asperger's syndrome and who might experience difficulty in making friends.[6] Understanding the building blocks of conversations and how interaction works will help them at home, at school, and in the playground.

One way to help children understand the sequential structure of conversations is to show them video vignettes of their own interaction. The aim is to create an open environment for talking about how interaction works and how it unfolds moment by moment. The idea is not to be dismissive or critical of what they have done, but for them to understand how people listen to what has just been said in the immediately preceding turn in order to appropriately respond. How a participant responds tells the speaker how the recipient received the preceding talk.

The following Extract 5 shows an 8-year-old girl playing with her friend of a similar age in the lounge room. This episode was discussed in Rendle-Short et al. (2014). Sarah who had been diagnosed with Asperger's syndrome had invited her friend (Ellie) over to play after school. Both children knew that they were being recorded. The video recording showed a lot of spontaneous play activities.

At the beginning of the extract, Ellie starts a spontaneous dancing activity (line 1). The images show Sarah closely monitoring her friend as she claps in time with the dancing. Even though the extract is very short and might initially seem inconsequential, it exemplifies an instance of interactional difficulty.

Extract 5 [Sarah and Ellie] (Rendle-Short et al., 2014)

```
 1.  El    we start (.) and we do some dancing.
 2.  El    one (.), two (.),
 3.        one two three four,
```

```
 4.        (1.0)
 5.  El    (cla:p.) huh huh.
 6.        (1.0)
 7.  El    (nuh,) (.) ♪ deh, (.) yeh, yeh, yeh
```

```
 8.  El    .hh ↑YEAH.
 9.  El    ♪ uh (.) uh (.) uh uh- (whoa,)
10.  El    (urrgh.)
11.        (1.0)
12.        °that hurt°
```

```
13.  →     (5.0)
14.  Sar   ((burp sound))
15.  Sar   hello prize dum dum¿ eheh,
16.  El    ee::::[:::::ew](groaning)
17.  Sar        [eheheh ]
18.  El    °how cn you keep on doing
19.        (sm) same thing.°
```

```
20.  El    I want to dance with the teddy bear.
```

The affiliative moment that was created at the beginning of the spontaneous dancing activity is lost when Ellie suddenly and without warning ends the activity (line 10). As she stumbles, Ellie says '*urrgh*', before pausing for 1 second and then saying "°*that hurt*°' (line 12). The only indication that Sarah might have understood that the activity is over is when she stops clapping, although she (Sarah) remains standing with flippers ready to continue clapping. She shows no sympathy for Ellie; instead, she looks at Ellie for 5 seconds (line 13) after Ellie has fallen down, clutches her stomach, and says "°*that hurt*°' (line 12).

In Extract 5, by not responding appropriately to the shift from playful to serious, Sarah is disrupting the social order (Maynard, 1985). Sarah gives no support or endorsement for Ellie's transition that marks the end of the dancing activity. When Sarah does respond, she burps (line 14) before saying '*hello prize dum dum*' (line 15), followed by laughter (line 17). These responses are not affiliative; instead they highlight the disruption.[7]

> **Important point**
> ! Due to the improvised nature of spontaneous activities, the children
> • are never quite sure what will happen next.

In a spontaneous activity, there is always the possibility of misunderstanding what is being proposed, what will eventuate, and when the activity (that may only be a few seconds long) will be brought to a close.

Being able to 'make sense of a social system' (Maynard, 1985, p, 220) is not always straightforward, and so a video vignette such as Extract 5 can be used as a teaching tool to help children understand how the social order is created. The child can look at it over and over again. In showing the extract to Sarah, it opens up a space to discuss how difficult it is to engage in spontaneous activities. The idea is not to admonish the child for not responding 'correctly', as per the deficit approach to communication difficulties, but to use examples of naturally occurring interaction as a way of understanding different possible ways of reacting to what had just happened, whether it be the previous talk or action. Different types of transitions or shifts can be used as a point of departure. For example: In Extract 5, Ellie challenged Sarah's inappropriate response when she said °*how can you keep on doing (sm) same thing*° (line 18).

Important point

❗ The important thing for the child to understand is how their response to the previous talk or action might be interpreted.

The structural framework of conversation provides an interactional predictability that can be harnessed for pedagogical purposes. Children can be taught how to respond to things such as FPPs, even when it is in the form of pain or an accident. In this case, Ellie kept on escalating the level of pain and hurt, possibly to achieve an appropriate reaction. In her responses to Sarah's behaviour, Ellie showed that an affiliative response was the most appropriate next action. Sarah's lack of response is an action for which Sarah could be held accountable in talk.

Some conversations have greater predictability than others and some conversational partners can take on more of the scaffolding responsibility than others (Rendle-Short, 2014). But the more that the child with Asperger's syndrome knows and understands how interaction works, the more they themselves will be able to successfully manage their own interaction. Interaction for children who have been diagnosed with Asperger's syndrome is like learning a second language.

Important point

❗ Interaction may not come naturally to children with Asperger's syndrome; they have to actively learn how conversations work, how utterances fit together, how previous talk links to subsequent talk.

Adjacency pairs are the key building blocks that enable them to understand the structural principles of everyday conversations and the pragmatic principles of interaction. The more they know, the more they will

---

Box 12.4 Reflecting on your conversations

Activity

Once more I would encourage you to pause and observe your own conversations. Observe what happens when you respond inappropriately to someone. You might say nothing, laugh at the wrong place, or talk loudly while they are trying to talk.
Be careful about doing this activity if someone has just hurt themselves!

---

become excellent manipulators of interaction, ensuring that intersubjectivity is maintained and that progressivity is not jeopardised. Even more importantly, they will ensure that friendships are not lost.

By this point in the chapter, you should be building a picture of how CA can be used as a pedagogical tool and why it is an important methodological approach for the study of ASD. In continuing your reflective position through the chapter, I would encourage you to do the activity in Box 12.4.

Summary

The chapter has looked at how conversation analysis can be used as a tool by the researcher interested in understanding some of the interactional difficulties experienced by children who have communication difficulties. It has focused on what can happen when a child who has been diagnosed with Asperger's syndrome pauses or is silent for longer than expected. It has examined different scenarios: when the silence is within a turn-at-talk (when initiating a topic); when the silence is following a FPP; or when the silence is in response to a pain announcement. The chapter demonstrates how detailed transcriptions and analysis can show what is actually happening interactionally and how practitioners, or even the children themselves, can better understand what it might mean to be someone who finds social interaction difficult. It also reminds practitioners that children who have been diagnosed with Asperger's syndrome may be very skilled interactionists. On the one hand, they may appear to behave like many of their unaffected friends or peers; however, they may also be vulnerable to pragmatic language challenges, which might mean that at times the interaction does not progress as anticipated.

One of the difficulties in understanding interactional difficulties experienced by children diagnosed with Asperger's syndrome is due to the context-specific nature of interaction. Context is both shaping and shaped by talk (Schegloff, 1992). This means that how a particular child behaves within a particular conversation is not easily generalizable—an utterance may never have been said in a particular way before, with those particular words, or with that particular intonation and other prosodic features. It may never have been said with a pause of that length in that place. Whether an utterance might be considered to be well-formed will depend on the context of the immediately preceding talk. As a result, it is not possible to prescriptively teach a child how to interact or to correctly engage in conversation. It is for this reason that using their own talk (video vignettes) and encouraging them to become mini-analysts provides children with the tools for understanding, and possibly changing, their own social behaviour. Such changes may have a positive effect on how they interact with peers and hopefully enable them to more easily make friends.

This chapter was designed to provide you with an empirical example of conversation analysis with children with ASD, or in this case more accurately, Asperger's syndrome. There have been several practical messages throughout the chapter and these are summarised in Box 12.5.

Box 12.5 Summary of practical highlights

Summary of practical highlights

1. Provides examples of how the conversation analytic methodology can be used to analyse naturally occurring conversations collected from children who have been diagnosed with Asperger's syndrome.
2. Provides examples of what might happen interactionally when a child pauses or is silent for longer than expected.
3. Provides an example of how conversation analysis can be used as a tool for children who have been diagnosed with Asperger's syndrome to become their own mini-analysts.

Appendix

Transcription conventions are based on Gail Jefferson's notation (presented in Atkinson and Heritage (1984) and Jefferson (2004)). The principal notions are as follows:

hello.	falling terminal intonation
hello,	slight rising intonation
hello¿	rising intonation, weaker than that indicated by a question mark
hello?	strongly rising terminal intonation
hel-	talk that is cut off
>hello<	talk is faster than surrounding talk
<hello>	talk is slower than surrounding talk
HELLO	talk is louder than surrounding talk
°hello°	talk is quieter than surrounding talk
he::llo	an extension of a sound or syllable
hello	emphasised talk
(1.0)	timed intervals
(.)	short untimed pause
.hh	audible inhalations
hh	audible exhalations
=	latched talk
[ ]	overlapping talk
( )	transcriber uncertainty

Notes

1. The DSM (American Psychiatric Association, 2000; American Psychiatric Association, 2013) is a manual prepared by psychologists for diagnosis of the full range of people with psychiatric disorders.
2. For discussion of key interactional features of CA, see Sidnell (2010a) or Schegloff (2007).
3. Extracts 1–3 were discussed in Rendle-Short (2014). The paper analyses predictable and less predictable environments and how interactional scaffolding can increase the likelihood that children with Asperger's syndrome

will be able make a contribution to the ongoing interaction within a more predictable environment.

4. Data was collected as part of a study investigating how children diagnosed with Asperger's syndrome interact within the home and school environment. All children are 8 years old; all gave permission for the recording; pseudonyms were used throughout.

5. This interaction highlights the difficulty of obtaining recordings of children with Asperger's syndrome within naturally occurring settings—Will knows that he is being video recorded and so this example starts off with him telling the audience of the recording what it means to have Asperger's syndrome.

6. A recent report from Autism Spectrum Australia states that "[w]omen appeared to be more socially isolated, with only around half (52%) stating that they were happy with their current level of friendships and social activities. In contrast 67% of men reported they were happy with their social life" (p. 3). https://www.autismspectrum.org.au/sites/default/files/ PDFuploads/Girls%20and%20women%20on%20the%20autism%20 spectrum.pdf.

7. Further evidence of the disruption is that the mother reported that the two children were not friends a week later.

References

American Psychiatric Association. (2000). *Diagnostic and statistical manual of mental disorders (DSM-IV-TR)* (4th ed.). Washington, DC: American Psychiatric Association.

American Psychiatric Association. (2013). *Diagnostic and statistical manual of mental disorders (DSM-5)* (5th ed.). Arlington, US: American Psychiatric Publishing.

Attwood, T. (2000). Strategies for improving the social integration of children with Asperger Syndrome. *Autism, 4*, 85–100.

Bauminger, N., & Kasari, C. (2000). Loneliness and friendship in high-functioning children with autism. *Child Development, 71*, 447–456.

Bruner, J. (1983). The acquisition of pragmatic commitments. In R. M. Golinkoff (Ed.), *The transition from prelinguistic to linguistic communication* (pp. 27–42). Hillsdale, NJ: Lawrence Erlbaum.

Cromdal, J. (2009). Childhood and social interaction in everyday life: Introduction to the special issue. *Journal of Pragmatics, 41*, 1473–1476.

Diehl, D. S., Lemerise, E. A., Caverly, S. L., Ramsay, S., & Roberts, J. (1998). Peer relations and school adjustment in ungraded primary children. *Journal of Educational Psychology, 90*, 506–515.

Dunn, J. (2004). *Children's friendships: The beginnings of intimacy.* Malden, MA: Blackwell.

Duranti, A., & Goodwin, C. (1992). *Rethinking context: Language as an interactive phenomenon.* Cambridge: Cambridge University Press.

Erwin, P. (1993). *Friendship and peer relations in children.* New York: John Wiley & Sons.

Fine, J., Bartolucci, G., Szatmari, P., & Ginsberg, G. (1994). Cohesive discourse in pervasive developmental disorders. *Journal of Autism and Developmental Disorders, 24*, 315–329.

Forrester, M. (2008). The emergence of self-repair: A case study of one child during the early preschool years. *Research on Language and Social Interaction, 41*(1), 99–128.

Garvey, C. (1984). *Children's talk.* Cambridge: Cambridge University Press.

Geils, C., & Knoetze, J. (2008). Conversations with Barney: A conversation analysis of interactions with a child with autism. *South African Journal of Psychology, 38*(1), 200–224.

Gillberg, C., & Gillberg, C. (1989). Asperger Syndrome-some epidemiological considerations: A research note. *Journal of Child Psychology and Psychiatry, 30*, 631–638.

Goodwin, C., & Heritage, J. (1990). Conversation Analysis. *Annual Review of Anthropology, 19*, 183–307.

Hale, C., & Tager-Flusberg, H. (2005). Social communication in children with autism: The relationship between theory of mind and discourse development. *Autism, 9*, 157–178.

Heritage, J. (1984). *Garfinkel and Ethnomethodology.* Oxford: Polity Press.

Heritage, J. (1989). Current developments in conversational analysis. In D. Roger & P. Bull (Eds.), *Conversation* (pp. 9–47). Clevedon; Philadelphia: Multilingual Matters.

Heritage, J. (2007). Intersubjectivity and progressivity in references to persons (and places). In N. J. Enfield & T. Stivers (Eds.), *Person reference in Interaction: Linguistic, cultural and social perspectives* (pp. 255–280). Cambridge: Cambridge University Press.

Heritage, J. (2009). Conversation analysis as social theory. In B. S. Turner (Ed.), *The new Blackwell companion to social theory* (pp. 300–320). Oxford: Blackwell.

Jefferson, G. (1989). Preliminary notes on a possible metric which provides for a 'standard maximum' silence of approximately one second in conversation. In D. Roger, P. Roger, & P. Bull (Eds.), *Conversation: An interdisciplinary perspective* (pp. 166–196). Clevedon: Multilingual Matters.

Jefferson, G. (2004). Glossary of transcript symbols with an introduction. In G. H. Lerner (Ed.), *Conversation analysis: Studies from the first generation* (pp. 13–31). Amsterdam; Philadelphia: John Benjamins.

Jones, C. D., & Schwartz, I. S. (2009). When asking questions is not enough: An observational study of social communication differences in high functioning children with autism. *Journal of Autism Developmental Disorders, 39,* 432–443.

Knott, F., Dunlop, A., & Mackay, T. (2006). Living with ASD: How do children and their parents assess their difficulties with social interaction and understanding? *Autism, 10,* 609–617.

Macintosh, K., & Dissanayake, C. (2006). A comparative study of the spontaneous social interactions of children with high-functioning autism and children with Asperger's disorder. *Autism, 10*(2), 199–220.

Margalit, M. (1994). *Loneliness among children with special needs.* New York: Springer Verlag.

Maynard, D. W. (1985). On the functions of social conflict among children. *American Sociological Review, 50*(April), 207–223.

McTear, M. (1985). *Children's conversations.* Oxford: Basil Blackwell.

Minshew, N., Goldstein, G., & Siegel, D. (1995). Speech and language in high-functioning autistic individuals. *Neuropsychology, 9,* 255–261.

Muskett, T., Perkins, M., Clegg, J., & Body, R. (2010). Inflexibility as an interactional phenomenon: Using conversation analysis to re-examine a symptom of autism. *Clinical Linguistics and Phonetics, 24*(1), 1–16.

Rendle-Short, J. (2003). Managing interaction: A conversation analytic approach to the management of interaction by an 8-year-old girl with Asperger's Syndrome. *Issues in Applied Linguistics, 13,* 161–186.

Rendle-Short, J. (2007). Catherine, you're wasting your time: Address terms within the Australian political interview. *Journal of Pragmatics, 39,* 1503–1525.

Rendle-Short, J. (2014). Using conversational structure as an interactional resource: Children with Aspergers Syndrome and their conversational partners. In J. Arciuli & J. Brock (Eds.), *Communication in Autism, trends in language acquisition research series* (pp. 212–238). Amsterdam; Philadelphia: John Benjamin Publishing Company.

Rendle-Short, J., Cobb-Moore, C., & Danby, S. (2014). Aligning in and through interaction: Children getting in and out of spontaneous activity. *Discourse Studies, 16*(6), 792–815.

Sacks, H. (1984). Notes on methodology. In M. Atkinson & J. Heritage (Eds.), *Structures of social action: Studies in conversation analysis* (pp. 2–27). Cambridge: Cambridge University Press.

Sacks, H., Schegloff, E., & Jefferson, G. (1974). A simplest systematics for the organization of turn-taking for conversation. *Language, 50*, 696–735.

Schegloff, E. A. (1968). Sequencing in Conversational Openings. *American Anthropologist, 70*, 1075–1095.

Schegloff, E. A. (1992). Repair after next turn: the last structurally provided defense of intersubjectivity in conversation. *American Journal of Sociology, 97*(5), 1295–1345.

Schegloff, E. A. (2007). *Sequence organization in interaction: A primer in conversation analysis*. Cambridge: Cambridge University Press.

Schegloff, E. A., & Sacks, H. (1973). Opening up closings. *Semiotica, 8*(4), 289–327.

Schieffelin, B. B. (1990). *The give and take of everyday life: Language socialization of Kaluli children*. New York: Cambridge University Press.

Sidnell, J. (2010a). *Conversation analysis: An introduction*. Chichester: Wiley-Blackwell.

Sidnell, J. (2010b). Questioning repeats in the talk of four-year-old children. In H. Gardner & M. Forrester (Eds.), *Analysing interaction in childhood: Insights from conversation analysis* (pp. 103–107). Chichester: Wiley-Blackwell.

Stribling, P., Rae, J., & Dickerson, P. (2009). Using conversational analysis to explore the recurrence of a topic in the talk of a young boy with autism spectrum disorder. *Clinical Linguistics and Phonetics, 23*(8), 555–582.

Tager-Flusberg, H., & Anderson, M. (1991). The development of contingent discourse ability in autistic children. *Journal of Child Psychology and Psychiatry, 32*, 1123–1134.

Wells, G. (1981). *Learning through interaction: The study of language development*. Cambridge: Cambridge University Press.

Wing, L. (1981). Asperger's Syndrome: A clinical account. *Psychological Medicine, 11*, 115–129.

Wootton, A. J. (1994). Object transfer, intersubjectivity and third position repair: Early developmental observations of one child. *Journal of Child Language, 21*, 543–564.

Wootton, A. J. (2003). Interactional contrasts between typically developing children and those with autism, Asperger's Syndrome, and pragmatic impairment. *Issues in Applied Linguistics, 13*, 133–160.

Wootton, A. J. (2006). Children's practices and their connections with "mind". *Discourse Studies, 8*, 191–198.

Wootton, A. J. (2007). A puzzle about please: Repair, increments, and related matters in the speech of a young child. *Research on Language and Social Interaction, 40*(2), 171–198.

Recommended reading

Rendle-Short, J. (2014). Using conversational structure as an interactional resource: Children with Aspergers Syndrome and their conversational partners. In J. Arciuli & J. Brock (Eds.), *Communication in Autism, trends in language acquisition research series* (pp. 212–238). Amsterdam; Philadelphia: John Benjamin Publishing Company.

Johanna Rendle-Short is Associate Dean at the Australian National University. She also lectures in linguistics and applied linguistics. In her research, she utilises the methodology of conversation analysis or talk-in-interaction within a variety of contexts, including language and learning, media studies, and children and adults who are communicatively impaired. She is particularly interested in how children with Asperger's syndrome or high-functioning autism communicate with those around them, both at home and in the school environment.

13

Animating Characters and Experiencing Selves: A Look at Adolescents with Autism Spectrum Disorder Constructing Fictional Storyboards with Typically Developing Peers

Kristen Bottema-Beutel, Laura Sterponi, and Rebecca Louick

Learning Objectives

By the end of this chapter, you will be able to:

- Describe how selves and others can be experienced through narrative activity, including fictionalized selves and others, hypothetical audiences, and actual audiences.
- Understand how the mental lives of characters can be indexed through character action.

K. Bottema-Beutel (✉) • R. Louick
Lynch School of Education, Boston College, Boston, MA, USA

L. Sterponi
Graduate School of Education, University of California, Berkeley, Berkeley, CA, USA

© The Author(s) 2017
M. O'Reilly et al. (eds.), *A Practical Guide to Social Interaction Research in Autism Spectrum Disorders*, The Language of Mental Health, https://doi.org/10.1057/978-1-137-59236-1_13

- Consider the various ways in which narratives can be designed so that they will be understood by an audience, and the forms of perspective taking involved.
- Critique the traditional Theory of Mind approach to intersubjectivity, especially as it relates to narrative and ASD.

Introduction

Our aim in this chapter is to examine forms of perspective taking and understanding of other and self as they emerge in the speech of adolescents with autism spectrum disorder (ASD) engaged in a structured group activity of narrative construction. We shall suggest that the experience of self and others is not only expressed in and through mental state language but also in and through the articulation of characters' courses of action and the enactment of genre conventions. In acknowledging enactive and sociocultural dimensions of perspective taking, we unearth autistic sensibility toward self and alterity previously unrecognized.

Individuals with ASD, including those who develop language, are often said to lack or be impaired in perspective taking and in the capacity to experience and express being a self in relation to other selves in interaction (Charney, 1981; Hobson, 1990). For a long while, the most accredited explanation related this difficulty to a deficit in mind-reading or mentalizing (e.g., Baron-Cohen, 1995). In recent years, however, an alternative account has emerged, grounded in phenomenological perspectives on subjectivity and intersubjectivity. Such an account contends that intersubjective understanding is grounded in embodied practices, which develop much earlier than mind-reading capacities, and are preeminently emotional, sensory-motor, perceptual, and non-conceptual (Hobson, 2010; Gallagher, 2005).

Human beings have an embodied propensity to 'identify with' another person—that is, "to relate to the actions and attitudes of someone else from the other's perspective or stance in such a way that the child assumes or assimilates the other's orientation towards the world, including towards the self" (Hobson & Meyer, 2005, p. 482). When such an embodied propensity to 'identify with' another person is impaired, which seems to be the case among individuals with ASD, self-other relatedness is jeopardized, with additional negative consequences on the development of a sense of self. As Hobson has pointed out, it is not the case that individuals with ASD are completely lacking in these abilities, but rather that they appear not to have the powerful pull towards relations that have the other-person-centred characteristics entailed in identification with the other (Hobson, 1995). In Hobson's own words: "[children with ASD] might be subject to lapses in the propensity to identify with others in role-appropriate ways [...] and they might be prone to experience themselves in a relatively 'uncommitted' manner" (ibid., p. 174). This phenomenological perspective is of relevance for us, not only because it provides a more compelling account of the aetiology of ASD, but also because it invites us to conceptualize self- and other-understanding as rooted in embodied interactional practices, which we navigate and make sense of without necessarily engaging in mind-reading (De Jaegher, 2013; Gallagher & Hutto, 2008).

Important point

> ❗ Another person's attitude, stance, or intention comes into being
> • through his or her embodied actions and expressive
> behaviours.

Grasping the attitude, stance, or intention of another does not require inference or speculation into the other person's mind. What we might reflectively or abstractly call her attitude, stance, or intention is expressed directly in her action and demeanour. Furthermore, others' actions are always situated in socioculturally stipulated practices and so is the subjective experience of those actions. The goals and motives that inform individuals' actions are thus articulated within cultural activities rather than abstractly in terms in presumed inner beliefs and intentions. Consequently, our perception of the other person, as another self, is never of an entity existing outside of a situation, but rather of an agent in a cultural context which shapes and makes intelligible actions, stances, and intentions.

These insights provide the basis and motivation for our investigation: we aim to examine enactive forms of perspective taking and understanding of other and self in ASD, that is, forms of understanding rooted in action and cultural practices. Our investigation focuses on narrative, a chief cultural locus for the construction and apprehension of the psychological life of self and others (e.g., Bruner, 1987; Hutto, 2007).

Context

As part of a counsellors-in-training summer programme, social groups comprising 1–2 participants with ASD and 2–4 typically developing peers were invited to create storyboards using photos taken over the course of the two-week camp session. The photos included several key people:

- The social group members
- Other counsellors-in-training
- Campers
- The camp director
- Camp management staff

Groups were instructed to create a fictional story using a minimum of ten photos. This activity revealed itself as a rich context for the study of perspective taking and the experience of subjectivity and alterity. Multiple selves and multiple others were mobilized in the creation of a storyboard:

- Selves as narrators
- Others as audience of the storyboard
- Selves
- Others as characters in the story

This multiplicity of subjectivities and alterities at stake might be closely related to the specific design of the storyboard activity: participants know that their work will be presented to the camp director and staff, which makes considerations around audience perspective salient. In addition, participants are instructed to use photos of themselves, other camp participants, and staff for the construction of the storyboard, which elicits fictionalization of self and others. We would contend, however, that a sensibility towards audience perspectives and multiplicity of self can augment our interpretation of children with ASD's performance on traditional tasks of fictional narrative constructions (e.g., Barnes & Baron-Cohen, 2012).

> *For example:* In many experimental tasks designed to elicit narrative, the child is required to tell a story on the basis of a strip of images to a co-present examiner. The examiner has direct access to the images and can be easily perceived as familiar with the story.

These contextual and interpersonal features dampen the need to account for audience perspective in the construction of the narrative, but have been disregarded by traditional research as possible influences on the child's narrative performance.

Methodology

Following a methodological approach to the study of ASD developed by linguistic anthropologist Elinor Ochs (Ochs, Kremer-Sadlik, Sirota, & Solomon, 2004), this investigation combines ethnographic and discourse analytic methods. Such an integrated methodology reflects a commitment to investigating social and communicative phenomena as they spontaneously manifest in natural settings. The data corpus included video data from a larger project on social interaction dynamics between adolescents with ASD and their typically developing peers in a summer camp workshop session for counsellors-in-training (also reported in Bottema-Beutel, Louick, & White, 2015; Bottema-Beutel & Smith, 2013; Bottema-Beutel & White, 2016).

The data corpus used in this study included approximately 7 hours of video recording of a certain workshop session in which groups created storyboards using photographs of themselves taken at camp. In all, 19 participants who were typically developing and 9 adolescents with ASD were involved in this study.

The first author attended each workshop session, and assisted Wendy,[1] the workshop facilitator. Video recordings were transcribed according to CA conventions, and all three authors reviewed the full set of transcripts. The first and third authors then identified segments of transcripts where the perspective of the characters, author, narrator, or audience was articulated. Discrepancies in the constitution of this collection of sequences were discussed by all three authors and resolved by consensus. All three authors were involved, independently first and then conjointly, in the analysis. Our discourse analytic approach focused on linguistic, paralinguistic, as well as nonverbal features through which perspectives get articulated.

Two spheres of perspective taking emerged from the analysis: one centred on characters and expressed through articulation of character action, and a second centred on genre, that is, the structural elements of the narrative including the multimodal presentation of the storyboard. Extracts that most clearly illustrate these themes were selected for presentation in this chapter and are given a more fine-grained transcription and analysis in what follows.

Thinking of these two research traditions, contrast the types of data

---

Important point

! 'Theory of Mind' views of ASD focus on the psychological dimensions of social encounters, while discourse and conversation analytic work focuses on the interactional dimensions.

---

relevant to each approach, and how these different data sources will lead to different conclusions.

Forms of Experiencing and Relating to Others

Indexing Mental States in Character Action

A range of research paradigms has indicated that children with ASD may more readily orient to action than to internal mental states, and to a greater extent than matched control groups (e.g., Hobson, 1994; Leslie & Frith, 1988).

> *For example:* When presented with a point-light display representing a person moving their fingers along their arm, they were more likely to describe the display as 'scratching' (an action) than 'itching' (a state). (Moore, Hobson, & Lee, 1997)

In research on narrative construction, findings are mixed as to whether children with ASD tend to use fewer mental state words as compared to their typically developing peers (Beaumont & Newcombe, 2006; Capps, Losh, & Thurber, 2000; Losh & Capps, 2003; Rumpf, Kamp-Becker, Becker, & Kauschke, 2012). Several studies have suggested that the use of emotion words in narrative retelling may be particularly impaired in this group (Kaushcke, van der Beek, & Kamp-Becker, 2016; Siller, Swanson, Serlin, & Teachworth, 2014). In contrast, there does not appear to be any such difficulty in signalling the occurrence of story events (Carnfield, Eigsti, de Marchena, & Fein, 2016; Kauschke, van der Beek, & Kamp-Becker, 2016).

Before you go any further, we invite you to critically reflect. It is helpful when reading the empirical example chapters in this book to critically reflect on what you are learning, and in Box 13.1 we ask you some questions to encourage this.

A propensity or *feel* for action[2] is not entirely at odds with the canonical structure of narratives. At a basic level, narratives are built upon transitions between physical events and mental acts (Ryan, 1985). Importantly, descriptions of physical events feature more prominently in most

---

Box 13.1 Critically reflecting

Activity

From what you have learned from the chapter so far, try to develop some responses in your research diary to the following questions:
• Must a speaker always use mental state terms to indicate that he or she experiences the perspective of others?
• How else might such experiences be indicated?

narratives as compared to mental acts. Literary critic and narratologist Marie-Laure Ryan explains:

> In a typical narrative, the representation of physical events is much more detailed than the description of states and mental acts, the reason being that the latter can be usually inferred from the former, while the converse does not hold true. (Ryan, 1986, p. 322)

Indeed, the participants in our study (both ASD and non-ASD) showed an orientation to action as a critical element in narrative construction. In the extract below, the group is formulating a story about 'blindfolded bandits'. Each scene in the story is represented by a photograph of the group members blindfolded during a previous workshop activity.

Wendy, the group facilitator, has just been introduced as a character into the storyboard. Once the group agrees that a photo of Wendy will represent a story character, they turn their attention to identifying something for Wendy to *do* (lines 1–4). The group displays a pronounced orientation for character action to drive the narrative, and specifically for action that is *tellable* (Norrick, 2007; Ochs & Capps, 2001): to justify Wendy's presence in the story, she must do something of significance worth narrating:

Extract 1a (Group 5)

```
1    Hal:    Wendy has to
2    Rob:    do something.
3    Wendy:  something awesomely awesome.
4    Rob:    something ninja-ish.
```

By focusing on action and 'doing', we do not intend to downplay the role of internal state references in narrative. According to Bamberg (1991), references to emotional states frame story events, signal how events are to be linked together, and provide the valence for how they are to be understood. In so doing, however, explicit references to emotions deviate from the plane of action and temporarily take the audience out of the event structure of the narrative (Ryan, 1986).

On the basis of our analysis, we suggest that characters' inner lives can be indexed within contextualized descriptions of character actions. These action descriptions are embedded in larger courses of action; that is, they are linked to prior action and project upcoming actions, and thereby work to create a landscape of action as well as a landscape of consciousness (Bruner, 1986).

The action descriptions in our data varied in the extent to which they linked to mental states. Some actions directly entailed mental states, while others provided more oblique references. Below, we illustrate the most direct connection between action and mental state, where a specific mental state is *entailed* by the action. This segment in Extract 1b occurs immediately after Extract 1a and focuses on a series of photographs that depict Wendy (the group facilitator) and Zane (a camp administrator). In lines 3 and 5, Randal, who is the group member with ASD, collaborates on this endeavour and describes a series of actions that tie the story events and the characters together:

Extract 1b (Group 5)

```
1    Randal:    then you can say um Zane
2    Hal:       she's definitely gonna come in from the sky.
3    Randal: →  [Zane     ] Zane has (been gettin away) with the
4    Hal        [(in this)]
5    Randal: →  bucket [but Rob's face] scares him away but then
                Wendy comes and catches him
6    ( ):                   [(         )]
7    Kristen:   ((laughs))[You gotta have the]
8    Hal:                  [See Rob takes  ] Rob takes off his
                blindfold and that's what he looks like.
9    ((laughter))
10   Hal:       that's why he wears a blindfold.
```

In line 5, the mental state 'scared' is entailed by the action clause 'scares him away'. To understand how this utterance works in terms of doubling, as both physical and mental action, it is worth deconstructing it a bit more: '*Him*' (a referential pronoun for Zane) is semantically the patient of the verb scared and syntactically the object, while '*Rob's face*' is the agent and subject. An alternative type of utterance, where Zane is the subject and scared is the predicate, as in '*he was scared*', would be a more direct description of a mental state. However, topicalizing the mental state would shift the narrative away from the plane of action and into the plane of consciousness.

Randal's syntactic format serves the narrative purpose of describing a mental event that provides a pretext for the next event, all the while remaining in the narrative frame of action. Randal's full utterance, in lines 3–5, includes transitions between physical events and mental events (Ryan, 1986): Zane attempts to escape with the bucket (setting event) → Rob's face scares him away (physical action entailing mental action) → Wendy pursues and catches him (subsequent event).

In the extract below, we illustrate the next level of linkage between mental state and action, where a specific mental state is *implied* by action, but is not directly stated. LeeAnne and Rob are negotiating a plot point around Viv, the camp director.

Extract 2 (Group 5)

```
1    LeeAnne:   Viv sends Zane out
2    Rob:       ((turns to Randal to explain)) the
3    LeeAnne:   [to find the blind (1.0) folded bandits.       ]
4    Rob:       [picture like after we capture the thing (.)
                that's a that's a                              ]
5    Randal:                            [((nods, looks down))   ]
6    Rob:       success picture.
7    LeeAnne:   she spots them (.) no.
8    Hal:       her trusty (.) [um]
9    LeeAnne:                   [so] Vi-<what should I say>
                Viv (2.0) ((looks to Randall)) °I need help°
                ((breathy, exasperated)) (2.0) what should
                we [say    ]
10   Rob:          [↑help↑]
11   Caleb:     orders that [the bandits        ]
12   Randal: →              [Viv discovered that] (.) the
                trophy is gone
13   Rob:       °↓yeah:[h°
```

	Research hint
❗•	Considering Extract 2, what does the developing story *index* beyond the semantic meaning of each group member's contribution? Think especially about words like 'capture' (line 4), 'trusty' (line 8), and 'orders' (line 11).

LeeAnne and Rob are trying to formulate a reason for Viv to 'send Zane out' (line 1), to go after the blindfolded bandits, when LeeAnne solicits input from Randal. In line 12, Randal supplies the requested motive with 'Viv discovered that the trophy is gone'. He uses the past tense action verb 'discovered'. The semantics of the verb *to discover* implies a change of epistemic state, and within the context of the unfolding discourse this verb construction signals the character's knowledge of a specific course of action, that is, that the trophy was stolen by the blindfolded bandits. As a reason for Viv's pursuit, Viv's discovery does not merely index her knowledge that the trophy is missing but implies that she knows it was stolen (as opposed to being misplaced or borrowed) and that the blindfolded bandits are the culprits (as opposed to some other thief). None of these mental state details are stated directly, but are implied by Viv's action of discovery.

The most rudimentary linkage between character action and mental state occurs when the action *indexes* multiple possible mental states, which are left up to the reader or audience to discern or conjecture. Returning to Randal's construction in Extract 1b, line 3, the action clause 'gettin' away with the bucket' could index a range of mental states. The fictional context in which the action occurs, in this case during a theft, is suggestive of several possible mental states, such as apprehension for being pursued, desire for the stolen item, or contempt for the owner of the bucket. Additionally, the sociocultural dimension of indexicality works to add depth to the character's mental life. 'Gettin' away with' bears an indexical tie to Bandit movie and television shows popular in the 1970s and 1980s, some of which continued to be regularly aired at the time of the data collection. In a well-known children's cartoon *Scooby Doo*, every episode concludes with the same protestation from the unmasked villain (emphasis added): 'and I would have *gotten away with it* too, if it weren't for you meddling kids!'

We do not have evidence in the sequence that Randal's usage of the colloquial construction 'gettin' away with' is performed as a quotation which relies on shared popular knowledge and links the storyboard character to villains that regularly appeared in media such as *Scooby Doo*. However, the fact that at least one participant in the interaction (i.e., Kristen) made such connection attests to the indexical potential of Randal's turn. In Randal's usage, 'getting' away with' links the storyboard character to *Scooby Doo* villains, whose mental lives were enacted in the cartoon by sour faces and harshly spat words.

In summary, we identified utterances that described character actions, but were linked to internal mental states to varying extents (see Table 13.1). It may be the case that individuals with ASD experience a pull toward action to a greater degree than their non-ASD peers, but it is not the case that these actions do not imply mental states. In our view, the preoccupation with whether or not individuals with ASD use, or fail to use, 'mental state terms' or 'internal state language' in their narrative constructions or retellings has been somewhat misguided insofar as it neglects forms of enactive understanding of self and others. The experience of fictional characters as others with inner lives is tightly tied with descriptions of character actions, not solely instantiated in a particular set of terms. To quote Ryan once more:

Table 13.1 Levels in the extent to which character actions link to mental states

Level	Extract from transcript	Description of action/mental state linkage
Specific mental state entailed by action	Rob's face scares him away	*Scares him away* entails the mental state *scared*
Specific mental state implied by action	Viv discovered that the trophy is gone	*Discovered* implies that Viv has the mental state of *knowing the trophy was stolen by the blindfolded bandits*
Multiple possible mental states indexed by action	Zane has been gettin' away with the bucket	*Gettin' away with* does not imply a specific mental state but could index a range of possible mental states, such as knowledge of pursuit, desire for the stolen item, contempt for owner of the bucket, etc.

[s]ince mental acts are triggered by physical facts, the various spheres of the mental domains form a system of satellites revolving around the actual world of the narrative universe. (Ryan, 1986, p. 320)

In other words, the depiction of actions and events in a narrative, and not the direct explication of mental activity, is the essential component of a fictional world, as mental domains are grounded in, and at times entailed by, physical events.

Accounting for Audience

In addition to experiencing characters as others, the audience of a narrative can also be experienced as 'an' other. The audience is a certain other whose understanding of the narrative as such can be considered critical to the narrative's success. This brings to bear phenomena similar to that of *recipient design* that informs much of CA research (e.g., Goodwin & Heritage, 1990). However, unlike in face-to-face interaction, the audience is not co-present in the production of the storyboard narrative. Because of this, there are fewer interactional scaffolds to ensure mutual understanding.

> *For example:* There are no raised eyebrows, interjections, or pauses, which can display troubles in understanding and trigger repair in face-to-face interaction.

This leaves at least two related, but somewhat distinct, strategies available for shaping a narrative in such a way that it will be recognizable to an audience:

1. Anticipating a specific audience
2. Relying on genre

Anticipating the Audience: In anticipating the audience, an author/narrator attempts to project and conform to his/her expectations about the recipients of the narrative. This strategy is most closely related to traditional theories regarding mindreading, and is particularly relevant here because the other in question is *not* co-present. At the same time, the storyboard activity we examined is interesting in that the participants could anticipate both a hypothetical audience and an actual audience. The former included anyone who would pass by the storyboard in the near or distant future, while the latter included Viv, the camp director, as participants were informed early on that the final product would be presented to Viv.

In the following extract, we observe an appeal to the audience as the group constructs a story about terrorists. Sayed, an adolescent with ASD, halts story production to assert that portraying the main characters as terrorists '*isn't really camp appropriate*' (line 1).

Extract 3 (Group 4)

```
1    Sayed: → ((to Wendy)) I think the idea of us being
                terrorists
                isn't really camp appropriate so (    )
2    ((laughter))
3    Lexi:    hey you still have uh Tommy's nametag.
4    Sayed:   yeah.
5    Lexi:    that's so cool mine got lost.
6    Will:    okay and you don't think we should be terrorists
7    Sayed:   [well]
8    Kristen: [it  ] it doesn't actually have to be totally
                camp appropriate, cause it's not like we're
                going to show these to the campers.
9    Sayed:   ((nods))
```

There are three points to be made about Sayed's utterance in line 1 that illustrate the multiple and intersecting selves and others that can be brought into being by the storyboard activity. First, Sayed's concern with *appropriateness* encodes a contextual and relational assessment, as actions and utterances are inappropriate based on situated criteria and insofar as they are taken up in certain ways by others. Sayed is therefore taking into account the audience as 'an' other who may have a perspective about their storyboard. Second, in the experience of the audience as 'an' other, there is a reciprocal experience of the self-as-author/narrator, a self to be evaluated by the hypothetical or actual audience. Given that the actual audience planned for the storyboard is Viv, Sayed's employer, Sayed enacts yet another self, that is, self-as-employee. Through voicing his concerns, Sayed experiences the integrity of his multiple selves as at risk. His author-self may be judged incapable of creating a 'good' story that is understood by others, and his counsellor-in-training self may be judged as unworthy of promotion or even retention. His apprehension in creating a narrative about an 'inappropriate' topic reflects an orientation to the power structure at camp, as well as his own and Viv's relational position within it. Viv's assessment of the topic as unsuitable would be consequential for the group members, possibly bearing on their status as employees.

It is noteworthy that Sayed's groupmates do not voice similar apprehension. Across the social groups, this was a recurring phenomenon. One interpretation is that, even while experiencing a self in relation to 'an' other, for many individuals with ASD the other is enacted on quite general terms. While it is true that Viv is 'the boss', the context in which the narrative will be presented to her will be at a private meeting without the campers. These contextual details mean (as Kristen explains in line 8) that their official roles can be relaxed, and Sayed will not be held to the same expectations as when he is overseeing campers. Sayed may less readily orient to these contextual details that modify explicitly stated norms.

There is one final self to mention: Sayed's use of 'us' to describe the terrorist story characters indexes his experience of a fictional self. Since the photographs depict the group members, the characters are imaginary versions of each group member. Sayed may feel tension in suspending his actual self to become a terrorist fictional self, a salient metaphor for evil.

Relying on Genre: The second strategy for constructing a recognizable narrative, which we identified in our data, consisted in drawing upon and enacting sociocultural knowledge about genre conventions. Genres can include broad types such as prose or poetry, or subtypes such as science fiction, romance, action/adventure, and drama among others. This strategy allows the author to circumvent anticipating general or specific expectations of the audience, and instead draw upon fidelity criteria for whichever genre is to be enacted. Relying on genre requirements, as opposed to anticipating a specific audience's expectations, appeared to be a more pervasive strategy for our participants, at least in the sense that it was more readily identifiable in group discourse. In the extract below, Sayed and Arthur, both participants with ASD, make critiques about whether or not the story elements sufficiently adhere to genre conventions. Sayed voices certain concerns about the fidelity of the characters to their respective story types (lines 1, 5, 10, 19). After several events have been featured in which terrorists are the central characters, they are subsequently referred to as 'evil villains from Pluto'. Sayed attempts to sort out the discrepant character identities, insisting that this distinction must be made before the story construction can continue.

Extract 4 (Group 4)

```
1.    Sayed:      [what are we are we                        ]
2.    Arthur:     [people are winging it. (the terrorists)]
3.    Sayed: →    are we five evil are we five
4.    Arthur:     [who's terrorizing who?]
5.    Sayed:      [evil villains or      ]
6.    Will:       we're terrorizing everybody.
7.    Wendy:      ((laughs))
8.    Lexi:       arright I said unaware [(              )]
9.    Wendy:                      [what did you say Sayed?]
10.   Sayed: →    [are we five evil villains from Pluto or ()]
11.   Will:       [(yes)                        unaware]
12.   ( ):          [(                              )]
13.   Will:       unaware unware [of the evil plot]-
14.   Wendy:                  [I'm gonna ask   ]
15.   Will:       going (on next door)
16.   Lexi:       (    )
17.   Wendy:      hey Sayed has a good question.
18.   ( ):            yeah?
19.   Sayed: →    are we are we five evil villains from Pluto or
                  or are we terrorists.
20.   Will:       we are (        ) from Pluto.
21.   Kristen:    terror villains from Pluto.
22.   Will:       we're the [terror villains from Pluto].
23.   Wendy:                [terror villains       ] that
                  should be your title.
24.   Sayed:      okay.
25.   Kristen:    [is that acceptable Sayed?         ]
26.   Will:       [() terror villains from Pluto.    ] in the
                  birthday room next door.
27.   (2.0)
```

```
28.    Lexi:     just (yards) away.
29.    (5.0)
30.    ():       [wait]
31.    Lexi:     [I'm ] writing this so sloppily. (1.0) okay um
32.    (5.0)
33.    Lexi:     okay what's next
```

Research hint

! Considering Extract 4, how is 'genre' relevant to the story
. production? Which story genres are being enacted by the
      group members, and how is this made evident by certain
      utterances?

Evil villains from Pluto and terrorists are characters that belong to different genres (roughly science fiction and action/adventure, respectively), which encode different conventions and expectations for character actions, and the inner lives that would be entailed by such actions. Sayed's attempts to clarify the identity category of the characters are not taken up until Wendy points out that Sayed's questions are 'good', marking them as worthy of response (line 17). This suggests that the non-ASD group members are not particularly concerned about the multiple and divergent ways in which the characters are depicted.

Along these lines, Kristen and Will advocate hybridizing the characters to represent multiple genres, as 'Terror villains from Pluto'. For them, genre requirements are flexible and can be blended or shirked entirely. Indeed, doing so is a potential source of humour. In line 26, Will further explicates genre violations, pointing out that many of the photos depict the 'terror villains from Pluto' in the 'birthday room'. This was a room on camp grounds where most workshop sessions were held (including the current session where the storyboards were being created). The room was small, and decorated with brightly painted balloons and hand prints of young children who had previously reserved the room for birthday parties— clearly not a setting where one would expect to encounter alien terrorists.

Other participants with ASD expressed concerns about adherence to genre conventions that were more general (also see Bottema-Beutel & White, 2016 for a discussion of orientation to rules for narrative). In the extract below, Arthur expresses dissatisfaction with the depiction of the story and the narrative that is being proposed to go along with the pictures. The extract begins with Lexi interpreting the narrative content of the first photograph:

Extract 5 (Group 4)

```
1.  Lexi:      all the campers were showing up for their
                first day at Blue Camp. [um ]
2.  Arthur:                      [but] how do we show
                that though. in the first [part of it   ]
3.  Lexi:                                  [welcome to   ]
                (parents and)staff appreciation day.
4.  Arthur: →  but wha- but this this if we're going this
                way we need a scene that will like convey
                that (blatantly) or write it and it can't be
                random.
```

Arthur appears concerned that the pictures do not sufficiently represent the story. For him, conveying connections between events need to be more explicit or 'blatant' and not 'random'. In traditional narratives, coherence is a salient aspect, so that the temporal sequence of the actual events can be delineated even if events are not presented in order. However, non-traditional narratives intentionally defy this rule, and prioritize the impression created by the narrative precisely by obscuring logical and temporal coherence (James Joyce's *Finnegan's Wake* is a most notable example). In the extract above, we see tension in the participants' orientation toward faithfulness to genre, with Arthur showing concern that their construction does not follow a more standard approach.

Anticipating the audience and relying on genre do overlap, as appeals to audience expectations entail presuppositions about which genre conventions are mutually known, and vice versa. Indeed, Arthur's appeals to narrative conventions are not completely separated from an experience of the audience. His turns in lines 2 and 4 include the words 'show' and 'convey', indexing the eventual audience to whom the storyboard will be shown and the narrative will be delivered. However, the psychological task of the author may differ depending on whether he orients primarily to the audience's perspective, or orients primarily to his own understanding

---

Box 13.2 Research tips

Research tips

1. While detailed descriptions of transcripts are an important part of discourse and conversation analytic work, this is just the beginning. After you have a detailed sense of the transcript, turn your attention toward identifying the interactional or discursive phenomena that are represented in the data.
2. Consider the *position* and *composition* of utterances. What is the sequential context of the utterance? What is the format of turn, considering syntactical, lexical, and prosodic features?
3. Look beyond the content of the talk; look to the *action* and *indexical* dimensions. What course of action is the utterance in service of, which may or may not be lexicalized? What indexical meanings does the utterance entail?
4. A good analyst will be able to explain how the analysis offers a new understanding of a phenomenon, the additional questions prompted by the research, and previous understandings that will need to be revised in light of the findings.

---

of socioculturally recognized genre conventions. In our data, reliance on and deployment of genre conventions afforded adolescents with ASD a good deal of competence in narrative construction. On the other hand, experiencing and projecting the other as a *particular* individual, with his/ her own specific, perhaps idiosyncratic, expectations that may defy sociocultural norms appears to be a more difficult task for individuals with ASD, who adhere more strictly to norms as anchors for intersubjectivity (Bottema-Beutel & White, 2016).

We have given you a lot of information in this chapter based on our own empirical analysis. In doing your own project, we provide you with some practical tips in Box 13.2.

Summary

Our analysis has discerned the ways in which the participants with ASD experienced self and others through the creation of a storyboard. We identified two main spheres within which adolescents with ASD experienced and related to others: the sphere of character action and the sphere of audience reception. We demonstrated that exclusively focusing on mental state language to investigate individuals with ASD's understanding of self and others is problematic insofar as it fails to consider enactive forms of self-other relatedness, towards which individuals with ASD exhibit a proclivity. The inner lives of fictional characters can be woven, to varying degrees of specificity, through character action. We argued that action descriptions are displays of enactive understanding of characters' stances and motives. We identified three levels of linkage between action and mental states in our data, which vary in degrees of explicitness in the action-mental state connection, while all three display an enactive understanding of others.

In addition, we have shown that in the creation of a storyboard, participants with ASD take into account the audience of their fictional narrative. The audience, whose expectations, knowledge, and taste can determine intelligibility and appreciation of the narrative, is a form of alterity that has remained largely unrecognized in research on narratives in ASD. Our analysis points to the relevance of the author/narrator and audience relationship in narrative construction, a form of self-other relatedness with which the adolescents with ASD in our study demonstrated an ability to engage. Our findings indicate that individuals with ASD have a propensity to mobilize genre conventions for securing intelligibility and appreciation of their storyboard by its audience.

Drawing from previous discourse analytic research on ASD, specifically the work of Ochs and associates (Ochs et al., 2004), we suggest that reliance on genre conventions is a form of sociocultural perspective taking. Ochs and colleagues delineated two distinct components of perspective taking, the interpersonal and the sociocultural. They contended that perspective taking encompasses "more than interpersonal inferencing about another's mental states, as codified in the concept of 'theory of mind'" (Ochs et al., 2004). In other words, perspective taking does not only require an understanding of the other's intentions, beliefs, and feelings, which they labelled interpersonal perspective taking, but also the ability to take into account culturally organized expectations regarding roles, stances, and conducts, which they referred to as sociocultural perspective taking.

Finally, taken together, our analyses suggest that it is not the experience of self or other *per se* that is at risk in individuals with ASD, but the flexibility with which self and other are brought into being. Too rigid adherence to explicit sociocultural conventions (such as the power hierarchy in an employee-employer context, or expectations around genre) may result in enactments of the other that are not aligned with the interlocutors' enactment of similar others. The forms of rigidity that we illustrate in this chapter may be a culmination of past experiences in interaction; individuals with ASD may more readily anticipate threats to intersubjectivity that could arise when conventions are *not* strictly adhered to, especially in interactions with relatively unfamiliar others. While strict adherence to genre conventions may present tension in the co-construction of a fictional universe, non-adherence may be even more risky for individuals with ASD who may have difficulty navigating a social world without the scaffolding provided by explicit norms.

In summary, it is not only mental state language into which we should look for insights about a sense of self and relatedness displayed by individuals with ASD. Autistic understanding of self and others is enactive and sociocultural; it is rooted in action and convention. It is within the manoeuvring of their characters and the articulation of genre-driven plots that autistic subjectivity emerges. And it is a sense of self that is full of investment and individuality, even if expressed in somewhat rigid formats, which wards off villains from Pluto and other uniquely imagined forms of subjectivity.

We conclude with a final summary of the practical messages from our chapter in Box 13.3.

Box 13.3 Practical messages from the chapter

Summary of practical highlights

1. This chapter investigates perspective taking and self-other relatedness in the interactions of a group of teenagers, some of whom have a diagnosis of ASD, as they created a storyboard. Joint construction of narrative is a rich locus for experiencing multiple others and selves.
2. Participants with ASD indexed the inner lives of characters, in varying degrees, by describing character actions.
3. Participants with ASD showed an awareness of audience in two ways: by anticipating audience expectations and by appealing to genre conventions.
4. Enacting genre conventions is a form of sociocultural perspective taking.

Notes

1. With the exception of Kristen, all names are pseudonyms.
2. We draw here from Bourdieu's (1990) discussion of a *feel for the game*, a concept whose relationship to the study of ASD has been discussed at length by Ochs et al. (2004).

References

Bamberg, M. (1991). Narrative activity as perspective taking: The role of emotionals, negations, and voice in the construction of the story realm. *Journal of Cognitive Psychotherapy: An International Quarterly, 5*(4), 275–290.

Barnes, J. L., & Baron-Cohen, S. (2012). The big picture: Storytelling ability in adults with autism spectrum conditions. *Journal of Autism and Developmental Disorders, 42*(8), 1557–1565.

Baron-Cohen, S. (1995). *Mindblindness: An essay on autism and theory of mind.* Cambridge, MA: MIT Press.

Beaumont, R., & Newcombe, P. (2006). Theory of mind and central coherence in adults with high-functioning autism or Asperger syndrome. *Autism, 10,* 365–382.

Bottema-Beutel, K., Louick, R., & White, R. (2015). Repetition, response mobilization, and face: Analysis of group interactions with a 19-year-old with Asperger syndrome. *Journal of Communication Disorders, 58,* 179–193.

Bottema-Beutel, K., & Smith, N. (2013). The interactional construction of identity: An adolescent with autism in interaction with peers. *Linguistics and Education, 24*(2), 197–214.

Bottema-Beutel, K., & White, R. (2016). By the book: An analysis of adolescents with autism spectrum condition co-constructing fictional narratives with peers. *Journal of Autism and Developmental Disorders, 46*(2), 361–377.

Bruner, J. (1986). *Actual minds, possible worlds.* Cambridge, MA: Harvard University Press.

Bruner, J. (1987). Life as narrative. *Social Research, 54,* 11–32.

Capps, L., Losh, M., & Thurber, C. (2000). "The frog ate the bug and made his mouth sad": Narrative competence in children with autism. *Journal of Abnormal Child Psychology, 28,* 193–204.

Carnfield, A. R., Eigsti, I., de Marchena, A., & Fein, D. (2016). Story goodness in adolescents with autism spectrum disorder (ASD) and optimal outcomes from ASD. *Journal of Speech, Language, and Hearing Research, 59,* 533–545.

Charney, R. (1981). Pronoun errors in autistic children: Support for a social explanation. *British Journal of Disorders of Communication, 15*, 39–43.

De Jaegher, H. (2013). Embodiment and sense-making in autism. *Frontiers in Integrative Neuroscience, 7*, 1–19.

Gallagher, S. (2005). *How the body shapes the mind*. New York: Oxford University Press.

Gallagher, S., & Hutto, D. (2008). Understanding others through primary interaction and narrative practice. In J. Zlatev, T. Racine, C. Sinha, & E. Itkonen (Eds.), *The shared mind: Perspectives on intersubjectivity* (pp. 17–38). Amsterdam: John Benjamins Publishing Company.

Goodwin, C., & Heritage, J. (1990). Conversation analysis. *Annual Review of Anthropology, 19*, 283–307.

Hobson, R. P. (1990). On the origins of self and the case of autism. *Development and Psychopathology, 2*, 163–181.

Hobson, R. P. (1994). Perceiving attitudes, conceiving minds. In C. Lewis & P. Mitchell (Eds.), *Origins of an understanding of mind* (pp. 71–93). Hillsdale, NJ: Erlbaum.

Hobson, R. P. (1995). *Autism and the development of mind*. London: Psychology Press.

Hobson, R. P. (2010). Explaining autism. *Autism, 14*(5), 391–407.

Hobson, R. P., & Meyer, J. A. (2005). Foundations for self and other: A study in autism. *Developmental science, 8*(6), 481–491.

Hutto, D. D. (2007). Narrative and understanding persons. *Royal Institute of Philosophy Supplement, 60*, 1–16.

Kauschke, C., van der Beek, B., & Kamp-Becker, I. (2016). Narratives of girls and boys with autism spectrum disorders: Gender differences in narrative competence and internal state language. *Journal of Autism and Developmental Disorders, 46*, 840–852.

Leslie, A. M., & Frith, U. (1988). Autistic children's understanding of seeing, knowing and believing. *British Journal of Developmental Psychology, 6*, 15–324.

Losh, M., & Capps, L. (2003). Narrative ability in high-functioning children with autism or Asperger's syndrome. *Journal of Autism and Developmental Disorders, 33*, 239–251.

Moore, D. G., Hobson, R. P., & Lee, A. (1997). Components of person perception: An investigation with autistic, non-autistic retarded and typically developing children and adolescents. *British Journal of Developmental Psychology, 15*, 401–423.

Norrick, N. R. (2007). Conversational storytelling. In D. Herman (Ed.), *The Cambridge companion to narrative* (pp. 127–141). Cambridge: Cambridge University Press.

Ochs, E., & Capps, L. (2001). *Living narrative: Creating lives in everyday story-telling*. Cambridge, MA: Harvard University Press.

Ochs, E., Kremer-Sadlik, T., Sirota, K. G., & Solomon, O. (2004). Autism and the social world: An anthropological perspective. *Discourse studies, 6*(2), 147–183.

Rumpf, A.-L., Kamp-Becker, I., Becker, K., & Kauschke, C. (2012). Narrative competence and internal state language of children with Asperger Syndrome and ADHD. *Research in Developmental Disabilities, 33*(5), 1395–1407.

Ryan, M. (1985). The modal structure of narrative universes. *Poetics Today, 6*(4), 717–755.

Ryan, M. (1986). Embedded narratives and tellability. *Narrative Poetics, 20*(3), 319–340.

Siller, M., Swanson, M. R., Serlin, G., & Teachworth, A. G. (2014). Internal state language in the storybook narratives of children with and without autism spectrum disorder: Investigating relations to theory of mind abilities. *Research in Autism Spectrum Disorders, 8*(5), 589–596.

Recommended Reading

Herman, D. (Ed.). (2007). *The Cambridge companion to narrative*. Cambridge: Cambridge University Press.

Hobson, R. P. (1995). *Autism and the development of mind*. East Sussex: Lawrence Erlbaum Associates.

Ochs, E., & Capps, L. (2001). *Living narrative: Creating lives in everyday story-telling*. Cambridge, MA: Harvard University Press.

Ochs, E., Kremer-Sadlik, T., Sirota, K. G., & Solomon, O. (2004). Autism and the social world: An anthropological perspective. *Discourse studies, 6*(2), 147–183.

Kristen Bottema-Beutel is Assistant Professor of Special Education in the Lynch School of Education at Boston College. Her research focuses on social interaction dynamics, language development, and classroom-based supports for students with autism spectrum disorder. Her work encompasses young children through adolescents, and who have a range of support needs.

Laura Sterponi is Associate Professor of Language, Literacy, and Culture in the Graduate School of Education at the University of California—Berkeley.

Merging her training in developmental psychology (Ph.D., 2002) and applied linguistics (Ph.D., 2004), she has developed a research programme that is centrally concerned with the role of language and literacy practices in children's development and education. Her studies have examined communicative practices in both typical and neurodiverse populations (specifically children with autism).

Rebecca Louick is currently a doctoral student at Boston College. As of fall 2017, she will be Assistant Professor of Special Education at St. John's University, the US. Her research focuses on adolescents with high-incidence disabilities, specifically in two key areas: communication and academic motivation. Prior to her doctoral studies, Rebecca spent eight years as a teacher of middle- and high-school students with learning disabilities.

Glossary

Adjacency pair A two-part exchange in which the second utterance is functionally dependent on the first, as exhibited in conventional greetings, invitations, and requests. The first utterance is called the first-pair part (FPP), or the first turn. The second or responding utterance is called the second-pair part (SPP), or the second turn.

Affiliation According with the demonstrated emotional stance of the speaker of a prior turn.

Alignment According with the expected next sequential turn, for example, following a question with an answer

Aphasia Refers to impairments with producing and/or understanding spoken language arising from damage to the brain.

Autism spectrum disorder ASD is a neurodevelopmental condition which is lifelong and causes impairments in communication, rigidity of thinking, and cognitive ability.

Collocate To utter a word or phrase alongside or in close proximity to another in a 'frozen' or semi formulaic way.

Communicative impairment This refers to limitations or difficulties in communication and would include, for example, speaking very little, and/or drawing on a very limited vocabulary.

Concrete competence Problem-solving strategies that are based on lived or concrete experiences.

© The Author(s) 2017
M. O'Reilly et al. (eds.), *A Practical Guide to Social Interaction Research in Autism Spectrum Disorders*, The Language of Mental Health,
https://doi.org/10.1057/978-1-137-59236-1

Conversation analysis This is an approach to analysing interactions that pays particular attention to the interactional work that words, body movement, gaze, and gesture are doing by considering where they are positioned in a sequence of interaction.

Critical discourse analysis An umbrella term that refers to a collection of discourse analytic perspectives that emerged in the early 1990s, which attends generally to criticality, power, and ideology, among other constructs. It often attends to the way in which power is produced in and through discourses and structures.

Critical discursive psychology This is an approach to analysing discourse that considers both the individual's psychological representation in how they talk and how they are politically positioned.

Deconstructionism Typically associated with the work of Derrida, it is a theoretical position that challenges the assumptions generally held about certainty and truth arguing that words only can refer to other words, and thus attempts to show how statements about text subvert their own meaning.

Discursive psychology A discourse analytic approach developed by Edwards and Potter (1992), which focused on the psychological language people use to describe mental states to perform a social action. This is a form of analysis of the details of interaction and how these are related to psychological concepts and ideas such as emotions and thoughts.

Discursive repertoires Frequently used phrases or explanations that a speaker might use to explain something.

Echolalia Refers to repeated phrases, words, or parts of words and is often understood as symptomatic of autistic spectrum disorders.

Enactivism A view of social interaction that rejects an appeal to inner mental states as the primary mediator of intersubjectivity. Rather, social actions are directly coordinated with others' social actions. Regularities in face-to-face interaction are not contingent on knowledge of preexisting social 'rules' that reside in the minds of interaction partners but on an outward orientation to the sequence structure of interaction, and participation in one another's sense-making activities. For further reading on enactivism, see Di Paolo and De Jaegher (2007), and for the application of this concept to ASD, see Klin, Jones, Schultz, and Volkmar (2003).

Epistemic resources Displays that express speakers' subjective assessment of the strength of reliability or certainty regarding the truth value of the information in their propositions.

Epistemology Relates to the theory of knowledge and what can be known, and by what means.

Eye gaze Refers to where one or other of the participants are gazing, often a concern within conversation analytic work where particular attention is placed on where, in the interactional sequence, specific gaze behaviour is located.

First pair part (FPP) A turn that initiates an action.

Forensic patient In the UK, this refers to a patient detained under the Mental Health Act (Department of Health, 2007).

Footing Refers to the way in which participants negotiate their relationships within a frame.

Forensic ward A ward in a secure psychiatric hospital. In the UK, secure psychiatric hospitals contain patients detained under sections of the Mental Health Act.

Foucauldian discourse analysis An approach to discourse analysis that studies historically based ideologies that are assumed to underpin dominant discourses.

Frame A structure of expectations which helps people to compartmentalise and recognise regularly encountered types of interaction in the world, for example, institutional discourse, sports, commentary, and so on.

Gaze avoidance This refers to those behaviours which reduce the chance of eye contact with others, such as gazing away from the other or at places other than their eye region. Gaze avoidance is often understood to be symptomatic of autistic spectrum disorders.

Genre A constellation of formal features and structures that functions as conventionalized framework for the production and interpretation of discourse, oral as well as written. For further reading, see Briggs and Bauman (1992) and Hanks (1997).

Indexicality A pervasive property of language that relates linguistic forms to the contexts in which they are produced. In addition to demonstratives, deictic adverbs, and pronouns, many other features of language bear relationship to dimensions of context. For further reading on indexicality, see Levinson (1983), and for an in-depth examination of the relationship of this concept to interaction in ASD, see Ochs, Kremer-Sadlik, Sirota, and Solomon (2004).

Interactants Those who are involved in a given interaction, by communicating or engaging in other shared behaviours.

Interactional action This refers to the things that might be accomplished by certain behaviours that are relevant to an interaction, for example the behaviour of gazing up at someone who is talking to you can demonstrate that you are attending to what they are saying.

Interactional sequence This refers to any period of time across which an interaction takes place. The concept is especially important for conversation analysis as any specific behaviour (such as gaze) is considered in terms where, in the sequence of interaction, it takes place.

Interactional sociolinguistics An approach to the study of discourse which analyses power within linguistic practices.

Interpretative phenomenological analysis A method of analysing data where the researcher tries to go beyond what their participants say and understand their experiences.

Intersubjectivity Coordinating or adapting one's subjectivity with other's subjectivity within interaction. A capacity that is embodied prior to becoming reflexive, that is, a theory of mind (Trevarthen, 1979). For further reading, see Duranti (2010).

Inter-turn pause or gap A pause that occurs between syntactic units at a possible transition relevance place.

Intra-turn pause A pause that occurs within a speaker's turn, but not at a possible transition relevance place.

Low functioning This term is sometimes used to distinguish people who are considered to be at a different point on the 'autistic spectrum' from those who are deemed 'high functioning'. The judgement is problematic, not least because there are several different criteria that may be employed. 'Low functioning' people with an ASD typically communicate less and are judged to have a reduced intellectual capacity compared with those who are 'high functioning'.

Minimal response A turn sequential to a question composed of vocal material which indicates little beyond acknowledgment of the prior turn.

Neurodevelopmental disorder These are a group of disorders where the brain has developed in a particular way that fundamentally changes the way the brain reacts to the outside world. In turn, this affects particular behaviours and emotions in the person.

Nursing assistant A non-qualified practitioner who works with patients under the supervision of qualified staff.

Ontology The underpinning theoretical position of a methodological approach. An ontological position is a position on the existence of reality.

Orthographic transcript A transcript that reflects what can be heard in the interviews, but does not include detailed prosodic transcription.

Paralinguistic Refers to the features which accompany words in a message to convey non-linguistic information, for example, tone, volume, rhythm, and so forth.

Post structuralism A label often used to characterise French philosophers and others who generated critiques of structuralism and also argued that for individuals to understand objects, they should study both the object and the systems of knowledge that produce the object—among other beliefs.

Recipient design The process in which speakers structure their talk in a way that is sensitive to the particular others involved in the social encounter. For further reading, see Sacks, Schegloff, and Jefferson (1974).

Register A variant of language, including both lexical and syntactic choices, associated and identified with a particular context, for example, scientific German, talk directed at pets.

Repair A correction of self or other in an interaction to clarify a misunderstanding. This refers to the set of practices whereby interlocutors attend to possible trouble in speaking, hearing, or understanding in conversation. For further reading, see Schegloff, Jefferson, and Sacks (1977) and Drew (1997).

Social constructionism This is a theoretical position positing that our understanding of the world is jointly constructed and forms the basis for a shared reality.

Social constructivism This is a theoretical position that posits that knowledge is constructed through interaction with others, which emphasises the learning that takes place through interaction.

Stereotypy This refers to repetitive motor movements often understood as being symptomatic of an underlying pathology and particularly associated with autistic spectrum disorders.

Subject positions Identities found in discourse, for example, Autism as a biological phenomenon that means a person might always be socially awkward, or an Autism position that suggests people can have high levels of social ability, they just do so differently.

Tellability The 'newsworthiness' of a story, as such a fitness criterion for narratives in everyday conversations (Sacks, 1992). For further reading on tellability and narrative in ASD, see Solomon (2004).

Theory of mind This is the appreciation of the views and perspectives of others, the ability to empathise.

Therapeutic alliance The collaborative relationship between patient and therapist which enables change.

Threshold concepts Concepts in learning a discipline that, once understood, change a student's way of thinking about a topic.

Turn construction unit This is a component of a speaker's turn after which the turn may be construed as complete.

References Referred to in the Glossary

Briggs, C., & Bauman, R. (1992). Genre, intertextuality, and social power. *Journal of Linguistic Anthropology, 2*(2), 131–172.

De Jaegher, H., & Di Paulo, E. (2007). Participatory sense-making. *Phenomenology and Cognitive Science, 6*, 485–507.

Department of Health. (2007). *Best practice in managing risk: Principles and evidence for best practice in the assessment and management of risk to self and others in mental health services.* London: Department of Health.

Drew, P. (1997). 'Open' class repair initiators in response to sequential sources of troubles in conversation. *Journal of Pragmatics, 28*, 69–101.

Duranti, A. (2010). Husserl, intersubjectivity and anthropology. *Anthropological Theory, 10*(1), 1–20.

Edwards, D., & Potter, J. (1992). *Discursive psychology.* London: Sage.

Hanks, W. (1997). Discourse genres in a theory of practice. *American Ethnologist, 14*(4), 668–692.

Klin, A., Jones, W., Schultz, R., & Volkmar, F. (2003). The enactive mind, or from actions to cognition: Lessons from autism. *Philosophical Transactions of the Royal Society of London B, 358*, 345–360.

Levinson, S. C. (1983). *Pragmatics.* Cambridge: Cambridge University Press.

Ochs, E., Kremer-Sadlik, T., Sirota, K. G., & Solomon, O. (2004). Autism and the social world: An anthropological perspective. *Discourse Studies, 6*(2), 147–182.

Sacks, H. (1992). *Lectures on conversation.* Oxford: Blackwell.

Sacks, H., Schegloff, E., & Jefferson, G. (1974). A simplest systematics for the organization of turn-taking for conversation. *Language, 50*, 696–735.

Schegloff, E., Jefferson, G., & Sacks, H. (1977). The preference for self-correction in the organisation of repair in conversation. *Language, 53*, 361–382.

Solomon, O. (2004). Narrative introductions: Discourse competence of children with autism spectrum disorders. *Discourse Studies, 6*(2), 253–276.

Trevarthen, C. (1979). Commuincation and cooperation in early infancy: A description of primary intersubjectivity. In M. Buolwa (Ed.), *Before speech: The beginning of interpersonal understanding* (pp. 321–348). Cambridge: Cambridge University Press.

Index[1]

[1] Note: Page numbers followed by "n" refers to notes

CPI Antony Rowe
Chippenham, UK
2017-11-28 22:22

Women and Wildlife Trafficking

Participants, Perpetrators and Victims

Edited by
Helen U. Agu and Meredith L. Gore

Routledge
Taylor & Francis Group
LONDON AND NEW YORK

earthscan
from Routledge

First published 2022
by Routledge
4 Park Square, Milton Park, Abingdon, Oxon OX14 4RN

and by Routledge
605 Third Avenue, New York, NY 10158

Routledge is an imprint of the Taylor & Francis Group, an informa business

British Library Cataloguing-in-Publication Data
A catalogue record for this book is available from the British Library

Library of Congress Cataloguing-in-Publication Data
Names: Agu, Helen U., editor. | Gore, Meredith L., 1977- editor.
Title: Women and wildlife trafficking : participants, perpetrators and victims / edited by Helen U. Agu and Meredith L. Gore.
Description: Abingdon, Oxon ; New York, NY : Routledge, 2022. |
Series: Routledge studies in conservation and the environment |
Includes bibliographical references and index.
Identifiers: LCCN 2021049258 (print) | LCCN 2021049259
(ebook) | ISBN 9780367640262 (hbk) | ISBN 9780367640286
(pbk) | ISBN 9781003121831 (ebk)
Subjects: LCSH: Wildlife crimes. | Wildlife smuggling. | Women. |
Conservation of natural resources.
Classification: LCC HV6410 .W66 2022 (print) | LCC HV6410
(ebook) | DDC 364.16/2859—dc23/eng/20211202
LC record available at https://lccn.loc.gov/2021049258
LC ebook record available at https://lccn.loc.gov/2021049259

ISBN: 978-0-367-64026-2 (hbk)
ISBN: 978-0-367-64028-6 (pbk)
ISBN: 978-1-003-12183-1 (ebk)

DOI: 10.4324/9781003121831

Typeset in Bembo
by codeMantra